Praise for The Youth Builder

The concepts presented in *The Youth Builder* are timeless. I love this book and you will also.

Stephen Arterburn
Founder, Women of Faith and New Life Clinics

Youth workers around the world often ask for basic youth ministry resources to help them establish their ministries and build from a solid biblical and practical base. I recommend them to *The Youth Builder* because it's principle based and lends itself to youth workers ministering in diverse cultures and contexts. The emphasis on relational youth ministry provides a framework on which effective youth workers develop fruitful ministry. I recommend *The Youth Builder* globally, and I recommend it to YOU!

Paul Borthwick
Former Director, The World Evangelical Fellowship Youth Commission and author, *Feeding Your Forgotten Soul: Spiritual Growth for Youth Workers*

The Youth Builder has been a handbook for youth workers for more than a decade. This new version of that book is even better; making it a must-read for anyone who takes youth work seriously.

Tony Campolo
Eastern College
St. Davids, Pennsylvania

Jim and Mike have been there and done that. They have a breadth of experience to be able to offer wise counsel to both the journeyman and novice youth minister. This book is jam-packed with creativity and fresh ideas. Jim and Mike offer practical insights and comprehensive ways of implementing them.

Les Christie
San Jose Christian College
San Jose, California

When the first edition of *The Youth Builder* arrived, everyone I knew in youth ministry devoured every bit of Jim Burns's history, heart, insight and passion for ministry to kids. It was *the* book to own and use. But like Jim and Mike's ministry the last several years, this edition is an even deeper, richer and more mature resource for youth workers, pastors, ministers and volunteers. It is filled with helpful and relevant resources, sage direction and time-tested, pragmatic advice for every level of youth ministry. But what is best about this new addition is the way Jim and Mike have cemented the most crucial foundations for solid youth ministry—just as Jesus Christ came to us with mercy, tenderness and love, so we too must approach our kids and ministry with incarnational compassion. I am so grateful that these two men have put on paper what God has built into them.

Chapman R. Clark, Ph.D.
Associate Professor of Youth, Family and Culture
Director, Youth Ministry Programs
Fuller Theological Seminary
Pasadena, California

There is no one whose council in youth ministry I trust as much as I do Jim and Mike's. Their transparent passion for mentoring the next generation of youth pastors breathes through every page of this book. Their words are well researched, practical, sensitive and Christ centered, offering veteran and novice youth leaders alike a book that is destined to become the standard youth ministry resource of this new millennium.

Mark DeVries
First Presbyterian Church
Nashville, Tennessee

Youth ministry leaders, like the youth they serve, are built from the inside out. In the pages of *The Youth Builder*, Jim and Mike have masterfully provided both the blueprints and the practical building tips necessary for crafting effective relational youth ministry leaders. As a mentor of youth ministry lay and pastoral leaders working on-site in a local church, I am thankful to have this invaluable leadership development tool added to my workshop.

Richard R. Dunn
Pastor of Leadership Formation and Student Ministries
Fellowship Evangelical Free Church
Knoxville, Tennessee

The Youth Builder is *the* comprehensive, practical and proven guidebook for youth ministry. It is a classic that deserves to be the cornerstone of any youth worker's library.

Paul Fleischmann
Executive Director
National Network of Youth Ministries

Many youth workers talk about relational youth ministry but fall far short of what it really is. Jim and Mike's passion for God and for teens is evident and brilliantly articulated in truly relational strategies that reach and minister effectively to youth. The revised version of *The Youth Builder* is, once again, a refreshing balance of theory and practice. This is a staple for any effective youth worker's library.

Dr. Steve Gerali
Chair, Department of Youth Ministry, Judson College
Elgin, Illinois
Director, Graduate Studies Program in Youth Ministry
Northern Baptist Theological Seminary
Lombard, Illinois

The Youth Builder drives right to the key of youth ministry—relationships. Of all the resources available to youth leaders today, *The Youth Builder* is without doubt our key to training and developing leaders to reach our nation's youth.

Walter Hoefflin
National Foursquare Youth Minister

Jim Burns touches on virtually all of the facets of youth ministry. Beginning youth workers will be challenged with the importance of thinking through the task, and veterans will be reminded of neglected areas that have become the source of conflicts and disappointment. All will benefit from an open and prayerful reading of this resource and a commitment to biblically based relational ministry. The principles and ideas presented come from a long and faithful hands-on experience in youth ministry.

Jay Kesler
Chancellor
Taylor University
Upland, Indiana

Many important changes were made to update *The Youth Builder* and modify it for a changing youth ministry environment. However, one very important thing did not change: *The Youth Builder* is still a classic and a necessity for anyone who strives to do effective, comprehensive and relevant youth ministry.

Mike King
CEO, Youth Front

I thank God for Jim Burns and Mike DeVries! This fresh new version of *The Youth Builder* is absolutely bursting at the seams with powerful tools for ministering to young people. I highly recommend it to anyone even considering youth ministry!

Josh McDowell
Josh McDowell Ministry

This new edition of *The Youth Builder* is your own personal youth ministry coach! As I read the book, I found myself putting sticky notes every few pages to use that week in my ministry. No book covers the basics so well with effective tools, current stats, relevant true-life experiences from recent hands-on experiences with students, and ministry methods you can apply the next day!

Jonathan McKee
National Speaker and Trainer
Jonathan's Resources

This comprehensive overview of healthy youth ministry is a training treasure for youth pastors, church youth workers and parachurch volunteers who want to reach kids in authentic, Christ-centered, relevant ways. Mike and Jim write out of a deep love for kids and a deeper love and dependence on Jesus. *The Youth Builder* will thoroughly prepare Christian adults to "be the conduits of God's healing grace in the lives of students" (from chapter 4). If you can buy only one youth ministry book, buy *The Youth Builder*.

Jennifer Morgan
National Director of Staff Development
Youth for Christ

As a student of today's rapidly changing youth culture, I am more convinced than ever of the essential role that healthy, caring relationships play in leading students to life-changing faith. In *The Youth Builder*, Jim Burns and Mike DeVries offer timely, practical and time-tested relational ministry wisdom for all of us who minister to kids. This is a book that a teachable youth worker won't leave on the shelf. Keep it nearby, as you'll refer to it time and time again.

Walt Mueller
President of the Center for Parent/Youth Understanding
and author, *Understanding Today's Youth Culture*

It is impossible not to combine the words "youth ministry" and "relational" in the same sentence. Jim and Mike have combined timeless principles with today's applications for reaching this generation for Christ. What a joy to recommend this to anyone whose heart beats for teenagers.

Helen Musick
Instructor of Youth Ministry
Asbury Seminary
Wilmore, Kentucky

Jim Burns and Mike DeVries have done it again in *The Youth Builder*. The material is practical yet profound. I recommend this to all youth workers. In a day when many youth ministries are program driven, *The Youth Builder* hits the nail on the head with the focus on relational youth ministry, something that many talk about but few implement. A must-read for those in the trenches of youth work.

Dr. David Olshine
Director, Youth Ministries Program
Columbia International University
Columbia, South Carolina

The Youth Builder delivers one of the best A to Z guides to youth ministry. If you're a rookie, read this yourself. If you're a veteran, read this with your team. Either way, you'll get answers to the what-do-I-do-now questions to help your ministry move from mediocrity to major impact.

Dr. Kara Powell
Assistant Professor
Azusa Pacific University
Azusa, California

I had one major problem while reading *The Youth Builder*: I kept daydreaming about how grateful my own church's youth pastor will be when I give him my copy! I can't think of another book that so thoroughly explores youth ministry while blending practical suggestions with thoughtful direction. Jim and Mike offer us the wisdom of a mentor in the encouraging tones of a friend. They demonstrate the sort of relational integrity in writing that they call us to in youth ministry. May thousands of youth ministers thank God for you both!

Dave Rahn
Director, Huntington College Link Institute
Huntington, Indiana

The best part of this book is its heart. Obviously Jim Burns and Mike DeVries have a real heart for Christ and a real heart for teenagers. But heart alone will not build a successful ministry. This book also takes practical care to give us authentic instruction in the handiwork and the head work that makes effective youth ministry possible. But what I most love about this book is its vision and intention. Mike and Jim have given us a book that takes the focus off of building a youth group and puts the focus back where it belongs on building youth and making disciples. I highly recommend this book.

Duffy Robbins
Chairman, Department of Youth Ministry
Eastern College
St. Davids, Pennsylvania

The Youth Builder has been an effective tool in the hands of youth ministers for the past 12 years. Recently it has been revised to better fit the grip of today's leaders. If you want to cut a lasting impression in the lives of kids today, read this book. It will tell you everything you need to know to leave a permanent impression of Jesus Christ on young lives.

Denny Rydberg
President, Young Life

Reading *The Youth Builder* reminded me of one of those 64-drawer roll-away tool chests with shiny chrome and red finish. This is the complete package! The dedicated youth worker/craftsman will have every tool needed for effective ministry to students and their families.

Tim Smith
Pastor to Family Life
Calvary Community Church
Westlake Village, California
Author, *7 Cries of Today's Teen*

Jim and Mike have taken a classic work and made it even better. A great resource for today's youth worker!

Dann Spader
Sonlife Ministries

In three words, it all boils down to relationships, relationships, relationships. This open-minded and creative book offers authentic help for the most inexperienced to the most veteran youth leader. It is a must-read for leaders who hunger to experience life change in this generation and insist on going to *the* Source for answers.

Barry St. Clair
President and Founder, Reach Out Youth Solutions

the YOUTH BUILDER

Today's Resource for Relational Youth Ministry

Jim Burns, Ph.D., & Mike DeVries

Gospel Light

Gospel Light is an evangelical Christian publisher dedicated to serving the local church. We believe God's vision for Gospel Light is to provide church leaders with biblical, user-friendly materials that will help them evangelize, disciple and minister to children, youth and families.

It is our prayer that this Gospel Light resource will help you discover biblical truth for your own life and help you minister to youth. May God richly bless you.

For a free catalog of resources from Gospel Light, please contact your Christian supplier or contact us at 1-800-4-GOSPEL *or* www.gospellight.com.

PUBLISHING STAFF
William T. Greig, Chairman
Kyle Duncan, Publisher
Dr. Elmer L. Towns, Senior Consulting Publisher
Pam Weston, Senior Editor
Patti Pennington Virtue, Associate Editor
Jeff Kempton, Editorial Assistant
Bayard Taylor, M.Div., Senior Editor, Biblical and Theological Issues
Kevin Parks, Cover Designer
Rosanne Richardson, Cover Production
Debi Thayer, Designer

ISBN 0-8307-2923-2

Printed in the U.S.A.

DEDICATION

FROM JIM

To Cathy—The most influential person in my life. Your support, sacrifice and consistent Christian behavior inspire me. Your faith, commitment and accountability motivate me to focus on Christ. He is the reason for our life together, our shared ministry and this book. Love, Jim

FROM MIKE

To Jamie—I've never been known to be at a loss for words, except for now. There are not enough words to describe all that you mean to me. Your example of a woman who loves Jesus inspires me to love and know Him more. You are the most authentic, genuine person I have ever met. Thank you for the way you love me. Ever since the day I met you, I have been the most blessed man on the face of the planet. I love you—and I always will. Love, Mike

To Joshua, Megan, Mikalya and Madison—I thank God for allowing me to be your dad. When He gave you to us, He blessed us beyond measure. You have brought so much joy into our lives. You make me laugh in so many ways and make me cry when I think about how much God has blessed me with you. May you know the love of God in your lives in such a deep way that you run to Him, like you do to me, calling out "Daddy!" Remember, I will always, always, always love you! Love, Daddy

Contents

Foreword by Doug Fields 15
Preface and Acknowledgments 17

Section I: The Foundation—Pillars for Ministry 22

1. What Is Relational Youth Ministry? 23
2. Preparing for Relational Youth Ministry 32
3. Understanding Today's Youth 42
4. Developing a Ministry That Lasts 53
5. Adolescent Development 62
6. Family-Based Youth Ministry 72

Section II: The Framework—Blueprints for Ministry 85

7. Relational Evangelism: Reaching a Generation in Need . . 86
8. Building Community Through Small Groups 99
9. Discipleship: Getting Kids Involved 109
10. Worship: Encountering the Living God 119
11. Camps and Retreats 127
12. Developing Student Leaders 135
13. Missions and Service 146
14. Developing a Dynamic Volunteer Team 156
15. Developing an Internship Program 171
16. Building Support Within the Staff and Church Leadership 178
17. Your Budget and You 188

SECTION III: PROGRAMMING—THE CREATIVE SPARK OF MINISTRY 196
18. Principles for Strategic Programming 197
19. Creative Teaching—So They'll Never Forget 205
20. Ideas for Creative Communication 218
21. Teaching on Sex and Sexuality 228

SECTION IV: PERSONAL RELATIONSHIPS—THE HEART OF MINISTRY 241
22. Building Self-Image in Students 242
23. Counseling Youth—Compassionate Youth Ministry 257
24. Working with Disrupted Families 268
25. The Crisis of Substance Abuse 282
26. The Crisis of Suicide 291
27. The Crisis of Sexual Abuse 300

Appendix 308
Endnotes 310

FOREWORD

Without a doubt, *The Youth Builder* is my favorite youth ministry book ever written. I can say that because I have firsthand experience that the words in *The Youth Builder* are life-changing. Here are three examples of what I mean.

I was a student in Jim Burns's youth ministry in the '70s when he was modeling the contents of *The Youth Builder* in the local church. Not only was he my youth pastor, but he was also my hero. The reason I am in youth ministry today is because of Jim and his influence on my life while I was a teenager. Jim hadn't yet written any books on youth ministry and he hadn't become a popular leader in the youth ministry movement. What he was doing was learning and practicing everything you'll read about in this book. During those years, he personified the essence of *The Youth Builder* in my life.

In the early '80s I was taught the principles of *The Youth Builder* while serving as an intern for Jim. As my boss, he modeled leadership, integrity and pastoral attitudes that taught me how to move from being a student in his ministry to being a youth worker. Together, we served in our church and partnered in the principles of *The Youth Builder*.

When Jim left the local church, I took over his position as youth pastor and maintained the thinking, philosophies and practices of *The Youth Builder*. Jim hadn't built a ministry on his personality (and he could have); what he had built was a solid foundation for ministry. I spent the next several years enhancing the healthy foundation he had developed.

Years later, equipped with Jim's teaching, thinking, youth ministry modeling and encouragement, I wrote *Purpose-Driven Youth Ministry* to complement all that I had learned from Jim and his first edition of *The Youth Builder*. My book is helpful in building a youth ministry strategy; *The Youth Builder* goes beyond the strategy and fills in the gaps that *PDYM* leaves behind. In addition to material on the five biblical purposes of youth ministry (evangelism, worship, fellowship, discipleship and ministry), *The Youth Builder* adds information on camping, creativity, suicide, adolescent development, counseling and so much more. If you own *PDYM*, you now have a great companion resource in *The Youth Builder*.

Over the last decade, Jim has been training youth workers all over the world and learning even more about youth ministry, youth workers, culture, students and transferable principles. While Jim has been on the road, his good friend, veteran youth worker, Mike DeVries, has been in the trenches applying *The Youth Builder* principles in the local church. With Mike's help, this new version of *The Youth Builder* has made a great book even better.

One of the reasons I continue in my third decade as a youth worker is because of what Jim's life has meant to me. He never said "Doug, follow me as I follow Christ." He didn't need to use those words; I watched a life that was worth following and chose to follow his model. Honestly, I feel like I'm one of the luckiest people on Earth to have had Jim Burns as a youth pastor, boss, partner in ministry and friend. I also believe that you too are lucky to hold in your hands Jim's words, his heart and his lifelong commitment to helping youth workers. Follow these words; they come from a man who knows and loves Jesus Christ.

A friend and fellow youth worker,
Doug Fields
Pastor to Students at Saddleback Church
Lake Forest, California
Author, *Purpose-Driven Youth Ministry*

Jim's Preface and Acknowledgments

I have just finished the final edit of the book you now have in your hands. This weekend as I read every word on every page, one more time, I was reminded again and again of the incredible, powerful impact you have on the lives of students. I was also reminded of the fact that the past 27 years of living and breathing youth ministry have gone far beyond what I ever dreamed when Cathy and I returned from our honeymoon and I started as the high school director at Yorba Linda Friends Church. For me, *The Youth Builder* is much more than another book. It is my lifelong work in the field of youth ministry. Within these pages are much of my heart and soul.

The original *Youth Builder* was written in 1988 and I was probably the most surprised of anyone to see it immediately become the biggest selling comprehensive youth ministry book in the world. I was humbled that colleges and seminaries across the globe used it as their text for youth ministry classes and that youth workers whom I knew to be more effective than I ever was, actually told me that they benefited from the book. This project has brought me great joy because through it, I share with you whom I respect so very much for your willingness to make a difference in the lives of students.

As the new millennium came I was approached about updating *The Youth Builder*. I realized quite quickly that while I am still intimately involved in the world of youth ministry, I would need the help of someone in the trenches doing outstanding work with students. Who could I find who was a great practitioner and also someone who knew the theory of youth ministry for this new generation of students? I could only think of one name to be my cowriter for this new addition—Mike DeVries. I told him there was nothing sacred and that I wanted to completely update the book to serve the new and even more-committed youth workers than a generation ago. I've seen for several years now that the old methods may not work, and with a new generation of students, so must we look at new approaches to doing youth ministry. Mike was the one person in the world I knew could come alongside me and make *The Youth Builder* absolutely relevant for this next generation. He did a great job. What is even more incredible is that we have both worked at the same church, Yorba Linda Friends Church, where some of these illustrations took place. I was on staff before going to graduate school and Mike served there for over 11 years.

There are simply too many people to thank for all their help and assistance. Cathy has been the greatest influence in my life. She has lived out the values in this book with sacrifice. Tic Long, Wayne Rice and Mike Yaconelli of Youth Specialties brought on a 25-year-old kid and taught me how to train youth workers. You are my friends, mentors and heroes. Thank you to Noel Becchetti for your macro edit on the first version when you were editor of *Youthworker Journal*. Thank you to the two very special "kids" from my youth worker days, Doug Webster and Doug Fields, both in ninth grade when I met you and now leaders in our movement.

I want to extend special thanks to the staff and board of YouthBuilders for your willingness to dare to dream. And thank you to Carrie Hicks Steele and Dawnielle Hodgman for your most incredible job on this manuscript.

Jim Burns
Dana Point, California

We loved you so much that we were delighted to share with you
not only the gospel of God but our lives as well,
because you had become so dear to us.

1 THESSALONIANS 2:8

He took a little child and had him stand among them. Taking him in his arms, he said to them, "Whoever welcomes one of these little children in my name welcomes me; and whoever welcomes me does not welcome me but the one who sent me."

MARK 9:36-37

Mike's Acknowledgments

I can still remember the first time I ever read *The Youth Builder*. I was a brand new youth pastor at Yorba Linda Friends Church. Fresh out of Azusa Pacific University and just starting my first full-time youth ministry position, I read every page. Over the years my first copy of the book has been read and reread. The jacket sleeve is ripped, the pages marked and folded. There is writing on almost every page. The book was foundational for me as a young youth worker. Now as a 16-year veteran of youth ministry, I am reminded of what really matters in youth ministry—being a part of what God is doing to touch the lives of students. May this book be for you, the reader, everything that it was and still is to me.

To Jim—I thank God for bringing us together some 11 years ago. You were a mentor from afar—now you are a friend up close. Thank you for allowing me the privilege of working on this project, to tinker and dream with your "baby." I appreciate you, my brother, and love you. Thanks for believing in me.

To the youth staff at Yorba Linda Friends Church—For 11 years I called YLFC my home. We served together, laughed together, cried together—and through it all we saw God do some amazing things. You all mean the world to me. God has so much in store for you. Keep seeking Him!

To the staff and board of YouthBuilders—Thank you for welcoming me in as a part of the family. I count it a privilege to be a part of the team. I can't wait to see all that God has for us in the future!

To Dawnielle Hodgman—I thank God that He brought us together at YouthBuilders. You came as my assistant, but you became my friend. Thank you for your encouragement, support and belief in me and this project. Thanks for your tireless work on the manuscript. You're the best!

To Jon Irving—"There is a friend who sticks closer than a brother" (Proverbs 18:24). Thanks for being the brother I never had. I love you.

To Ryan and Alyssa Low, and Jay and Deanne Hoff—Our couple's group has been such a wonderful place of encouragement, transparency and growth. Thank you for standing with Jamie and me through the writing of this book. We love you dearly.

To Mom—As I write this acknowledgment, it's May 14, 2001, Dad's birthday. He would have been 67 today. I miss him. I wish he could have held a copy of this book. Thank you for all the things I've thanked you for, and thank you for the ones I haven't. I love you so very much, Mom. I'm so proud of you. Dad would be too.

To my God—May all this be done for Your glory and Your fame.

Mike DeVries
Mission Viejo, California

Yes, LORD, walking in the way of your laws, we wait for you;
your name and renown are the desire of our hearts.

ISAIAH 26:8

SECTION I

THE FOUNDATION—PILLARS FOR MINISTRY

CHAPTER 1

What Is Relational Youth Ministry?

Your young people are making major decisions that will affect them for the rest of their lives. Adolescence is a time of transition that brings long-lasting effects. As a youth worker, you play a powerful role and have great influence in the lives of your students. In one survey, students on a secular high school campus were asked, "Who would you turn to in time of trouble or for help in life decisions?" The number one choice was parents, but the second choice was youth workers. Not too many years ago, youth ministry in the church was either a glorified baby-sitting service or an insignificant event on the church calendar. Today, however, youth ministry is viewed as one of the key ministries within the church.

But what is effective youth ministry? What does it look like? In the past, good youth ministry was often seen as primarily program-oriented: rallies, events and other elaborately orchestrated gatherings. However, today we have come to realize that long-term influence with lasting impact comes from significant relationships and role models. Of course programming has its place in youth ministry, but the long-term positive influence on the lives of students comes from people, not programs. Programs are a framework in which ministry exists. Programs don't minister—people minister. The part of ministry that will change the lives of the young people we work with won't be our speaking or our creative programming. Long after the events are over, long after our messages are forgotten, it will be relationships that are remembered and have the greatest influence.

I (Jim) recently asked 1,000 youth workers at a conference to list the five most influential sermons or programs in their lives. One minute later, no one had come up with five sermons or programs. In fact, the vast majority of the workers could remember only one or two sermons or programs at best. Then I asked them to list five of the most influential people in their lives. After one minute, most of the people in the conference had listed four or five people who had influenced their lives in a significant way. Some listed teachers, some listed youth workers, and others listed parents and others who had taken the time to invest in their lives. Very few were public figures—almost none were famous. Most were ordinary people, like you and me—people who cared about them enough to invest time and energy in their lives. That's our calling. My guess is that you are where you are today because of a few significant individuals who cared for you on a personal basis. It was those significant relationships that have shaped who you are today. Years from now, if I were to ask the same question to a room full of youth workers, would your name be on that list?

In order to have an important influence in the lives of young people, you do not need to be a dynamic speaker, know all the latest music, or even dress in the latest fashions. You must, however, love kids and be willing to spend time with them, which is what effective, relational youth ministry is all about. Effective youth workers may never be polished, dynamic communicators or highly creative programmers; but they do need to have a heart of compassion, a listening ear and a willingness to get to know the students in their youth ministry. *Genuinely caring for your students is the primary prerequisite for working with them.*

Incarnational Ministry

After I (Jim) had finished speaking to a group of youth workers in Kansas, several of them came up to talk. The particular issues varied, but the question was the same: "What program can I use to keep my group enthusiastic about their faith?" My answer was probably disappointing to some people. There are a variety of proven methods; many different youth ministry organizations, denominations, books and individual churches use every type of program imaginable—and they all seem to work. Yet at the same time, any method can also fail!

However, there is a way to build a youth group spiritually and numerically—contrary to what some might say, youth go where other kids are, so numbers can at times be important. There is one word that stands out above all others—"relationship."

Our Christian faith is sealed in a personal relationship with Jesus Christ. Theologically, Jesus is the *incarnation* of God. He is God in the flesh (see Colossians 1:15). As the ministry of Jesus was incarnate in the Gospels, so our life must be incarnate in youth ministry. Jesus stepped into our world to identify with us: to walk as we walk, to experience what we experience, to talk and relate to us in relationship. So it is with us as we enter into an incarnate relationship with our students. If we are ever to have a positive influence on our young people, we must build relationships with them and live out our faith in their midst.

Young people tire of shallow and hollow programs or manipulative methods. They can see through false pretenses. They are looking for something deeper, something real and something authentic. While building relationships we become the hands and feet—and even the voice—of Jesus in their lives. As we seek to build relationships with the students we minister to, they will see us as real and approachable, genuine in faith and a friend to be trusted. By building genuine relationships with them and allowing them to see healthy adult staff relationships, we will be considered friends and mentors. We believe that the students who remain active in the youth ministry will stay, not because of our creative programming, but because of healthy and genuine relationships. Students who are connected to their peers and adults stay, and staying power is created by mixing the six basic ingredients of an effective relational youth ministry.

Team Ministry

Young people are looking for role models to imitate. The adult staff (whether comprised of scores of youth workers or a husband-and-wife volunteer team) must build toward a loving, unified team before any young person will stand up and take notice. We believe that the first commitment that a new youth worker should make in the church, even before developing a ministry with students, is to develop a youth ministry team. Relational youth ministry starts with a relational youth staff. Jesus told His disciples:

> A new command I give you: Love one another. As I have loved you, so you must love one another. By this all men will know that you are my disciples, if you love one another (John 13:34-35).

In other words, the youth in your church and community will often judge the attractiveness and validity of the gospel by the relationships that the staff members have with one another.

Take time to build significant relationships with your staff, and encourage affirming friendships between them. You will be creating a wonderful role model for your students. You will also be cementing the volunteer staff's involvement in youth ministry. The youth group is watching, listening and at times imitating the relationship role models of the staff.

A unified staff is one that prays and shares with each other. A unified staff plays together. Some of the best quality times for building staff unity can be done in the very same manner as with students: through playing together, shopping or other "fun" activities.

Be as proactive and intentional in building and nurturing relationships with your staff as you are in building and nurturing relationships with your students. It is an area of ministry that is often neglected because we are so focused on our ministry to students, but it is one that will expand our ministry's effectiveness. As your youth staff develops a mutual love, support and respect for each other, your young people will notice and respond.

Modeling

Most likely, your greatest influence will not be in what you teach through your words; rather, it will be through your actions, reactions and lifestyle.

The most effective teaching that takes place is usually not during the formal teaching times but, rather, when students get to know their youth worker on a relational level. What students need today is not an adult that dresses like they do, knows all the latest trends in youth culture or even talks like they do. What students need today are adults that are crazy about them and are willing to share their lives with them. Students need models. They will be watching your life and mine—what will they find?

Every year our group has a senior banquet. It's a time for our seniors to share what God has done in their lives over the past four years. For years, I (Mike) kept waiting for students to say that it was our great programming that changed their lives. Perhaps it was all the creative messages we gave. Rather, what we heard time and time again was about significant relationships. For example we might hear something similar to "It was the time when my parents were getting a divorce and I needed someone who understood what I was going through. I thought of Megan. She let me spend the night and told me all about her struggle and how God had helped her. She listened to me, cried with me and prayed for me. I'll never forget that." Students need role models of what Christianity looks like lived in the context of life's issues. They need to see a model—not a perfect one, but one that can show them the way.

Unconditional Love

The truth of the gospel is that God loves us not for what we do but for who we are. God loves us unconditionally. His love is sacrificial and deep. Grace permeates our relationship with our Lord. We also must love our students with an unconditional, no-strings-attached love. We must accept the fact that kids will fail. When they miss the mark, they need our love and encouragement to keep trying. They need to know that no matter where they've been or what they've done, our love for them remains unchanged. In a world that is marked by conditional love, our unconditional love can make all the difference.

Your actions of unconditional love will often be the determining factor in solidifying the faith of your students. How can they know God's grace and love if they don't see it firsthand from significant others? The apostle John's words are so important for youth workers: "Let us not love with words or tongue *but with actions* and in truth" (1 John 3:18, emphasis added). In other words, actions really do speak louder than words.

Once while chaperoning a party for one of the local high schools, I (Jim) watched one of our core leadership kids literally being carried out of the party because he had passed out from drinking too much. I was hurt; he was embarrassed. Of course, on Sunday he didn't come to our group. I decided I had to go to him and let him know I loved him and still wanted him in our group. He had to learn that even though he made a mistake, he was still accepted by our group and leaders. Even through this negative experience, he would understand the *grace* of God in a stronger, more meaningful way. Recently this young man told me that if we had not loved him with unconditional love, he probably would never have come back to church. Don't miss the opportunity to demonstrate God's grace to your students.

Nurturing

There is no such thing as instant spiritual maturity. Sanctification is a continuing process. Just as newborn babies need constant care and nourishment, so young people need our consistent attention, time and presence. Effective youth ministry with a lasting and eternal impact takes time and nurturing.

The reason we have so many young people with stunted spiritual growth is because we have not given them the nurturing needed to produce vibrant spiritual lives. One of the major goals of youth ministry should be to move the students from dependence on us—the youth workers—to dependence on God. Yet we need to remember that the process takes time. Many youth workers have been guilty of manipulative methods to produce quick fixes or instant spiritual maturity, only to see in the long run that this tactic failed to produce healthy and genuine spiritual fruit.

The Christian life is not a sprint but a marathon. Students need to know that their youth leaders will walk *with them* through the Christian journey and nurture them to become all that God desires them to be.

Meeting Students on Their Territory

We live in a fast-paced culture. If the Church stands still and waits for youth to come to it, then the Church will have a long, quiet, empty and frustrating wait. Meeting students on their territory is vital because it breaks down the often imposing walls of the Church. To get a response from young people, it is important to go out to the schools and hangouts in order to interact with them. For many youth workers this means watching a high school soccer game or helping with decorations for the school play, rather than spending time in the office. It's finding out where students are and making a decision to enter their world.

By going into the students' world, you will show them that you are interested in them as people, not just as church participants. One of the most important aspects of ministry is to let them know you care. Your presence and commitment to be in their world communicates care and concern.

Entering their world can become a great tool for evangelism. Young people will introduce you to their friends, and eventually as new friendships evolve, others too will want to see what the youth group is all about.

Contact work—meeting your students on their territory—is one of the most rewarding aspects of youth ministry. When we show up at a school event, game or even lunch, they will usually react with enthusiasm because they see that we were willing to take time out of our busy schedule to take an interest in them.

While working with Young Life, I (Jim) remember going to soccer games and practices. Eventually the coach asked me to help with the team for the last few games. Actually, I was more like an adult water boy. At the time we had two guys on the team coming to our Young Life club. Before the season was over a majority of the team had come to one of our club meetings. There was nothing more effective that entire year than spending a considerable amount of time on that soccer field.

You can learn a great amount about the youth culture when you invade young people's territory. Be a student of their world; watch and listen. If you want to really understand the world students live in, spend a day on a local campus. Your life will never be the same.

Spending Time with Students

Students need significant adults to give them time and attention. It takes both quality and quantity time to do effective relational youth ministry. Some time ago I (Jim) called up two high school guys one Saturday morning and asked them to go shopping with me at the mall. I already knew what I wanted to buy, but I thought it might be good to spend some time with those two guys. After finding what I wanted to buy, we walked around the mall for an hour and went to the food court. During lunch we had a very nonthreatening, open conversation about the Christian life. As I look back, the investment of those few hours and the conversation that took place were far more productive than all the Sunday School classes I had ever taught those two students.

Educators talk about the idea of hidden curriculum, which means that we must look for every opportunity, or teachable moment, outside the classroom setting to teach our students. When you spend time with kids in your ministry, you are showing them that they are important and that you really care. A friend of mine plays basketball with a group of guys every week. He told me that he talks more about God before, during and after the weekly basketball game than at any other time during the week.

Jim Rayburn, the founder of Young Life, used to say, "It's a sin to bore a kid with the gospel." The gospel of Jesus is the most exciting news the world will ever hear, yet young people often drop out of the church because it's boring. In truth what many are saying is not so much that church is boring, but it's unengaging. They left without significantly connecting with anyone. We believe that one of the major reasons kids drop out of church and call it boring is because no one was willing to take an interest in or spend time with them. Students stay when they have built relationships and connected with others.

Reaching Out

We can't compete with the latest technology in media to keep kids' interest. Producers and advertisers spend millions of dollars to gain and keep the attention of adolescents. However, there is one thing that television, the Internet or any other competitors for kids' attention cannot give—a real flesh-and-blood relationship. Students will respond to someone who genuinely cares about them and is willing to spend time with them.

Relationships are the *key* to effective youth ministry. The greatest programs will fail and the most interesting curriculum will never be absorbed if the primary focus in youth ministry is not building solid, encouraging, positive relationships with students. The great news for most of us is that it isn't necessary for us to be an excellent communicator or to produce incredible programs; rather, what we truly need is a willingness to spend time with kids and let them know we care.

CHAPTER 2

Preparing for Relational Youth Ministry

One of the saddest commentaries on youth ministry today is its overwhelming turnover of professional and volunteer youth workers. The odds are incredibly high that most of the youth workers in churches today will not be in the same churches three years from now. Furthermore, the majority of volunteers won't be involved in the youth ministry next year. Burnout and frustration are chronic roadblocks in our mission to reach students.

We believe the high turnover rate in youth work is often due to a lack of personal preparation and spiritual care in the life of the youth worker. How can we, who have been called to work with students, prepare ourselves to be effective for the long haul? Begin with a good look in the mirror.

The area of balance and renewal is one of the most vital in our ministry to students. We've heard it said, "You can't give from an empty well." But isn't that exactly what we do? We give and give, watching our spiritual reserves used up, like gas from our gas tank. We give and give, without thought to our own personal spiritual lives; then one day we awaken to the emptiness of the soul. In looking at our personal preparation for ministry, we need to keep in mind three truths.

1. **Balance starts and continues with a daily choice.** It is a choice that we make daily to be a part of exercises and habits that keep us in balance. The undisciplined life is never kind to the areas it neglects.
2. **Balance is maintained through constant evaluation.** It means asking yourself some difficult and sometimes painful questions, such as, *How balanced am I really? Where do I need to make some changes in order to be more balanced?*
3. **Balance requires a plan.** We need to be proactive in placing safeguards in our lives that will help us pursue balance and therefore long-term ministry with students. A good plan will take into account six areas of balance: spiritual, family, relational, emotional, physical and leadership.

Spiritual Balance

I (Jim) once heard it said, "Untended fires soon become nothing but a pile of ashes." One intern involved at my church said, "I can't afford to take the time to have a quality devotional time with God." My reply was simple: "You can't afford *not* to have a quality devotional time with God."

Many youth workers are high on energy and enthusiasm. We can wing a program and Bible study with some degree of success. We can't wing spiritual depth. Over the long haul we often run out of gas and burn out spiritually because we have neglected to fuel the fire of our faith.

Most Christian leaders have their most effective ministry impact in their 40s or older. They are mature and have set a foundation for their faith. Unfortunately, many youth workers never make it in ministry to their 40s (or older), because their lack of personal time with God catches up with them. They fade away before God can use them to their greatest potential.

Paul's advice to Timothy was to "train yourself to be godly" (1 Timothy 4:7). A disciplined devotional life is not an option for spiritual growth; it is a necessity. As we read the biographies of great men and women of God, there is one common thread visible in all of their varied lives: they all met with God on a daily, intimate basis.

It is essential that we who minister be ministered to first. Our calling is not first to the students to whom we minister; it's to God Himself. When was the last time we approached God as a beloved child of His, rather than as a youth worker trying to finish our Bible study? With proper priorities, there should be no excuse strong enough to keep us from a daily, disciplined devotional time with God. The length of time spent with the Lord is not as important as regularity and expectancy. We wonder why we feel powerless and spiritually drained when in reality less than 1 percent of those who call themselves Christians spend 30 minutes or more a day with God.

Our lives should be marked by a daily time spent seeking the face of God. Reading the Scriptures, prayer, personal worship and even reading spiritual classics will bring a depth to our lives that will keep our spiritual fires burning and impact our ministry. It's exciting to see the sudden upsurge of interest among Christians to take a sabbath. The Old Testament Sabbath is a form of rest, reflection, a change of pace—a solo time with God. Even God rested on the seventh day! It is time away from the office for extra time with God. When I (Jim) go on a solo, I try to be away for five hours. I bring my Bible, my journal and a pen. I spend my time reading, praying, journaling, singing, worshiping and walking. I've even been known to take a short nap! I want my solo to take place in nature. I will go to the beach, a park, a lake or somewhere else where I can be away from people and in God's creation. It's a time of reflection, worship and refreshment. The purpose is to refresh me so that when I'm with people, they will have my full and refreshed attention. If you've never taken a solo, try it. You'll be amazed at the impact it can have.

Family Balance

After the first year of our marriage, Cathy and I (Jim) decided to review the year. We talked of our joys and discouragements. Cathy's biggest complaint hurt: "You give all you have to the youth and their families, and you have nothing left for me." The truth was that she was absolutely right. Through the years I've had to make adjustments to insure a healthy, solid marriage and family relationships. We need to proactively plan for and guard our time with our families. Here are a few suggestions:

- Make a weekly date night a nonnegotiable item in your calendar.
- Be sure to take at least one 24-hour period off a week from work.
- Look at your day in thirds: morning, afternoon and night. Schedule work for only two of the three. If you need to work at night, take off the morning. If you must work morning through night, make up for the time on another day during the week.
- Schedule your personal life in advance of the ministry schedule. Don't let the ministry schedule always dictate your personal life.
- Give your spouse veto power over your schedule. Plan nothing for the youth ministry without consent from your spouse. It will save you that haunting feeling of a lack of unity and agreement with your spouse.
- If needed, plan regular business meetings with your spouse to talk about the business of your family, including calendar, finances, projects and other issues that we seldom find the time to discuss.
- Daily phone calls are a must when you are traveling and are away from each other.
- Take periodic overnight trips with your spouse.
- Take vacation times for building up your relationship—and not always for visiting the relatives!
- If you have children, be sure to plan regular dates with them, letting them choose what they want to do.

Give your family your prime time, not just the time when you are exhausted. If your family life is suffering, then it is certainly time to reevaluate your ministry and make the necessary adjustments before both your family *and* your ministry dissolve. The most important ministry you can ever have is to your spouse and children. There was a youth worker before you, there will be one after you—but you are the only spouse or parent your family will ever have!

Relational Balance

Unfortunately, many youth workers are lonely, isolated people. Supportive relationships are not an option; they are a necessity. If all our relationships are with students and the people we minister alongside, we are setting ourselves up for difficulty and burnout. We need to develop relationships and friendships, especially adult friendships, that are outside the realm of ministry. It is questionable how long you will last in youth ministry if you are not in a support group. These are strong words, but we believe them to be true. Working with students is both a joy and a strain. We need the support and accountability of peers who love us and encourage us but aren't afraid to question our motives and help us grow.

In my own personal growth, I (Mike) need to be in relationship with an accountable support group in order to share my hurts and joys. I need to feel a sense of community. My accountability group meets on Thursdays; we've met together for the past five years. Over the years, this group has been a place of community, encouragement, support and conviction. I need to be in a place where I am loved enough to be asked tough questions. I also need a *mentor relationship*. I've had to find more mature and wiser Christians from whom I can learn and grow in a mentorship capacity. I also need a *Timothy* in my life—someone to whom I can give myself in a ministry of discipleship and training and to whom I can be a mentor. More than you might realize, the longevity of your ministry often relates to having a support group.

Emotional Balance

An important question to consider in the midst of ministry is, *How am I recharging my batteries?* Emotional balance seeks to recharge our batteries, not only for ministry, but also for life. To be people of balance we need to have healthy recreation in our lives. "Recreation" is an interesting word. It literally means to re-create. Positive, healthy recreation in our lives serves to help us maintain balance by *re-creating* and refreshing our spiritual and emotional battery reserves for ministry.

All of us need a healthy diversion from life and ministry, something that emotionally restores us. Hobbies, passions and loves that keep us fresh and alive need to be a part of our life profile. We need to proactively make room for those passions in our lives. Schedule times of refreshment and renewal through your hobbies and passions. Be it reading, going to the movies or taking in a baseball game—find something that disengages your mind from the demands of ministry. Seek out whatever it is that replenishes your life and find time for it in your schedule.

Physical Balance

Paul reminds us in 1 Corinthians 6:19, "Do you not know that your body is a temple of the Holy Spirit, who is in you, whom you have received from God?" God has given us our bodies and we are to take care of them. Often one of the most neglected areas of balance in our lives is the area of our physical well-being. Our bodies were meant to be cared for. Part of caring for the temple of the Holy Spirit is proper exercise and rest, which bring spiritual and physical benefits. Time spent working out relieves stress, energizes, clears the mind and helps us feel better about our physical shape. We need to schedule regular times of exercise to keep our bodies and minds in order.

Rest is another often neglected area of physical balance. If you are not taking at least a 24-hour period of rest in your week, most likely your primary relationships are out of order and you are not functioning in balance as a Christian. Rest heals; rest soothes; rest gives us perspective. Without a definite time of rest each week, our lives become more and more confusing and disordered. If you can't finish all you need to get done in five or six days, then you are doing too much and are most likely not listening to the Spirit of God in your life.

Leadership Balance

In order to stay fresh in ministry, especially in dealing with volunteer leaders, we must proactively seek growth in many areas such as scheduling, training, equipping and administration.

Scheduling

The deadliest sins of the youth worker are perhaps overcommitment and fatigue. Youth workers burn out because they tackle too many responsibilities and commitments without enough rest. Professional football coach Vince Lombardi used to tell his team, "Fatigue makes cowards of us all." Many youth workers burn out because they simply can't say no.

The sooner we learn that we must say no, the more productive our ministry will be. Consider overbooking your schedule as a sin, not a sign of success. Busyness does not equate to godliness. Workaholism is an addictive sin in our lives similar to any other addiction. Leave room in your schedule for rest, flexibility, freedom to be available and fellowship. The best advice I (Jim) ever received in seminary was from a friend who upon my graduation wrote these words on a card to me: "If the devil can't make you bad, then he will make you busy."

Training and Equipping

Most youth workers are undertrained for working with adolescents. Not only are we undertrained, but also our culture and the needs of adolescents are constantly changing. In order to be effective, we need to be learners, always growing. Planned times of training provide leaders with the opportunity to strengthen skills, gain needed education and be spiritually refreshed. We strongly believe that the church should give a youth worker two weeks a year for continuing education and should pay for the expenses. (Of course, we must keep it reasonable. Study leave to cruise the Caribbean islands is probably not wise stewardship of church funds!)

As you look for training and equipping experiences, search for types that will fit your particular needs best. Here are four different ideas:

1. **Pursue continuing education.** There is an abundance of high-quality continuing-education experiences emerging in all shapes and sizes. Many Christian colleges and seminaries offer short-term classes, summer sessions and weekly classes in youth ministry or counseling. There are excellent organizations putting on conven-

tions and conferences all across the country. Explore what's available on tape, CD, video and the Internet. There are incredible organizations which are passionate about encouraging and equipping youth workers.

2. **Visit other ministries.** If you are tired of seminars, conferences and conventions, an excellent idea is to plan your study leave to visit effective youth ministries. Plan your trip carefully so that you can visit with a few ministries in a single area of the country. Be sure to make time to attend their student programs. Visiting other ministries can give you fresh and new inspiration about ministering to your own youth.
3. **Spend time alone.** I (Jim) have found that one of the most efficient uses of time is to find a motel or a friend's cabin away from the phone and other interruptions. In a few days alone I can set vision, develop ministry ideas, plan my messages, work on scheduling, come up with ideas and study curriculum. Two to four days of uninterrupted time frees me up to spend more time with students when I'm back home.
4. **Bring in an expert.** You may not be able to afford to pay for an expert to be your personal consultant, but many people today are gathering a number of church youth workers and bringing in experts to train and equip them. When a few churches come together, it really reduces the cost of the program. If you offer to drive to the airport to pick them up (or, better yet, invite them to dinner), you'll find that the special one-on-one times will be well worth the time and effort. Don't be intimidated about seeking out experts. Be proactive in developing relationships with others.

Administration

Vision usually isn't the thing that hinders most youth ministries; it's a lack of administration that sinks many of them. Administration does not appear to be a common spiritual gift among most youth workers. Often the strength of a youth leader is that he or she is flexible and spontaneous. Sometimes that strength can become a weakness when it comes to administering a youth ministry. In reality, a well-administered ministry will provide more valuable time to spend with your students. Good administration builds support and belief in the ministry and its leadership in the eyes of students, parents and volunteers, as well as church leaders. Here are a number of suggestions:

- Before your week begins, plan it out! Block out the time needed to accomplish the goals you know must be done that week.
- Begin each day by reviewing what you plan to accomplish that particular day.
- Leave room in your schedule for flexibility.
- Plan out meetings in advance. Have a purpose and know what you're trying to accomplish with each meeting. Have an agenda. Finish each meeting with a recap of the decisions made and the action steps that will be taken.
- Schedule times to return phone calls and e-mails. Don't let the phone or e-mail interrupt or dictate your schedule.
- Touch your mail *once*. Answer it, file it or throw it away.
- Organize certain times of the week for projects. For instance, every Tuesday morning plan your message, with no other interruptions. Make Thursday a study day; then work your projects around your schedule.
- Set up the calendar for an entire year. There is no reason why you can't know in September who will be in charge of an event in February.
- Learn how to delegate versus dump. The difference? Delegation involves support, assistance, availability and evaluation. Dumping means you hand it to someone and walk away, letting him fend for himself.
- Read a good book or attend a seminar on time management and administration.
- Seek the advice of others who appear to be organized. Ask them how they do it.

The ultimate goal of every good leader is to be replaced. Our job is to work ourselves out of a job. We need to be continually developing others to take over areas of ministry, while we explore new avenues of ministry ourselves.

For a list of some of our favorite youth ministry training organizations, visit YouthBuilders at www.youthbuilders.com.

CHAPTER 3

Understanding Today's Youth

The adolescent world is changing rapidly; it is virtually impossible to keep up with every new fad and movement within the culture. I (Jim) recently looked out at an audience of several thousand young people after another act of campus violence and said, "I wouldn't want to be your age today. I believe you are living in a more dangerous culture than I did." Yet our goal stays the same—helping students make lifelong, positive decisions about their values and their lifestyle from a Christian viewpoint.

In Jeremiah 29:11, the prophet states, " 'For I know the plans I have for you,' declares the Lord, 'plans to prosper you and not to harm you, plans to give you hope and a future.' " This verse contains one of the most powerful promises in the Bible. When God looks at this generation, what He sees is a generation with hope and a future. God has plans for our young people. This verse also contains two words that are foreign to today's society: "hope" and "future."

What happened on April 20, 1999 changed a generation. At Columbine High School in Littleton, Colorado, two students walked into their school and completely changed the face of a culture. Before turning their guns on themselves, the two teens killed 13 people—12 classmates and 1 teacher—and wounded 23 more. It was the seventh school shooting since October 1997, and there have been more since then. For some it was a random, irrational shooting. For others, it was a sign of the times—a sign of what type of world our young people are growing up in. Considering the statistics accentuates the challenge of ministry in today's culture. In the next 24 hours in America,

- 1,439 teenagers will attempt suicide;
- 2,795 teenage girls will become pregnant;
- 15,006 teenagers will use drugs for the first time;
- 3,506 teenagers will run away;[1]
- 10 children and youth will be killed by firearms;
- 3,544 babies will be born to unwed mothers;
- 2,911 high school students will drop out of school;
- 17,297 students will be suspended from school;
- 1 young person under the age of 25 will die from an HIV-related infection.[2]

The Revolution of Change

The young people we work with today are different from those of any previous generation. They are more knowledgeable, have greater opportunities and are filled with greater potential than people of any other time in history. However, they also deal with more stress, anxiety and pressure than those of any previous generation. Their world is a maze of continuing transformations. In a real sense, today's young people are like ships on the open sea, facing the raging storm of the culture with little to guide or protect them. They are making choices and getting involved in things that have an eternal impact on their lives. Many are doing these things without a safe harbor or a lighthouse to give them guidance. In order to meet the important needs of this generation of young people, we must keep our ears and eyes carefully tuned to the rapidly changing storm of the culture. There is a revolution of change taking place in the youth culture. Youth workers can help make a positive influence amid the frightening changes taking place. Let's take a look at the landscape our students are living in.

The Family Revolution

Although we don't want to sound too pessimistic, the stable underpinning of the family is not just buckling—it is collapsing all around us. Families are experiencing an unprecedented amount of stress and conflict today. Divorce, addictions, lack of father figures, domestic violence and abuse—like never before, all of these issues are influencing the students to whom we minister. Even those young people whose parents are not divorced are not free from anxiety. Every time their parents have an argument, they wonder, *Is my family next?* The adolescent of today has been deeply affected by this family revolution. Consider the following snapshots of today's family:

- 40 percent of kids will go to bed in homes without a father tonight.[3]
- A 1999 study by Barna Research Group discovered that 57 percent of teens live in the same house with both of their natural parents.[4]
- Teens are emotionally closer to their mothers than their fathers—57 percent versus 39 percent.[5]
- In the United States, there is a divorce every 27 seconds—approximately 1 million a year. The fastest growing marital status category is "divorced." The number of divorced adults more than quadrupled from 1970 (4.3 million) to 1994 (17.4 million).[6]
- Unfortunately, the Church has little or no influence. According to Barna Research Group, born-again Christians are slightly more likely than non-Christians to go through a divorce—27 percent versus 24 percent.
- Among people attending mainline Protestant churches, 25 percent have been through a divorce; 29 percent of Baptists and roughly 34 percent of nondenominational Protestant church members have gone through a divorce.[7]
- Half of all children in the United States will witness the breakup of their parents' marriage. Of these, close to half

will also see the breakup of a parent's second marriage.[8]
- Divorce in America is a $28 billion-a-year industry.[9]

Family dysfunction and instability have a direct impact on adolescents today. In the past, the family was stress reducing; now the family is stress *producing.*

Many studies tell us that the greatest place of violence in America is inside the home. It's no secret that the home is no longer a happy place to be in the majority of teenagers' lives. Physical abuse and neglect have become major issues for far too many families. We can't assume that the kids in our churches are doing OK at home.

Much of our youth ministry must be geared at helping families succeed. We firmly believe in a family-based style of youth ministry. The family is, by God's design, the center of life and even of our students' Christian education. Youth workers cannot neglect the fact that one of their major goals must be to help families succeed—to promote the family in the midst of a culture that is ever-changing and even negative toward the family. We can no longer ignore the family within our youth ministries. We need to equip families to be the nucleus of spiritual experience.

The Sexual Revolution

In a 1999 national study conducted by the Center for Disease Control, half of all high school students surveyed reported having sex. The study went on to break down the percentages by grade. The results were alarming.

- 38.6 percent of ninth graders have had sex.
- 46.8 percent of tenth graders have had sex.
- 52.5 percent of high school juniors have had sex.
- 64.9 percent of high school seniors have had sex.[10]

The same study found that of those having sexual intercourse, 8.3

percent had initiated the act by age 13. Equally alarming was the finding that 16.2 percent of all students had experienced sexual relations with more than 4 partners.

Approximately 12 million teenagers are sexually active—by the time current high school students have graduated from high school, 7 out of 10 girls and 8 out of 10 boys will have had sexual intercourse. What are the consequences of all this sexual activity?

- The suicide rate among teenage mothers is 10 times that of the general population.
- There are more than 1 million teenage girls who become pregnant in the United States every year—that's 10 percent of all young women ages 15 to 19, and approximately 19 percent of young women who have sexual intercourse.
- 30 percent of teenage pregnancies end in abortion.
- There are 3 million new adolescent cases of sexually transmitted diseases occurring every year (that's approximately 1 of every 4 sexually experienced teens).[11]

Who says there is not a price that is paid in the sexual revolution? While the Puritans did not want anyone to know that they had sexual feelings, this generation is ashamed if it does not openly express its sexual feelings. There is an overwhelming sexual barrage from almost every aspect of our society. Although this is not new, its impact is growing steadily.

The Church must take a strong stand for morality. In a world of instant intimacy, the Church must teach and live the values of commitment and fidelity taught in the Scriptures. Because sex is a dominant issue in the minds of young people, the Church can no longer remain silent. We must let our kids understand that God is not disgusted by sex! He cares about their sexuality. God created sex, and within His biblical guidelines He sees it as good. It's time for the Church to provide a healthy view of sexuality and teach honor and respect for relationships with the opposite sex. (Chapter 20 discusses the issue of sex and sexuality in depth.)

The Media Revolution

The influence of today's media is alarming. Modern television holds teenagers' attention through sophisticated technology and fast-paced visual images. Visual stimulation is a high to the mind similar to that of a chemical high. Today a young person's morals, values and thought processes are molded as much by the media as by relationships. The media is profoundly affecting our society.

Young people today are constantly being bombarded with messages and images from the media. Students aged 12 to 17 watch an average of 22 hours of television per week. By the time the average student graduates from high school, he or she will have watched 23,000 hours of television, as compared to 11,000 hours spent in the classroom.[12]

What about music? Students listen to music an average of over two hours a day during the weekdays and over five hours a day on the weekends. The question begs to be asked—who is educating and influencing our students?

We need to accept the fact that the media is not neutral. Every television show, movie or lyric carries a message from its creator. Robert Pittam, the former president and CEO of MTV, put it this way: "Early on, we made a key decision that we would be the voice of young America. We were building more than a channel. We were building a culture."[13]

The power of the media is seen in the messages it carries. Advertising tells us that our life is in need of something. If only we had a certain product, life would be more fulfilling. Movies and television give us windows into what life really should be like. Music moves its listeners, challenging their values and philosophies about what matters in life. In the midst of all these media messages, positive models of what Christianity is all about are rarely found.

Is all media evil? Just as most things in this world, it can be used for good as well as evil. Youth workers have two important roles to play in helping students make good media choices. First, they must be willing to keep up with the changes in order to know what is influencing the people in their own ministry and community. To think that a church's weekly one to four hours of influence is overpowering the media's 30-plus hours is to be naive. Second, youth workers must help students learn how to view the media with discernment. Since young people are and will continue to be influenced by the media, a good youth ministry program will help them learn to filter what comes into their lives. We must teach them that they have a choice; they do not have to be unduly influenced by the media.

The Technological Revolution

Technology is the main source of influence and connection in the lives of this generation of youth. By the year 2005 over 1 billion users will be connected to the Internet.[14] This generation of students uses the Internet an average of 8.5 hours a week for chatting and e-mail, compared to 1.8 hours spent for schoolwork.[15] Today, an estimated 18.8 million kids under the age of 18 have access to home computers.[16] According to Barna Research Group, 60 percent of teens use the Internet. The following are the most common uses among adolescent Internet users:

- Finding information—56 percent
- Checking out new music or video releases—51 percent
- Participating in a chat room or other online discussion—51 percent (with teens 13 and 14 most likely to participate)
- Making new friends—34 percent (most common among girls)
- Playing video games—33 percent
- Keeping up existing relationships—28 percent[17]

Technology has also brought a host of images into our homes. According to Enough is Enough, an advocacy group against pornography, a recent survey found that 63 percent of teenagers unintentionally found pornography on the Internet. As of March 1998, there were 100,000 commercial pornographic websites—with an estimated 200 new sites added *every day*.[18] Our country now has over 20,000 outlets selling prosecutable, hard-core pornography. The largest consumer group of pornographic material in this country is adolescent boys 12 to 17.[19]

With the increased use of the Internet, what we thought would bring about the incredible isolation of interpersonal relationships has done just the opposite: it has created a cyber reality in which students can assume whatever identity they want within that reality, assuming any personality they wish and fitting in wherever they want to fit in.

A dangerous product of cyber reality is the development of cyber romances. These romances often occur between people who have assumed chosen identities and met online, allowing teens to date before they even meet each other in person. Oftentimes these cyber romances are incredibly emotionally charged and often sexually oriented. There have been far too many cases in which students have begun a cyber romance only to find out that they have been interacting with an adult sexual predator.

The Internet, just as all other forms of media, is not all evil. There are many wonderfully positive aspects of the Web. The Internet has begun to evolve into a great tool for ministry. However, in youth ministry we need to help students understand the power of the Internet and encourage them to use it responsibly.

Anger and Violence Revolution

One of the most disturbing revolutions in current youth culture is the trend of rising anger and violence among teenagers. The past few years have seen scores of incidents occurring across America's school campuses. From students who are made to feel like outcasts to those seeking violent revenge—anger and violence have increased with ferocious intensity on campuses and in communities.

How bad is it? According to a study by the American Psychological Association, every year nearly 1 million students in the United States took guns to school—resulting in 1 in 12 high school students being threatened or injured with a weapon each year.[20] One in five high school students say they personally know a student who's brought a gun to school. Of those, only 83 percent ever reported it. Similarly, a third of students have heard a classmate at their school threaten to kill someone, with 78 percent choosing to do nothing about it.[21] In just the past few years the homicide rate among 14- to 17-year-olds has increased 165 percent; for 18- to 24-year-olds the rate has increased 65 percent. These increases have now placed youth between the ages of 12 and 24 at the highest risk of being a victim of violence.[22]

Factors Leading to Teen Violence

The question being asked today is, What has caused this generation to seek violence as an expression more than any other generation before? The answer is a complex one. There are many factors that contribute to the trend of anger and violence that we see across the country. The following are just a few:

- The need for attention or respect
- Constantly being degraded or attacked verbally
- Feelings of low self-worth/self-image
- Early childhood abuse or neglect, leaving the student feeling powerless or a lack of control
- Peer influence toward violent acts
- Witnessing acts of violence at home, in the community or in the media[23]

> By the age of 18, the typical American will see 40,000 dramatized murders.[24]

Warning Signs of Teen Violence

As these random acts of violence seem to be increasing, there are common warning signs that we as youth workers must be sensitive to in our students. If there is one thing that we have learned from the school shootings of the past few years it is that no community and no school are immune to the threat of violence. The following are a sampling of warning signs that should at least alert us to the possibility of violence:

- Has a history of tantrums or uncontrollable angry outbursts
- Uses abusive language or calls people names
- Makes violent threats when angry
- Has brought a weapon to school
- Has serious disciplinary problems at school or in the community
- Abuses drugs, alcohol or other substances
- Has few or no close friends
- Is preoccupied with weapons or explosives
- Has been suspended or expelled from school
- Is cruel to animals
- Has little or no supervision and support from parents or a caring adult
- Has witnessed or been a victim of abuse or neglect
- Has been bullied and/or bullies or intimidates other kids
- Prefers TV shows, movies or music with violent themes
- Is involved with a gang or an antisocial group
- Is depressed or has significant mood swings
- Has threatened or attempted suicide[25]
- Prefers reading materials dealing with violent themes, rituals and abuse
- Reflects anger, frustration and the dark side of life in school essays or writing projects
- Tends to blame others for difficulties and problems caused by him- or herself

Teen violence is not just an issue for schools or for our homes; it is an issue for our churches as well. If we are to help families succeed, we need to be ready to address the issue and offer support to families. Students and parents are scared. They are looking for answers. We need to help students and families work through the process of dealing with anger and conflict resolution. We must equip them with practical ways in which to deal with the emotions and conflicts that arise in life.

Making a Difference

Given the reality of the influence and transformation of our culture, many youth workers feel paralyzed, asking "What can I do in my little church?" That was precisely the feelings of the Israelites when they encountered the Philistines and particularly Goliath. The Israelites were paralyzed with fear. The young shepherd boy David came out to the battle, at his father's request, to bring supplies to his older brothers. When David observed Goliath mocking the people of Israel and the living God, he decided to do something about it. Armed with five smooth stones, a sling and his faith in the living God, he killed the giant Goliath. While everyone else's philosophy was, *He is so big I can't win,* David's belief was, *My God is so big I can't miss!* With God's help, David prevailed. We look at the realities of the culture and often see them as too big to overcome. Yet in actuality, with God's help we can make a difference that lasts for eternity.

What can we do? For starters we can begin to help students experience life on a different level. Through our ministries—moreover through our relationships with students—we can slay the giant of the influence of our current times. We believe we can develop a ministry with long-lasting results, as seen in the next chapter.

CHAPTER 4

Developing a Ministry That Lasts

It would be easy for us to walk away from the previous chapter feeling defeated. Much like the Israelites viewed Goliath, we seem to be faced with a task that is beyond our influence—helping students navigate the seas of the current culture. The Israelites chose to back down from the battle, hoping help would come. David, however, had a different plan. With the help of God, he knew that there was nothing that could stand in the way of victory, not even Goliath. The same choice is ours to make. Will we choose to stand by, hoping help will come, or will we echo the attitude of David and believe, *My God is so big I can't miss!*?

As youth workers, we have an advantage. There is something that we possess that current culture cannot defeat. It's not found in programs; our programming will not enamor the students of this culture. They can stay at home and watch programming on television that is 100 times better. However, as our society continues to move toward becoming more impersonal, our advantage is in the relationships we can build with students. The following are essential ingredients for developing life-transforming relationships that will help students navigate the current times. We *can* make a difference—with God's help.

Acceptance

Students today are asking themselves: *Who am I? Who do I want to be?* At the heart of these questions is the desire for acceptance. They are bombarded with messages that tell them that worth and acceptance are given conditionally—that you have value *if* . . . , and you are accepted *if* . . . Nothing can be further from the truth. One of the greatest gifts we can ever give students is the gift of unconditional, loving acceptance.

God's love is based on who we are and not what we do. His acceptance is based purely on the fact that we are His precious creation—nothing more, nothing less. When we communicate that type of acceptance to our students, we are communicating the unconditional love that Jesus has for all of us.

Acceptance is shown in remembering names; in a smile and a word of encouragement; when we remember a prayer request, pray about it and care enough to check back in with that student. Acceptance is shown in taking the time and having the willingness to listen to students pour out their hearts in honesty; in giving value to a student who may have never seen his or her value in the eyes of God.

Our youth ministries should foster an environment of honesty and transparency where even doubts are accepted. We often make the mistake of pressuring kids into conformity and of not respecting their unbelief. Accepting, yet not agreeing, with young people's unbelief can be a very positive witnessing tool.

AFFIRMATION

Students are starved for affirmation and encouragement. If the truth be known, we all are. Often we rise or fall to the level to which we are encouraged. But what does affirmation look like? How can we give our students life-altering affirmation, rather than just an emotional shot in the arm?

Often affirmation is based on how students look or how they perform on the field, on the court or in their classroom. But what happens if they don't score the winning touchdown? What happens if they don't measure up physically to others around them? What happens if they fall short of making the grade? Is their worth wrapped up in those things? Do we unwittingly wrap their worth to God and us in temporal things?

There will always be someone better looking, someone with better grades or someone who is a better athlete. What do they do when they realize that?

True affirmation is seeing what God sees and what He is doing in their lives—and expressing it to them. The art of affirmation is catching our students doing something right and celebrating with them. It is looking for those opportunities to affirm character and growth in Christ. It is looking for opportunities to point out what God is doing and who He is molding them to be. It is affirming the eternal transformation in their lives.

Affirmation is seeing what God sees and what He is doing in the lives of students. It's seeing who He is developing and transforming them to be and expressing it to them. We need to affirm our students publicly, privately and perpetually!

Attention

Young people are also desperate for attention, for anyone to notice and give them value and significance. To give students our attention means giving them time and touch.

Love is spelled T-I-M-E. Your very presence in students' lives communicates care and concern for them. All those hours spent at sporting events, dance recitals, community events and even junior high band recitals—all communicate that we care about the lives of the students we minister to. Spending time with students is like making a deposit into the bank account; the more time spent, the greater the balance grows. There will come a time, however, when we will need to make a withdrawal on that account: sharing a hard truth, saying the tough thing, challenging students about where they are going in life or in their journey with Jesus. But if we haven't invested anything, there's no account balance from which to minister.

We also need to touch students—relationally, as well as appropriate physical touch. Relational touch comes as we take the time to do the small things that students remember. Phone calls, notes and e-mail are all ways of staying relationally connected with students. Anything that shows personal touch in the life of a student communicates value. We also need appropriate physical touch within our ministry to students—a handshake, a high five or an appropriate hug communicates a love and concern that students are desperate for.

Linda was a heavyset, unpopular, melancholy eleventh grader who was on the fringe of our youth group. She was quiet, shy and unresponsive, and her home life was less than desirable. One day I (Jim) went up to her and told her how much I appreciated her presence in our youth group. I then felt by her response that it was okay to give her a hug. It was an awkward hug but nevertheless a hug. At a senior dinner a year and a half later we were sharing important youth group events. Linda stood and, with tears in her eyes, shared with the group that the time she felt loved and cared for the most was when I hugged her. Frankly, I had forgotten all about this experience until she brought it up.

Modeling

Students are searching for role models. They are looking for people they can pattern their lives after. From dress and language to values—they are looking to musicians, athletes, actors and other celebrities to see what their lives should be like. Students need God-honoring role models and mentors who will invest in their lives and point them in the right direction.

Our calling in youth ministry today is to provide a working model of what the Christian life looks like in the real world. More than hearing about Christianity, students need us to come alongside them and daily live out our Christianity, to show them what it looks like in real life.

Discipleship is not a program; it's a modeled relationship with Jesus. Young people don't need adults who act like kids; they need adults who care about them and open their lives to them to see Christianity at work. They may never remember the events you planned, but they will always remember you. Students are watching our lives—what will they see?

Hope and Healing

There is an incredible amount of pain, burden and brokenness in the lives of kids today. Disrupted homes, fear, loss, loneliness, disappointment and guilt seem to be the norm for students today. A youth ministry that has lasting impact is one that gives hurting students hope and healing for their broken lives.

Mindy was in junior high when I (Mike) met her. It was at summer camp after a seminar on suicide that she stopped me and asked if she could talk. The story she told me left me speechless. She had seriously contemplated suicide earlier in the summer and desperately needed some hope. Years ago, she had been a victim of abuse by a family member, and I could tell that it still haunted her. We talked for hours that weekend. We talked about God, the abuse and where she saw hope for herself. One night at camp, while the speaker was giving an invitation for commitment, he had the youth leaders line up in front of the platform. He said that if anyone needed hope and needed a deeper relationship with Jesus, they should come to their youth leader. Mindy was the first one out of her seat. She ran forward and buried her face in my chest and began to cry.

The days ahead weren't easy. She still struggled to deal with the abuse, wondering why God allowed it to happen and if there was any reason for it. Three years later, she was on a mission trip to Guatemala with our group. We were going to be in public schools throughout Guatemala, spending half the day in classes and the other half presenting an assembly that shared the truth of the gospel. In every school we had a different person sharing about his or her faith. At our first school, in Guatemala City, Mindy was chosen to share her story. As she was getting ready to stand in front of the entire school, I told her, "Mindy, God is going to use you in incredible ways if you allow Him to."

As Mindy finished telling her story of the abuse and the hope she found in Christ, dozens of girls surrounded her. She had struck a chord with those girls in a deep way. Everyone of them had experienced some form of abuse and were looking for what Mindy had: hope and healing. Mindy is now attending a local Christian college and God has done an amazing work in her life. She has a ministry to sexually abused girls in our youth ministry, as well as on her campus. God took a broken, fragmented life and made it whole again.

Youth workers can literally be the conduits of God's healing grace in the lives of students. But they need us to be the hands and voice of Jesus in their lives, helping them to experience and receive forgiveness, healing and hope.

Responsibility

Students need to know that we believe in them and see their God-given potential. When we take the time to notice and develop students' potential, they discover their value and significance. Unfortunately, we are often the ones who stand in the way.

God has placed within students certain gifts and talents that need to be unlocked for His glory. We should strive to develop opportunities and responsibilities that can help them develop their gifts and talents to serve God. It begins with us looking beneath the surface, beyond what is there, to what could be.

Jesus was the master of seeing beneath the surface. Take Simon Peter for example. In John 1:42 when Jesus met Simon, He said " 'You are Simon son of John. You will be called Cephas' (which, when translated, is Peter)." Most of Peter's friends and family must have laughed. In the Aramaic, "Peter" would be translated as "a rock." No one would have believed that one day this fisherman would be the leader of the Church in Jerusalem. Jesus looked beyond Peter's problems, personality quirks and sin. Jesus saw Peter not only for who he was but also for what be could become. Even three years later when Peter so blatantly denied Jesus, Jesus forgave him and put him in charge of the sheep (see John 21:15-17). Simon became what Jesus knew he could become. Who are the Simon Peters in your life? What positive steps are you taking to believe in them and help develop their God-given potential?

In addition to seeing what lies just beneath the surface, we need to be proactive in creating hands-on responsibilities for students that will allow them to develop their gifts. Gift-developing responsibilities have four qualities.

1. **They are *meaningful.*** Give them roles and responsibilities that are truly meaningful to the ministry as a whole. More than cheap labor, students deserve roles that have meaning and purpose.
2. **They are *gift appropriate.*** Provide roles that express and develop individual spiritual gifts. Preaching, encouragement, leadership, administration and mercy gifts are just a few examples of gifts that need to be developed and expressed.[1]
3. **They are *timely.*** There needs to be a sense of urgency to their roles. Responsibilities need to be essential for the running and health of the ministry. Assign roles and responsibilities that students can look at and say, "We really need to pull through with this. This is important to *our* ministry."
4. **They are *challenging.*** The responsibilities that we give our students should not be so hard that they give up yet not so easy that they can do it without relying on God's strength and power.

COMMUNITY

Students long to belong to something—a sense of community. Within the body of Christ, students can encounter a community that is radically different from what they have ever encountered before. They need to walk away from our youth ministries and say, "That was totally different that I ever expected, and I want that in my life!" Students may be attracted to our programs, but lasting life change comes when they are having their needs met—something that can happen powerfully in a community that is focused on Jesus.

Students today don't need us to imitate the world in order to attract them; they need something far deeper—a community that has substance. It has been said that this generation of young people is more spiritually hungry and sensitive than any other preceding generation. The incredible growth of worship in youth ministry in the past few years is evidence of this need for substance. Students are looking to connect with the almighty God in a personal and meaningful way. Our call as youth workers today is to help foster an environment where true Christian community exists—with hallmarks of honesty, transparency and genuineness.

Authentic Encounters with God

Recently, after speaking at a youth event in Atlanta on the issue of authentically seeking God, a student came to me (Mike) and said, "I never thought it was okay to be real with God. I thought God was like a big policeman in the sky waiting for me to make a mistake. Now I want to know God, not just know about Him!"

Students need authentic encounters with the true God of Scripture. What has been offered is all too often something less. They ask questions, struggling to understand who God is and what it means to be a passionate follower of Christ. Many of us have failed, giving them the same tired answers they have heard for years. Rather than showing students the massive reality of God, we have given them a mere glimpse of God. After feeding them this fragmented view of God, we somehow wonder why their faith can be shallow, lacking real obedience to Him.

Our students need to encounter God in a fresh way. They need to see and understand the character of who God is and how that impacts their everyday lives. Their morality and Christianity must be founded, not on rules and regulations, but on who God is. As followers of Christ, we know that we shouldn't steal, cheat and lie—not simply because those things are bad but because we know that being a Christian means being transformed into the likeness of Christ (see Romans 8:29; 1 Corinthians 15:49; 2 Corinthians 3:18).

Are we offering the almighty creator of the universe to our students, or the servant god whom we call when we need Him to do something for us? We are called to give students an authentic view of God in all His majesty, mercy, love, forgiveness, judgment and holiness. Take that seriously and guide them into authentic encounters with God; they will never be the same.

Spiritual Challenge

What many teenagers lack is a moral compass, something to guide their lives. Our calling in youth ministry is to help students be transformed more into the likeness of Christ. The unfortunate fact is that we often lose sight of that goal. We get so caught up in the programming or in the details of the ministry that we miss the very purpose and end result of youth ministry: to see our students become lifelong, passionate seekers and followers for the glory of the living God. Sadly enough, we build great relationships, but we sometimes forget to turn the spiritual corner with our students.

What they truly need from us is spiritual challenge. They need us to be encouragers, mentors and guides for them on their spiritual journey. What they need to successfully make that journey are guides and mentors who are seeking God themselves. It is out of the overflow of our own lives that we will minister to youth. It comes from being in touch with their lives, spending the time necessary to build relationships. It comes from taking the opportunity to speak into their lives as we walk together, challenging them in areas where they need to be made more like Christ. It's saying, "I will walk with you because I love you and believe in all that God has in store for you!"

The choice is ours to make. We can stand by like the Israelites before their enemy Goliath and say, "He is so big I can't win." Or we can echo the heart of David and say, "My God is so big I can't miss!" We truly can make a difference in the lives of young people.

CHAPTER 5

Adolescent Development

It's been said that the only thing normal about adolescent development is that there are very few norms. Just when you think you have the wonderful world of teenagers figured out, you meet one who doesn't fit the pattern. Stephanie, a 14-year-old girl, is four feet eight inches tall, weighs 86 pounds and measures 26-24-26. Her best friend, Katie, also 14, is five feet eight inches tall, weighs 125 pounds and measures 34-26-34. Brian, a friend of Katie, started shaving last week, while his best friend, Trevor, is still intently gazing in the mirror hoping to find even a remote sign of facial hair. At age 14, Brandon was the most serious Bible scholar in the entire church. He was so together that you considered firing the senior pastor and hiring Brandon. Now at age 16 he seldom comes to church and has lost complete interest in the youth ministry.

Anyone who spends much time with teenagers has often asked, "Why do they act the way they do?" Unfortunately, most youth workers, teachers and parents have forgotten the changing developmental world of the adolescent. *Adolescence is a time of transition and change.* It is very easy as adults to simply forget what it was like to be a teenager.

Teenagers move rapidly from childhood to adulthood. Not only their bodies but also their minds, emotions, friendships—even their faith—are making major transitions. Most of the decisions teenagers face today are over issues that we seldom had to deal with at their age. They are forced to grow up too fast and too soon, and their decisions may impact them for the rest of their lives. It's no wonder that many adolescents struggle during these teenage years. Each day brings them a new round of unexpected and sometimes bewildering changes. The chemical makeup of our students changes almost daily, and students can be significantly different from week to week.

Many youth workers do an excellent job of working with students, but they could do an even better job if they took the time to understand the important areas of adolescent development.

Physical Development: Body Under Construction

The advance of puberty carries with it the difficulty of coping with all the physical changes that are occurring. The adolescent's body grows in rapid spurts and then slows and finally stops growing. Even muscles and bones are growing at an uneven rate. Coordination problems sometimes exist. Casey was the outstanding leader in the junior high group. During the summer between junior high and high school Casey grew seven inches taller. He now slouches in class and has a bored look on his face. Is it a spiritual problem? Probably not. Casey is tired; the other aspects of development haven't caught up with his bodily growth spurt.

Students are very much aware of the physiological changes taking place in their lives, becoming totally self-absorbed in the transformations happening regularly within their bodies. You and I may know that the normal skin problems of adolescence will eventually disappear and be forgotten, but try explaining that to a 15-year-old who refuses to come to the youth ministry because of acne on her chin, forehead and nose.

Both young men and young women are extremely aware of their sexual development. Hair is growing where once only skin lived. The size and shape of their sexual organs are very important to most teenagers. After a talk I (Jim) gave at a conference center years ago, a beautiful young girl came to me after the talk and asked to talk to me in private. She was sobbing uncontrollably. I wondered what horrible event had happened in her life. Finally she gained her composure and shared with me what she had never shared with anyone else: "I'm frightened. You see, I have one breast that is larger than the other." Not understanding adolescent physical development and having only brothers in my home, I had absolutely no idea what to say. Finally I asked her if she would be willing to tell her trauma to my wife. When she told Cathy the story, Cathy smiled and explained to her that this problem was extremely common and assured her in a short amount of time that everything would be normal again. The young girl left jubilant!

Another very important matter in physical development to remember is that teenagers have an extreme concern that their physical appearance measures up to the cultural norm. As much as kids want to be different from their parents, they do not want their physical appearance to be dissimilar from their peers. The implication for our youth ministry is that students are painfully aware of the physical changes inside their bodies, as well as their outer appearances. We can help them begin to wade through the emotional minefield by helping them understand that their bodies are the temple of God, and at the same time their bodies reflect the wonderful truth of Psalm 139:13-18:

> For you created my inmost being; you knit me together in my mother's womb. I praise you because I am fearfully and wonderfully made; your works are wonderful, I know that full well. My frame was not hidden from you when I was made in the secret place. When I was woven together in the depths of the earth, your eyes saw my unformed body. All the days ordained for me were written in your book before one of them came to be. How precious to me are your thoughts, O God! How vast is the sum of them! Were I to count them, they would outnumber the grains of sand.

In these words of the psalmist we are reminded that God is our master creator and that we are an original masterpiece in His eyes. He is the creator of our bodies. He formed us in our mother's womb. As students go through these physical changes, they need to anchor their hearts in the fact that God is forming them into the person He desires for them to be. They are in process. God isn't finished with His original masterpiece yet; He is still molding them into finished products.

Social Development: "Everybody's Doing It"

Adolescents are social by their very nature. It is during the teenage years that their social lives begin to blossom and develop, often becoming the most important area of their lives.

The need for acceptance and belonging drives some young people into lives of moral compromise. Unfortunately, the desire to belong can sometimes be greater than the desire to live a life of noncompromise. So strong is the desire to belong that students will fall into temptation and influences that seem like a step backward in their faith. They view the compromise as well worth it if the end result is that their social group will accept them. If we are to effectively minister to our students, we must understand their social world and its influence.

It is important to note that today's campuses, and often our own youth ministries, are broken up into *social groupings*. The average high school is a maze of social groupings within the student body. From athletes to intellectuals, from band members to computer techies, from skaters to other myriad of social groupings—students live and move in social groups. This is also where the majority of students are the most influenced. No longer is there just one popular crowd, with the rest outside looking in. Today, within each of these social groupings there are people who are the leaders and influencers, while the others are followers.

Ever hear the response "Everybody's doing it" or "Everyone's going to be there"? Is it true that *everyone* does that? Is it true that *everyone* is going to be there? What is meant is that everyone who is of influence in that young teens' world or social group is involved in or values this or that or is going to be at this or that happening. Sociologists tell us that kids build their world and values around these social groupings and that their most important influence comes from a still smaller, more intimate group of two or three best friends. It is no secret that you become like the people you spend the most time with—even Paul warned that "bad company corrupts good character" (1 Corinthians 15:33).

The implications for youth ministry in this area of social development are that we not only need to be a friend to students but also to understand the social friendship groupings at their schools and within our own youth ministry. As youth workers we must do all we can to help unify the different social groups into one community—the Body of Christ. We will also need to develop our student leadership out of a variety of social groups because students from the same social group will tend to have a greater influence on their own group. Although we cannot tear down the strong groupings that make up the social landscape, we must strive to do everything we can to help students see that there is life beyond their own small sphere of influence. We should help students see their sphere of social influence as a mission field.

Programming and contact ministry should be influenced by the social groupings of students. Investigate where your students hang out and what they like to do. Know where to be and when to be there in order to meet them on their territory. Knowing what activities your students enjoy, you will also be able to plan more effective events. Take the time to learn the whats and wheres of your students.

Emotional Development: The Roller Coaster of Extremes

Until Alyssa turned 13, she seemed to be a joyful, positive young girl. Then, seemingly overnight, on her 13th birthday she changed. Her parents told me (Jim), "Alyssa has no self-control; she lives her life in extremes. Sometimes she's the loving daughter we've always known, and the very next minute she's sobbing uncontrollably for no good reason at all."

Few young people come out of adolescence without a time of intense emotional responses. For many teenagers this period of life can be summarized by an increase in chaotic extremes and contradictory, intense inner feelings. Emotions like anxiety, worry, anger, inferiority, passion and fear can occur with ferocious intensity.

Sometimes if we are not careful, youth workers will overlook the strong emotions of teenagers and fail to channel those emotions. In a time of emotional intensity and instability, teenagers need role models of emotional stability and consistency. An effective youth worker should not be frustrated by the emotional swings of youth. We need to listen to their hurts and feelings because they are real, but we also need to help balance out their tendency toward emotionalism. There are some youth leaders who believe that in order for students to feel close to God, the students need to be worked into an intensely emotional state on a weekly basis. The danger we face is reducing the Christian journey to a series of emotional experiences needed to remain intimate with God. Students need to express an emotional side to their faith—it's a part of who God has created them to be. However, they need to experience God in other less volatile realms as well, having their faith anchored beyond the emotional, which can be easily manipulated.

Intellectual Development: Exploring the Mind

One of the greatest areas of change from preadolescence to adulthood is in the area of cognitive, or intellectual, development. The people in your youth group are moving from concrete thinking to a more abstract way of thinking. The students in your group who are always asking "Why?" (or at times even seem argumentative) are testing their new intellectual development in the world of abstract thinking.

During this stage adolescents tend to be curious, adventuresome, open to new ideas, inventive and, often, a bit idealistic. Jean Piaget, the father of cognitive development, defines these two stages as concrete operations (between 7 and 12 years) and formal, or abstract, operations (after age 12).

This new period of intellectual development has important implications for the Church because kids are beginning to ask themselves questions like, *Who am I? Who do I want to be? What is true and real in life?* and *What is life all about, anyway?* In elementary school, teachers can get by with just talking to their students. However, in the adolescent years, discussion becomes a necessity for good learning. Youth ministry is a time of enabling the students to learn on their own. We must *ask* rather than *tell.* It's a time to unleash creativity and develop leadership. Students learn best when they talk and discover truth for themselves, not when we give them easy answers.

One of the best youth ministry speakers I (Jim) know asked me to evaluate and consult with him about his youth ministry. I watched him deliver an excellent message to his students. After the meeting he shared his concern that he was losing numbers in his group. My response was that his speaking was fine for a younger group, but he never gave high school students the opportunity to interact and dialogue. A spoon-fed discipleship program or a message without interaction will leave the students empty. In order to stimulate their newfound abstract thinking, we must find a Christian education approach that involves the students, isn't afraid to ask questions and even accepts some differences of opinion. (See chapter 19 for more information on creative teaching.)

Faith Development: "Who Is God and Where Does He Fit into My Life?"

There is much research today addressing the issue of faith development. James Fowler's *Stages of Faith* is probably the foundational work in this area. Oversimplifying Fowler's six stages can be misleading, yet it may be important to do so in order to help youth workers grasp at what stage of faith development their students may be involved.

Fowler's Stages of Faith

Stage One—Intuitive

At this stage students have simply taken on their parents' faith. They believe what their parents believe because their parents believe it.

Stage Two—Literal

The literal stage moves students from only their parents' faith to their extended family and perhaps their church's faith. They believe what they believe because their primary influencers in their world believe it.

Stage Three—Conventional

This is still an unowned faith. The conventional stage is the church or denomination's faith. Students have still not personalized their faith. This is often the stage for students entering junior high youth ministries.

Stage Four—Individual

Students' faith becomes their own. They have moved outside the faith of the significant people in their lives. However, it is usually very close to the faith of their family. It is a simplistic yet serious commitment.

Stage Five—Consolidating

The consolidating stage is relatively complex and reflective and students are aware of paradoxes. This stage of faith does not shatter at the apparent suffering and evil in the world, unanswered prayer, etc. A consistent commitment has developed.

Stage Six—Universalizing

This is a more complex stage. Students have developed a world vision. They have a mission in life. Their life, faith and call from God make sense. Their faith impacts the way they see the world and others and how they live their daily lives.[1]

We live in an instant society, one in which we tend to want instant spiritual maturity. This is definitely not God's plan. Faith develops in stages. Sanctification is a lifelong process. Our goal in youth ministry should be to help young people own their faith and enable them to grow in Christian maturity. Just as their physical development comes at different stages, so too does their intellectual development. Because of this, we must present faith to students by using both concrete and abstract methods. Young people need spiritual experiences that will give them the opportunity to explore the Christian life, both concretely and abstractly.

Parents and significant adults play an important role in the faith development of adolescents. We can no longer allow the Church and the family to assume that their tasks are mutually exclusive. The youth worker's role as an equipper must focus on parents as well as teenagers because both live in a relationship together. In a society that continues to put stress on the traditional family structure, the youth worker must remain committed to recapture the family as the context in which faith is primarily formed. Given the reality of faith development, what does it mean in practical terms for the youth worker?

Lead Students to Experiential Faith

A firsthand faith—one that is experienced and is not just their parents' faith—is essential. Students need to touch, feel and handle the Christian life. That is why mission and service projects are so necessary in youth ministry. Through experiences like these, students can gain faith through personal, practical involvement. When teaching, we also need to use terms that are understandable and can be practiced. When we speak and teach, we need to give them clear instruction and application for living the Christian life.

Help Students Learn to Integrate Their Faith into Their Daily Lives

Many adolescents have great difficulty relating their spiritual life with the other important areas of their life, such as home, school, work, relationships and dating. It seems as if their spiritual life has no bearing on how they live their lives. It's as if every area has been compartmentalized; i.e., this is my life at home, this is my life at school, this is my life at church. One of our main callings in ministry should be to help students see that their faith *is* their life, in its entirety. To follow Christ is to follow Him with every part of our lives. Through our teaching, modeling, interaction and conversations, students must see the Christian journey as the major theme and framework for their lives.

Help Students Act on Their Natural Spiritual Interest

Because their moral, intellectual and faith developments are in a state of constant change, we sometimes wrongly suppose that there is no interest in spiritual things. Even though there is a great deal of doubt and even lifestyle inconsistency, adolescents today are very interested in spirituality and spiritual things. Many are disillusioned with the world, modernity and the temporary. Many are looking for something more, something transcendent. Our goal is to facilitate movement from an unowned faith to an owned one that brings maturity and growth in Jesus Christ. In fact, one of the reasons we stay in youth ministry is because we believe that when adolescents are given the right kind of opportunities, they will make lifelong decisions to be lovers of God and passionate followers of Jesus Christ—in a stronger manner than any other age group.

CHAPTER 6

FAMILY-BASED YOUTH MINISTRY

I (Jim) never thought I would publicly say this, but I actually miss one of the rowdiest and most hyperactive students I have ever worked with. Danny could not sit still; he interrupted almost every lesson I ever gave while he was in our ministry. His foot was tapping at all times, he talked loudly, and he talked fast. He was a bundle of energy. His family did not attend our church, so I reluctantly became Danny's personal chauffeur after meetings. It never failed that as the group was dispersing to head for home, Danny would come bouncing up to me and ask me for a ride. He couldn't even sit still in my car. He fidgeted and talked during the entire ride to his house.

One evening after attending a seminar on family ministry, I decided that it was time to meet Danny's parents. When we pulled up to Danny's house that night, I asked Danny if I could meet his parents. He said sure and ran inside (Danny never walked), leaving me at the door. Finally his mother came to the door and invited me in. She was a beautiful woman who practiced true Southern hospitality. For some reason I couldn't put Danny's hyperactivity together with his mother's slow, calm spirit. His mother then called for her husband, Dan, to come out of the back room to meet the youth pastor. Literally bouncing out of the back room came Dan, pumping my hand and talking even louder and faster than Danny. I couldn't help but smile and think, *So that's where Danny gets it from.*

Sometimes we in youth ministry forget that our students have parents and that they are part of a family system. Their values, beliefs and actions are all intertwined with their family. Family heredity and environment play the most significant roles in who we are and who we are becoming. Because of this truth, youth workers are involved in family ministry whether it is in their job description or not. Youth workers can no longer afford to compartmentalize their ministry to work only with the students. The family plays too much of an important role in the spiritual, mental, emotional and physical development of students to just ignore it. If we are to be successful with our students over the long term, we need to be able to impact and minister to the family as a whole. One of the healthiest paradigm shifts in the last 20 years of youth work is into the area of family-based youth ministry.

It is obvious that today's family is caught in incredible turmoil. The nuclear family—mom, dad and child(ren)—is now a minority in the United States. Parents are no longer secure about their parenting ability. They are often paralyzed with fear, and because of this fear, they quit parenting altogether. Instead of preparing for this new world of adolescence, they give up and let their children guide themselves. You don't need to look very far in your ministry to see exactly what we're talking about.

No matter what a student's family situation is like, you can never take the place of the parent. Don't even try. Your task is to support and strengthen the *existing* family unit. Our response as youth workers needs to be timely and proactive. Ministering to the family unit is not something that should be left to someone else or a good idea that we'll get to someday. Most youth workers believe that family ministry should be a priority, but the fact is that for many ministries it is just one more thing added to the already too long list of good ideas to get to.

The reality is that in order to have long-term success and effectiveness in ministry, we cannot neglect the family unit. We as youth workers can have an incredible influence and impact in the lives of our students. However, we must realize our impact pales in comparison to the influence of their families. After our combined 40-plus years of youth ministry experience we must admit that many of the students who were the strongest and most vibrant in their faith were nurtured and mentored not by the youth ministry, but by their families. One of the greatest common denominators in the long-term development of a loving, intimate relationship with Jesus is not the quality of our programming; it is the influence and nurture of the family. We in youth ministry would do well to understand and heed that truth.

The Needs

If we want to be serious about our commitment to minister to the family, it will take proactive vision and planning. It may even necessitate a shift in philosophy. For most of us it will not mean increasing programs but rather rethinking how we program and what is the priority in our program. We must look toward helping families succeed. There are four main needs that we should address in ministering to families.

Informing Parents and Families

Parents are in need of accurate, available and advance information concerning the ministry and events. We cannot assume that students are passing on important information to their parents. One of the main complaints that parents have about youth workers in their church is in the area of communication and keeping them informed. They want to know the direction of the ministry, as well as the details of events. I've (Jim) been asked numerous times, "Why didn't we know that the money was due yesterday?"

I would reply, "I sent a letter to your daughter and reminded the entire ministry every time we were together for the last month."

More often than not, the response would be, "Well, I'm sorry, but I never heard about it."

It's also important to keep parents informed about events and programming to let them know who you are and what your role is. As a parent myself, I (Jim) don't blame parents for being interested in who is spending time with their kids. I also don't blame them for wanting to know the role we play in their children's lives. It's very important that you let them know that you are there to support—not compete with—them.

Parents need avenues in which to dialogue with the ministry about the needs and issues that they are facing with their children. This dialogue can help us as we seek to be a support and encouragement to parents. When parents and families have an avenue to openly share, doors are opened and we as youth workers gain insight into the lives of our students' families.

Encouragement and Support

Parenting is tough. Parents need all the support and encouragement they can get as they endeavor to raise their children. When I (Mike) was first starting out in ministry, and without children of my own, I remember that whenever students came to me complaining about their parents, I'd almost automatically side with them. "You know, you're right. Your parents don't understand you. They need to give you more freedom." As the years passed by and I became a parent myself, I had a slightly different perspective. "You know what—give your parents a break! It's tough being a parent. Your parents may not understand you, but you are hard to understand!" All right, so maybe I was a little biased. What families need is an advocate for overall health in the family, not someone who will choose sides. Make a choice to be an advocate for the family system.

Parents also need a place where they can talk with others about the issues going on in the family so that they can see that they are not the only ones dealing with an issue of crisis. "We're struggling here—is that normal? Are other parents going through what we're going through?" More often than not the answer is yes. Just knowing that fact and being able to dialogue about it, frees parents up. Whether as a part of support groups, parent prayer groups or parent seminars, allow parents the opportunity to dialogue and find encouragement and support from one another. Parents need to connect with one another.[1]

Equipping

Parents genuinely want information and equipping on parenting issues and other needs. As a youth ministry, one of the most immediate wins you can have with parents is to host a Parents' Night Out forum, where you bring in a parenting expert to talk about family issues and concerns. Issues such as adolescent development, spiritual growth, adolescent culture, sex and sexuality, parenting with positive discipline and communication with teenagers are all topics you can deal with as a service and encouragement to parents within your ministry. There is a deep need for a forum where parents can discuss the nuts and bolts of parenting. One idea for determining the content for a parenting forum is to go directly to the parents themselves. Poll parents to find out what issues and subjects they would like addressed.

Students, too, need to know how to live and survive in a family. From learning how to truly honor and obey their parents to understanding God's view of their family and learning how to communicate with their parents, students need a forum in which to delve into topics related to family. Sometimes those forums need to be without their parents, but there are some powerful ministry times that are missed by not discussing these issues together as a family unit.

Evangelism

One often forgotten role in youth ministry is the evangelizing of the family itself. Many times, parents who don't go to church or don't have a relationship with Christ are open to support and encouragement from their local church in the area of parenting. A Parents' Night Out can be a great means to help those parents begin to view the church as a positive, supportive place which can lead to opportunities for us to share our faith with them. Sometimes the best ministry we can have with a family as a whole is to see the members surrender their lives to Jesus Christ. That alone can initially help a family get on the right path, moving toward good solutions to issues and struggles within their family system.

The Plan

Any successful ministry must take its vision and put it into a practical plan. The following are just a few ways in which you can begin to minister to the families that are represented in your youth ministry. Begin slowly; don't try to tackle all of these suggestions in the first month. Take time to lay the groundwork and the foundation first; then you can start building a ministry that impacts the family unit. When it comes to family ministry, you need to realize that you will never be able to do all you want to do. However, this should not keep you from providing excellent resources and opportunities for family ministry.

Meet with the Families in Your Youth Ministry

It should be the goal of every youth ministry—whether done by you or by a small-group leader—to attempt to meet with every family in the youth ministry. This allows the parents to get know the person who will be spending time with their child and will undoubtedly help them to feel more comfortable about the mystery person at church who their son or daughter talks about so often. While most youth workers are much younger than the parents of students in their group, don't let this age difference stop you or your other adult volunteers from developing meaningful relationships with parents. You can learn a lot about families from being in their homes and observing how they relate to each other, and if you've been in their homes, they will feel more comfortable about coming to you with their problems.

Teach About the Importance and Priority of the Family

There are four important truths every student needs to understand about their parents in order to take more responsibility in building positive family relationships.[2] (Note: These ideas are for normal families; they do not necessarily apply to families with intense or complex problems.)

Parents Aren't Perfect

We should ask students to walk in their parents' shoes and look at some of the pressures and struggles that their parents are facing. Adolescents can be very self-absorbed and sometimes need to be reminded that there are other people in their families besides themselves!

Our (Jim's) high school ministry once invited a panel of parents to participate in a series called "Getting Along with Your Parents." We chose a divorced mother, two sets of married parents and my wife for the panel. We asked each of them to share some of the problems and struggles they faced as parents. What a response! The parents shared deep feelings about loneliness, insecurity at work, financial pressures, relational struggles and problems communicating with their kids. It was an eye-opening experience for our students to hear that parents have many of the same problems that they have.

Communication Is the Key

Most parents want to communicate with their children; they simply do not know how, and their children are not much help. A typical conversation between a parent and a high school student usually goes something like this:

> "How was school today?"
> "Okay."
> "What did you learn?"
> "Nothing."

We need to challenge students to initiate communication and conversation, especially with their parents. We need to give them encouragement and the tools to help them discuss their feelings and not just give robotic one-word responses.

God Gave Us Our Parents

God had an intricate part in bringing parents and their children together. Psalm 139:13-16 reminds us:

> You created my inmost being; you knit me together in my mother's womb. I praise you because I am fearfully and wonderfully made; your works are wonderful, I know that full well. My frame was not hidden from you when I was made in the secret place. When I was woven together in the depths of

> the earth, your eyes saw my unformed body. All the days ordained for me were written in your book before one of them came to be.

It's important to recognize that although this passage reminds us that God has our lives completely in His hands, teens in truly difficult family situations may think that this verse is a cruel joke by God. Most will understand the fact that no parent is perfect, but we need to help students understand that even in difficult situations, God can be a part of their relationships. A very mature junior in high school said to me (Jim), "I've finally accepted the fact that even though my father is an alcoholic, he loves me; and God has used me to help other kids who have alcoholic parents."

We Should Honor and Obey Our Parents

Exodus 20:12; Ephesians 6:1 and Colossians 3:20 tell us that honor and obedience are pleasing to God. Students need to be reminded that God's desire for them is to honor and obey their parents. This does not mean students should blindly obey; it means that—with God's help—they should always seek to honor and obey their parents.

Parents have problems too, and some of the most influential healers in a parent's life can be his or her own children. Gently reminding students that they can be instruments of God in leading the way in building a more positive environment at home is an important ingredient in our ministry to families.

Encourage Families to Spend Time Together

With today's hurried lifestyles, some parents and teenagers cross paths at only a few meals each week. Why not encourage our young people to take the initiative to take Mom out for dinner or invite Dad to attend a ball game? Often the best communication takes place in a neutral environment, such as a lunch date or shopping at the mall.

Some of the best times with my (Jim) dad during my adolescent years were when we would work in the yard together or when I would go with him to help at his office. This usually gave us some quality time alone and a meal together with his full attention.

Let's challenge students to initiate a date with each parent. We can brainstorm creative student-parent dates at a group meeting. Here are just a few ideas that students and parents can do together:

- Play a sport.
- Go to a play or movie.
- Go out to lunch or dinner.
- Go bowling, miniature golfing or shoot pool.
- Volunteer at a local hospital.
- Read a book.
- Take a special interest class at a community college (i.e., photography, crafts, Web design, etc.).

Your Own Family

Attention Singles: Although this section is about ministry and marriage, it is well worth reading and storing in your memory for future reference. You can learn some important tips that will help you to prevent much of the heartache that some of your married peers are experiencing! Besides, even as a single youth worker, you need to develop balance between your personal and professional lives.

After a recent talk to youth workers on the issue of family ministry, one youth worker asked, "Working with families is well and good, but how can I add that to my high school ministry when my own family relationships are in shambles?"

Most of the ministry workers we know are so overcommitted and completely stressed that relationships with their own families are mediocre at best.

We can become so emotionally spent that we have little or no time (much less, energy) to spend building our marriages—despite the fact that our greatest ministry is our own marriages. Before I (Jim) came to South Coast Community Church, I told the board of elders that if they wanted me to come, they had to understand that I believed one of my primary witnesses to the students in our ministry was a healthy marriage. That meant I was willing to work only three nights a week. (Most youth workers spend at least four to five nights a week out of the house.) Having discussed it beforehand, it was easier for the church board to understand when I couldn't attend every evening function.

If you're not giving time and energy to your spouse, then we question your witness to your students and your own children. A healthy marriage is a strong model for your children and will give them a sense of security.

Dealing with Fatigue

What undermines the building of a youth worker's marriage is overcommitment and fatigue. It's not likely that the heavy turnover and burnout of youth workers is due to lack of education or low finances as much as it is fatigue. Overcommitment and fatigue will always cause tension in a family. In order to nourish our ministries and our marriages, we probably need to cut back our outside activities and do less.

In order for us to live up to everyone's expectations, *someone* is going to come out the loser—someone is going to come out feeling cheated. Who is it going to be? It was Andy Stanley at the Youth Specialties National Youth Worker Convention who said it best: "There's not enough time to get it all done. You're going to have to cheat somebody. Who are you going to cheat? The ministry? Or your family? You always, always, always cheat the ministry!"[3]

There will be another youth worker at your church after you. The youth ministries at the churches we have been a part of are still operating today and, in some senses, operating better. The truth of the matter is there will never be another husband or wife or mother or father to your family. You cannot minister effectively in the name of Jesus Christ if your family is getting leftovers. Your first ministry truly is to your family. I (Jim) keep two questions written in the back of my prayer journal: (1) Is the work of God I'm doing destroying the work of God in me? (2) Is my family receiving only my emotional scraps?

OK, now that we know the dilemma, what's the answer? *If you are married, make your marriage and family the top priority in your life.* If you are not, as a couple, taking at least a 24-hour period at a different pace at least once each week, then your marriage—and ministry—may be in jeopardy. I've (Jim) used every excuse in the book—and then some. "It'll get better after this one retreat," I've said. "Just wait until we get past this season; then things will slow down—I promise." Year after year, the excuses sounded flimsier and flimsier.

Building Your Relationship

If the answer is to make your marriage of greater priority, what can you do to make your relationship with your spouse strong? Here are a couple of very practical ideas that have worked for us.

Date Night

Plan a weekly date. You've got to continue dating your spouse throughout your life, and a weekly looked-forward-to date helps inhibit the creeping peril of a stale marriage. We can always find time for weekly Bible studies or one-on-one discipleship ministry; we can always find time for one more school event or one more really important counseling appointment—so what makes us think that we can't find the time for a two-hour date with our better half?

Pacing

Youth ministry has a tendency to move so fast from one event to another that we take little time to reflect or debrief. Cathy and I (Jim) are learning what we call pacing. Even though I feel drawn to the office after a big event, we try to take the next day off. If we know I'm going to be out of town for a few days, we try to make the week before my departure less hectic than usual. If I'm going to be out late a particular night, then I try to stay home until lunchtime and maybe go to the office a little later the next morning.

Positive Modeling

During a seminar that Cathy and I (Jim) taught on ministry and marriage, we were surprised by the intensity, even the anger, of most youth workers' opinions about the poor role modeling they receive from their workaholic senior pastors. Let's face it: Role models for a strong, happy marriage may be uncommon among your pastoral staff. Andy Stanley again wisely stated, "Don't let your senior pastor's dysfunction become yours."[4] The unfortunate truth is that most youth workers gauge their success and effectiveness on their busyness. If that's true for you, find an older couple who really work at making their marriage and family the top priority in their lives and learn from them.

Phones and E-Mail

Youth workers usually work long hours and consequently find it difficult to communicate with their spouses. This is where the phone and e-mail can be your best friend. Call and communicate *daily*. When we are away from home, our wives and children get a phone call every day. Even when we are home and in the office, we try to communicate with our wives at least once during the day. The phone calls simply communicate "I love you and was thinking about you; you are important to me."

Growing Spiritually Together

I (Jim) wish I had an easy answer for growing together spiritually. There are no magic formulas. However, let me suggest three helpful ideas.

1. **Solos**—A solo is a spouse's regular time away from the routine hassles of life in order to have an extended period of devotion, reflection and quiet time with God. Do whatever it takes to free up your spouse, so he or she can take a solo; then take time together soon after in order to share with each other any thoughts from your solo times with God.
2. **Support Group**—With the hectic pace of life that a youth worker lives, we cannot understand how couples can grow spiritually without the help of a support group. We have our separate weekly support group meetings as well as a weekly couples' Bible study group. Our separate support groups help us keep our perspective

and vent feelings and receive encouragement from someone other than our spouses. If you don't have a support group or a Bible study for you as a couple, find or create one.

3. **Overnighters**—One night away from the routine hassles really helps couples gain a clearer perspective on things. Overnighters can also be incredible times for spiritual growth. They can be programmed with reading and prayer, or you can have a more spontaneous time together. If you have children, it's even more vital to have periodic overnighters. You need those times to be able to connect with each other amidst the flurry of being a parent. As an idea, trade baby-sitting with another church couple who also need overnighters.

Keeping the Fires Burning

One of the tragedies of youth ministry is the trouble that so many ministry marriages have gotten into, and the culprit is often an emotionally drained youth worker so emptied by his or her work that proper attention cannot be paid to his or her family. What Gail MacDonald wrote in *High Call, High Privilege* relates perfectly to this epidemic: "Untended fires soon become nothing but a pile of ashes."[5] If you're concerned about ministering to families in your church, you can't afford to neglect your own fires at home. For the sake of your family and for the sake of your students and their families, take the time necessary to minister to the needs of your *own* family first. It is a priority that we simply cannot let slip away.

> For ideas on creative family events and devotional times with your family, visit YouthBuilders at www.youthbuilders.com.

SECTION II

THE FRAMEWORK— BLUEPRINTS FOR MINISTRY

CHAPTER 7

RELATIONAL EVANGELISM: REACHING A GENERATION IN NEED

Following one of my high school Bible studies, I (Jim) was talking to one of our adult sponsors who had been an overseas missionary. I was telling her that sometimes I feel guilty for not being a missionary to another culture. She shot back, "You are a missionary to a different culture. These high school kids"—she pointed to a few kids who were still left after the youth group meeting—"live in a different world. You've chosen to infiltrate that world to give them the message of Jesus."

I had never before looked at ministry to high schoolers as missionary work, but she was right. We're working with kids who are different from the way we were when we were in high school and junior high. As one youth worker put it, "We were never their age. Yes, we were 14, 15 and 16; but we were never their age." Life has changed for high schoolers since our adolescent days, and if we're going to reach them with the good news of Jesus Christ, it's time to take on a missionary perspective.

People ask me periodically why I continue to work with students instead of getting a real job, like the senior pastorate. I always tell them, "Adults have already made just about every major decision in life. For the most part, they have already set their priorities and their values. I work with high school students because they're still in the process of making their major life decisions—ones that will affect them for the rest of their lives. They are still forming their thoughts, values and priorities in life." In fact, a majority of our staff working with us at YouthBuilders made his or her commitment to Jesus Christ while in high school or younger. That's not atypical. The Barna Research Group reminds us that "the majority of Christians accept Jesus Christ as their Savior before they reach the age of 18."[1] With that truth in mind, youth ministries should make quality outreach and evangelism a top priority.

The sad reality, however, is that too many of us spin our wheels when it comes to evangelism. As we've evaluated our own outreach programs, we've seen that we often wasted time, effort and money on activities that didn't accomplish the goal of reaching unchurched students in our community. Instead, we developed evangelistic meetings for Christians.

A few years ago, for example, our (Jim's) high school group sponsored a concert that attracted well over a thousand students. Our paid and volunteer youth staff invested weeks putting the concert together, and our student leadership poured out an incredible amount of time and energy into making it a success.

Was it a success? Our hard work helped the concert to come off smoothly. Our senior pastor was ecstatic over the numbers, and our students enjoyed themselves. Our goal, however, had been outreach. And to my knowledge, no unchurched students became a part of our (or any other) church because of that concert. We had an evangelistic concert without evangelism. I don't believe the evening was worthless, but we came to the conclusion that we could have used the hours and what the event cost us to reach out more effectively than by putting on a one-night concert for our current students.

It is statistically staggering how few people respond to Jesus Christ and the Church through mass evangelism. Most people become Christians through influential friendships and family relationships. People respond to mass evangelism appeals usually because of a positive relationship with a Christian person. You can call it what you want—lifestyle evangelism, earning the right to be heard or relational evangelism—but good, influential and responsive evangelism is based around a relationship with someone or a group of people who are modeling a vibrant, genuine Christian lifestyle.

Caring as Evangelism

A ministry that genuinely cares for students is involved in a ministry of evangelism. Loving and caring for students unconditionally fulfills the often unmet need for acceptance. Young people, regardless of whether they have a relationship with Christ or not, have the same needs. As we strive to meet those needs, opportunities for evangelism happen.

Vanessa was a girl that I (Mike) will never forget. She was sitting in our student leadership meeting one night when we asked the question, "How did you become a Christian—what led you to surrender your life to God?" Vanessa's response was a lesson in evangelism that I'll never forget.

> I surrendered my life to Jesus because Mike remembered my name. I had just come to the youth group and felt really out of place. I was wondering how I was ever going to fit in. I didn't like myself very much and was here just because my mom wanted me to be here.
>
> One day, I came in and Mike introduced himself and talked with me for a few minutes. The next week, he found me. We talked and I shared with him that I was going through a rough time with my mom. We were arguing and not getting along very well. He said that he'd pray for me. During the week I got a note card from Mike saying that he was praying for me.
>
> The following Sunday, I found Mike. We talked more about my relationship with my mom. For the first time in my life I felt like I mattered. I felt like someone was there for me. I started to think, *Maybe this God thing is for real.* I decided that I would stay. Over the course of time, I heard about Jesus—and His love for me. After one Sunday morning, I decided that I needed Jesus to forgive me, to help me with my relationship with my mom, to fill the loneliness and the hurt that was in my life.

The best evangelism starts with a relationship, not a program. The best evangelism is when we strive to meet the needs of students, loving and accepting them just as they are. Those moments of ministry, even the ones that seem insignificant, can make all the difference in the world.

Friendship Evangelism

Over 15 years ago Canadian sociologist and youth culture expert Donald C. Posterski wrote, "The majority of teenagers are *clustering* together and enjoying their small circle of friends."[2] We believe this is absolutely right for this new generation as well. The typical student's life is centered around his or her social group. In fact, for most teens there is nothing more important or significant at this stage in their lives than their friendships. On each campus today, there are hundreds of small friendship groupings that constitute the sociological makeup of any school. Groups of three, four or five students hang out in the hallways before going to classes; they meet for lunch in the same spot every day; they pass notes between classes; and they wait for each other to walk home together. Out of this friendship cluster comes much of what is influencing students' decisions. We cannot underestimate the value students place on their friendships.

One of our chief tasks, then, must be to equip teens to become evangelists to their peers. Sharing their faith can be scary, so they need lots of encouragement and modeling from us. As young people learn to share their faith, we will see great spiritual growth in them as well as an impact for the kingdom of God.

In order to create a healthy atmosphere of peer evangelism, we must understand the world in which teenagers live today (this is discussed in depth in chapter 3). Years ago, Posterski put together a very important study on Canadian adolescents, filled with startling information extremely important for the world of youth ministry. Imagine a "ladder of values." The highest rung of the ladder represents values that young people consider very important in their lives, and the lowest rung represents those of lesser importance. Here are Posterski's findings, indicating that high school students are replacing traditional family relationships with their own family of friends:

- 91 percent ranked *friendship* on the top rung of their value ladder, with 9 out of 10 high school students ranking it as their highest value.
- 87 percent ranked *being loved* next on the value ladder (i.e., looking for friends and family who will love them).
- *Family life* ranked a comparatively low 65 percent.
- Rather surprisingly, only 21 percent considered *being popular* as very important on their ladder of values. General popularity has been replaced by being accepted in a friendship cluster or social grouping.[3]

The bottom line for your youth ministry program is that if your students don't develop a significant connection with other students in the youth ministry, they won't stay.[4] As we develop a relational evangelism ministry, we need to keep in mind the idea of peer relationships and help students see their relationships as a potential mission field of people who need Jesus.

Contact Work Evangelism

Contact work is one of the most effective forms of evangelism in youth ministry. It means meeting students on their territory, outside the walls of the church. Contact work is identifying with young people where they are and penetrating their culture.

Throughout the New Testament we see Jesus identifying with people on their own territory. Even the well-known words about the incarnation of God found in John 1:14 help us understand the power of a contact ministry: "The Word became flesh and made his dwelling among us. We have seen his glory, the glory of the One and Only, who came from the Father, full of grace and truth." Jesus was not afraid to be seen with sinners (see Luke 5:27-32; 15:1-2).

Similarly, the powerful effect of the apostle Paul's ministry was based on his willingness to identify with people. We see Paul as a minister who lived among his people, urging his followers to imitate his actions.

Paul truly shared his life with the people he ministered to. Contact work is merely following the example of those before us who understood and penetrated the culture of those they wanted to influence with the good news of Christ.

The possibilities of being a part of a student's world are almost limitless. Wherever students congregate should be seen as an opportunity for contact work. Athletic events, school functions, choir and band concerts, student hangouts, recreation centers, shopping malls and lunch hours at the school are great starting places for contact work. Also use your imagination to plan or attend events conducive to contact work, such as waterskiing trips, snow-skiing trips, pizza feasts, professional athletic events, school events and all-nighters. Volunteer to help out at the schools.

One of the great Christian youth ministry organizations, Young Life International, has developed a relational contact style of ministry that is second to none.

Follow-Up Evangelism

Many studies on church growth show that the reason people don't stay at a church is because they haven't connected with anyone in the church. The dramatic increase of numbers in several of the cults is because they have an extensive calling, visitation and follow-up program. Every Christian youth group needs some form of follow-up with both non- and new believers, as well as those who are a part of the group, as an important part of its evangelism program.

As you create a follow-up program, it is always best to begin with an easy-to-follow plan. We believe there are four principles that should be incorporated into any plan. These four timeless follow-up principles may be simple, but they are profoundly impacting. When we take the time to apply these principles to our ministries, visible results are usually not far behind.

Have One-on-One Contact at Least Twice a Year

The most effective way to have an avenue for spiritual challenge with someone is to get better acquainted with him or her. Despite the size of your group, every member should have at least two one-on-one contacts a year. If your youth ministry is small, then you are fortunate because you can do much of the one-on-one time on your own. If your youth ministry is large, then other leaders will need to be in on the program. The goal of the one-on-one is to get to know the student in a more personal setting, finding out more than you would with a brief interaction at a program. Here are some helpful questions to ask during your one-on-one time:

- If you had three hours to do anything, what would you do?
- What's one word that you would use to describe your relationship with your parents?
- Do you have a job? What do you like best (and least) about your job?
- What would be the dream job in your future?
- If you could be anyone else for a day, who would you want to be and why?
- What is one word that you'd use to describe how God fits into your life?
- If you could ask God any question, what would it be?
- If you could do anything for God and make an impact, what would you want to do?

Some inactive students may wonder why you are getting together with them. Our suggestion is to state up front that you are trying to get together with everyone in the youth ministry in order to get better acquainted with him or her. A note of caution should be made here. Be sure that you establish and maintain clear boundaries when meeting with students. We believe same sex one-on-one relationships are best whenever possible. If that is absolutely not possible, then make those meetings in very public places, arriving separately if at all possible.

Develop a Method for Gathering Visitor Information

We can't do follow-up without getting some kind of contact information on new people. Whether it's through a visitor information card, a registration card or a sign-in table, we need to think through how to gather information on new students in a nonthreatening way. Tell them up front that you will be sending them junk mail from the group to keep them informed on upcoming activities.

Many database programs today have features for adding digital pictures. If your program has this feature, be sure to take advantage of it. Help put a face with a name by taking each student's digital picture when they sign in at the table. Add the pictures to the appropriate names in the database. If you don't have the capability in your church to take digital pictures or don't have the software, don't worry; simply take pictures with any camera and when the pictures are developed, write students' names on the back of their pictures. You can use those as flashcards in learning new names. For instant pictures, use a Polaroid camera. Whether the pictures are taken digitally or more traditionally, think of the impact we can have when a student comes back a second week and you've already remembered his or her name.

Follow Up with Visitors Within a Week

Far too many young people slip through the cracks because no one responds to them from their initial visit to the youth event. If they are willing to visit the church or youth ministry, then the overwhelming odds say that they will come back if relationships are built and they are asked back. Within a week of their visit they should receive a handwritten note from one of the leaders. The note should be short, positive and personal—mention the name of their friend if they came with one. Tell them you hope to see them again. In addition, within the week they should be contacted by phone or personally at school and invited to attend the next youth group event. Many churches have effectively used peers to make the phone or personal contact. When you invite them, be sure to offer them a ride if they need one. Sometimes students don't come only because they don't have a way to get there.

Develop Students to Reach Out to Their Peers

Don't try to do it all on your own. Develop a team of adults and students who have a heart and passion for reaching out to new students. Let them be in charge of a sign-in table: developing the visitor information card, taking the pictures, writing follow-up letters and notes and making phone calls to new students. Let them explore new and innovative ways to reach out to new students. The goal is to come up with a plan that makes every person who walks through the door feel significant, valued, welcomed and celebrated.

Event Evangelism

Students like to be in the middle of a happening. For a number of years, organizations such as Youth for Christ and other parachurch organizations have shown us that non-Christian young people will come to special events if we are willing to put the time into making it a significant experience for them. Many churches make the fatal mistake of putting together the world's greatest event, only to be disappointed because the results turned out to be mediocre at best.

If you are going to try evangelism through special events, then make sure you have the time, energy, finances and leadership to pull off a very successful program. Our suggestion is to make the event high quality or else don't do it. Honor the students with thorough preparation and excellence, and don't forget a well-planned follow-up program.

A well-planned evangelistic event doesn't have to be large—more important than size is the focus of the event, one that students can get behind and bring their friends to. It should be an event in which we honor our students, as well as their friends, with excellence in planning and creativity. A well-planned evangelistic event is also one in which students are given the truth of who Jesus is, what He has done, how what He did impacts our lives, and what we need to do because of that truth.

When you decide to put together a community outreach event, be sure to combine forces with other churches and organizations. Many youth groups never get together with the other churches in their community because of insecurity on the part of the leadership. Unfortunately, the greatest evangelistic opportunities in many communities have been missed because no one ever came together to do something worth raising the attention of students in the community. Here are some ideas to consider:

1. **Christian Concerts**—Music draws students more than any other activity. A well-done Christian concert can be an excellent outreach. The most difficult hurdle to face is the style of music. Because many students listen to such a wide variety of music, it may be difficult to find one genre of music that will have broad-based appeal. This may mean that you go after a certain segment of the youth population with a certain musical genre, rather than trying to please everyone's musical taste.
2. **Special Speakers**—Non-Christian students will not usually attend a seminar unless the subject draws them or the speaker is a famous personality. A sports figure, musician or actor will usually be your best evangelistic draw. If you bring in an unknown Christian speaker to the kids, make sure you talk up the subject. Have your speakers talk on sex, dating, music and other subjects important to teenagers.
3. **Special Events**—Community-wide events can also be an exciting way to pull in students. Whether it's an all-nighter or nightly events using musicians, broom hockey or an amusement park—ask students what would be a draw for their non-Christian friends. What works for one youth group may not work for another. Be sure to check in with the experts: your students. Use them in the planning, promotion and program; have them be a part of the event from the beginning to the end; and have students deliver the testimony or message.
4. **Camps and Retreats**—Whether it's summer or winter camps or retreats, make the sole purpose one of evangelism. Waterskiing trips, snow skiing/snowboarding trips, rock climbing, white water rafting and other retreat venues can be a great opportunity to gather together our students and their unsaved friends. As in special events, ask the experts—your students—what would work best. Also be sure to utilize students who have a passion for evangelism to be a part of the planning and program for the camp or retreat.

Campus Ministry Evangelism

When I (Jim) first started in youth ministry, I accidentally started a campus ministry. Fresh out of seminary and a Young Life ministry, I went to work at a church with a handful of students and a desire to develop a strong youth ministry. Every Thursday I visited the same campus after school. I played tennis, went out to eat with students, watched football games and was the only person who sat through the band's rehearsal for homecoming. Every Thursday the few kids in my church would look for me, and as the weeks turned into months, I met their friends. We eventually started getting together just to talk every Thursday afternoon. The second semester I suggested that we start a Bible study after school. Most of the students said they were too busy—they had not realized I had taken their Thursday afternoons for months! We ended up with a great Thursday afternoon Bible study. In fact we started four Bible studies at four different high schools that year.

When youth workers decide to have a campus presence, the first thing we must do is meet with the principal and the administration of the school. It is a time to leave our Bibles in the car and spend the time getting to know each other. It's important that we let them know who we are and that we care for students just as they do, and that we can offer our services as chaperones and in other ways we can serve the school. I (Jim) usually let the principal know I will be attending games and school functions and would love to serve in any way I could be used. I may ask if he or she minds if I eat lunch with a few of the kids on campus, and I make it clear that these lunch dates would not be for Bible study. Principals can be nervous about religious people being on campus. However, as you get to know each other and as you never take advantage of the system but instead serve the school, you will usually be openly received on campus.

The interpretation of the law of equal access on public school campuses will continue to be debated, but you have every right to make your presence known on the campus. You may not be able to be on campus, but that doesn't diminish the impact we can have on a campus by serving and equipping students to reach their peers. There are some wonderful organizations who are helping both youth workers and students to reach their campus for Jesus Christ. The Challenge Alliance is helping youth ministries target campuses in their area as mission fields. The National Network of Youth Ministries and See You at the Pole are being used to raise awareness that our campuses are in need of prayer and spiritual influence. The Coaching Center is an online ministry that assists youth ministries as they raise up students to be campus missionaries. You may want to think about contacting one of these organizations to see how you can be involved in the efforts to reach your local campus with the good news of Jesus Christ.

Listed below are a number of simple suggestions for making a difference on campuses in your area.

- Sponsor a campus club.
- Host a training event for campus ministry leaders.
- Link arms with parachurch ministries in your area (Youth for Christ, Young Life, Fellowship of Christian Athletes, Student Venture).
- Become an assistant coach, lunch supervisor or tutor.
- Help with drama, band, cheerleading or any other clubs on campus.
- Chaperone school activities.
- Join the PTA.
- Help decorate for school parties and functions.
- Get involved in peer counseling programs or speaking to classes on at-risk issues: drug and alcohol abuse, sexuality, teen pregnancy, suicide and school violence.

Every youth worker, in a small or large way, is an evangelist and a missionary. The fields are ripe for harvest. No doubt we will need different and innovative methods of outreach to minister to the particular kids in our area, but we are convinced that they will be open to the gospel if we enter into their world—bearing love, care and the life-changing message of hope in Jesus Christ.

For a description of principles for contact work and a sample information card for first-time visitors, visit YouthBuilders at www.youthbuilders.com.

CHAPTER 8

BUILDING COMMUNINITY THROUGH SMALL GROUPS

Pastor and author Bruce Larson made this very profound statement about community:

> The neighborhood bar is possibly the best counterpart there is for the fellowship Christ wants to give His Church. It's an imitation, dispensing liquor instead of grace, escape rather than reality, but it is a permissive, accepting and inclusive fellowship. It's "unshockable." The bar flourishes *not* because most people are alcoholics but because God has put into the human heart the desire to know and be known, to love and be loved, and so many seek a counterfeit at the price of a few beers.[1]

One of the most glaring needs for teenagers is the need for community and relational connection with others. How many young people find the same feeling of acceptance and community within the church as people who frequent the neighborhood bar?

The degree to which students will stay in the church, get involved and make significant life decisions for Christ is directly dependent on their sense of belonging to the community. If they connect significantly with peers and adult leaders, teenagers are more likely to stay in the church. Spiritual impact is the same. It's been said that students are not theologically aware until they are sociologically comfortable.

A healthy, impactful youth ministry is one that strives to develop a deeper sense of community. To do so increases the chances of students being lifelong followers of Jesus; in failing to do so, we take the risk that students will seek that sense of community elsewhere. Many students compromise their faith and values in order to fill their desire to belong. They get involved in all kinds of areas and activities that leave them scarred and broken, including sexual promiscuity, drugs, alcohol, eating disorders and the occult.

In a questionnaire, I (Jim) once asked 160 high school students, "Why do you come to the youth group?" The vast majority replied that they came because they felt loved and accepted. They were not coming to hear me speak or because our facility was so nice; they came because of a sense of community. Whether a teenager decides to go on a retreat or stay home depends largely on who else will be attending the event. Of all the student retreats I've taken, *not once* has a student asked me what I'll be speaking on; however, almost every student has asked *who* will be there.

Religious Socialization

The goal of youth ministry is to have community (relationships) with God and with other people. Whether or not youth workers have ever heard the phrase "religious socialization," that is precisely what we are trying to do with our kids. Religious socialization consists of the accumulated experiences that bring students to the exact place they are in their spiritual life. It is accomplished through family, friends, church, community and other shared experiences. Your job is to help make this process a very positive and growing one. Many studies on death and dying reveal that when on their deathbed—with all other priorities and agendas put aside—the majority of patients desire two things: a relationship with God and a relationship with loved ones. Similarly, our youth ministries must focus on developing in students a vital, trusting, loving relationship with God and a healthy sense of community and support.

Youth ministry cannot be compartmentalized to meet only the spiritual needs of the people in it. Good religious socialization in youth ministry means developing a whole-person approach. In order for a person to be growing spiritually, he or she must be dealing with other areas in his or her life as well. A good youth group will have a healthy balance of physical, mental, social, emotional and spiritual activities. Acts 2:42 shows us that the early Christians balanced their time together in prayer, fellowship, food, teaching, worship and serving. We've already discussed in chapter 4 that peer influence is one of the strongest elements in building self-identity and socialization for an adolescent. This is also true in building a teen's Christian self-identity and healthy religious socialization; students need positive peer influence. Some questions to ask yourself when thinking about how your ministry addresses this issue are

- *Is there a true sense of community and support in the youth group?*
- *Does our youth group minister to the whole person?*
- *What can I do to enhance a deeper commitment to community within the youth group?*

Finding Community in Youth Ministry

There are a number of great community-building models for youth ministry. The one that has been most useful to us to understand and work toward as a goal is Lyman Coleman's (of Serendipity) model for community. This model involves a gradual process of community development that begins on a simple, nonthreatening level and grows toward a deep sense of belonging and trust. Coleman describes the process by comparing it to a baseball diamond.[2]

Coleman's Model for Community

First Base—History Giving

Who I am. Before you develop intimacy, you must get acquainted. This level deals with the facts about the person and his or her general history. Using a "this is who I am and where I've come from" approach, students begin to share their stories.

Second Base—Sense of Warmth and Affection

I feel cared for and valued. When students begin to know each other's stories, they begin to have a sense of acceptance. There is a sense that "I matter to these people—they have accepted me for who I am and for where I've come from." When students feel cared for and accepted, they will begin to open up.

Third Base—Deeper Sharing

I feel safe here. Once students have shared their stories and sense that they are accepted and cared for, then they begin to test the waters with sharing deeper issues. Deeper sharing brings with it some vulnerability. As students feel safe and begin to share deeper issues, it is imperative that they encounter a community that continues to be unconditional. If students don't feel safe, they won't venture out to share deeper issues and struggles. Joys, frustrations, dreams, fears and even doubts are shared openly within this level. Achieving this level of intimate sharing takes time.

Home Plate—The Depth of Christian Community

I belong here. Within this level, students are connected deeply with one another. It is developed in smaller groups that have traveled the course of the first three levels; therefore, it is never fully reached between everyone in the group. This is the community and fellowship that students deeply long for. It is characterized by a sense of belonging that is so deep that students see this grouping of people as family. It is these relationships that will have an eternal impact on their lives and the decisions that they make. This grouping is the type that develops a lifelong commitment to each other that says "No matter where we go, we will always have this connection with each other."

Our goal in youth ministry is for students to find their identity in

Christ and their belonging in the people of God. Outstanding youth ministries proactively and purposefully move students through all four levels. Although we can help students through the initial levels of the model in a large group, to fully see students attain the depth of Christian community, small groups are a necessity. Small groups are the vehicles that can get students to the level of community that their soul longs for.

Small Groups

In youth ministry today, much of the philosophy of ministry is bigger is better. Unfortunately, this philosophy doesn't work when developing community. One of the true blessings of the small church and small youth ministry is that even though the programs are usually not as overwhelmingly dynamic, there is a much greater atmosphere in which to develop community. The goal of large youth ministries should be small—looking for ways to break into smaller, more intimate groups. True community cannot be developed until we get smaller. Small groups and more intimate shared experiences are at the heart of building community within a youth ministry.

Many churches are finding that small groups designed specifically to share and encourage one another have become the backbone of their ministry. Even breaking up the whole group into smaller segments during meetings often becomes more conducive to spiritual growth and community. However, leading a small group can be difficult. We've all experienced those times when no one spoke or when one person monopolized the entire conversation. Leading a small group takes a certain amount of skill that may not come easily.

Two common mistakes in developing community are that we either try to sidestep the importance of history giving and affirmation in favor of going straight to deeper sharing, or we spend all our time at the first stages of developing community and provide little opportunity for developing intimacy in a group.

Students will be much more vulnerable after they sense that your group knows and accepts them. For example, I (Jim) sat in on a small group of high school students led by one of our volunteers. She opened the group by saying, "Why don't we go around the room and share what God has been doing in our lives?" First, she received blank stares (you know, that deer-caught-in-the-headlights look) and then everyone looked down and proceeded to count the spots on the carpet. Even after she shared her own victorious story, no one had anything to say. She was asking for deeper sharing than students were ready for. Too much, too soon.

On the other hand, I've (Mike) seen too many small groups in which students knew each other well but were missing something. I remember one small group of guys in particular. Their leader came to me in frustration and said, "I just don't feel like God is using me in my small group." After sitting in on his group for a while, the problem was apparent right away; even after three years together, students in the group still functioned together on a very shallow level. What they needed was to get unstuck and move on to their next level by being more transparent and sharing some deeper issues.

The Purpose of Small Groups

Without initiative, small groups can become just another place to socialize, and there is not much development of community or life change. Regardless of what type of small group ministry we have—growth groups, support groups, fellowship groups or discipleship groups—all have a few characteristics in common. Healthy small group ministry is a ministry in which C-A-R-E is happening.

C = Connectedness

Small groups are the primary place where students can connect with a few people—a place to know and be known, to love and be loved. True community can only start to form as students connect with one another. There needs to be consistency for relationship and connection to occur. You need to ask yourself, *How are students in this group doing at connecting with one another? Are they beginning to bond?* Small group activities outside of the church walls will begin to foster connectedness.

A = Accountability

Spiritual application plus accountability equals dynamic spiritual growth. Small groups are the best places for accountability, a necessity in helping each other grow. Accountability is tough in a large group. It is better served in small groups where we can know each other well enough to be honest and transparent, giving others the right to ask us the tough questions that will foster our accountability and growth. You need to ask yourself, *How transparent is this group? Are we moving toward deeper sharing? Where does each member need to grow in his or her spiritual journey? What can we do as a group to help keep members accountable?*

R = Relevancy

Students today need to see God's Word as relevant. Far too many times we've heard students say, "The Bible just doesn't make sense to me!" Small group ministry is where God's Word can be made relevant, applying it to the everyday lives of our students. It is in the context of small groups that we can deal with in-depth questions, doubts and struggles, showing how God's Word is as current today as it was the day it was written. Small groups can dig into passages, explore application and apply God's Word with accountability.

E = Encouragement

Perhaps one of the greatest benefits of small groups is found in the area of affirmation and encouragement. If it is true that affirmation is the art of seeing what God is doing in the life of a student and pointing it out, then it must be true that there is no better vehicle in which to do this than in a small group. In a smaller community, we will have a front-row seat to the work of God in the lives of our students. As long as we keep students in large groups, we will lack the necessary relationship to truly know each student and see the work of God in their individual lives. In small groups we can know the dreams, fears, desires and goals of our students. We can enter into their lives and have the platform to be able to encourage them, not with surface encouragement, but with affirmation that changes the heart and perspective.

Ten Commandments for Dynamic Small Groups

As we seek to be about C-A-R-E, there are some tools that we need to have. We've come up with 10 small group principles that will help in leading and using small groups to a gain a deeper sense of community in your youth ministry.

One: Thou Shalt Ask Dynamic Questions

Dynamic questions are open-ended (not answered by yes or no), surface breaking (probe beneath the surface to deeper issues) and thought provoking (not always easily answered). Questions like "Do you struggle with praying?" may not lead to discussion. A better question would be "Why does it seem like God doesn't hear our prayers?"

Two: Thou Shalt Realize That Atmosphere Is Everything

The atmosphere that we create is paramount to helping students feel comfortable, open up and grow in a small group setting. We need to strive to have an atmosphere filled with unconditional love and acceptance, where students feel safe enough to share what they think and feel.

Three: Thou Shalt Not Be a Dictator

Students learn best when they talk—not when you do. Facilitating discussion and interaction is what will help students open up and grow. Every time a student says "This might be a dumb question, but . . ." what he or she really means is "I have a question, but I'm afraid to share it for fear of what others will say or do."

Four: Thou Shalt Not Fill Each Moment with Talking

It's okay to have silence in the midst of a discussion. Silence can mean that students are thinking. Silence can give students time to process and formulate their thoughts and opinions. If you come across a time of silence and students are really wrestling with a tough question, send them to be alone for five minutes and have them write down what they are thinking.

Five: Thou Shalt Be As Transparent and Open As Possible

We can't ask students to share something that we wouldn't share ourselves. The key to helping them open up in the midst of a small group is to lead by example. Being transparent shows that we are in process of growing too, giving others hope that God isn't done with them, or us, yet. Being open with students frees them to be open with us.

Six: Thou Shalt Create Tension

Too many students today are practicing agnostics. They say they believe one thing, but their lives don't reflect it. Most students have never been taught to think on their own about what they believe and how that really impacts their everyday lives. Tension forces students to think and consider the consequences behind the choices they make, and how those decisions reflect their values and convictions. Using real-life scenarios, case studies or stories can help students apply their convictions to their lives.

Seven: Thou Shalt Know and Use Scripture

When dealing with a subject, we should know what the Bible has to say about it. Likewise, we need to know what the Bible doesn't say about the subject. It's okay to say "I don't know, but I'll find out for you" when it comes to questions about the Bible. Better to admit that we don't know and find the answer than to give a wrong answer to a tough question. Today there are excellent Bible study curriculum guides to help you.

Eight: Thou Shalt Always Be Sensitive to the Circumstances

You may have planned to talk about one subject, but someone in the group may be going through a divorce situation in his or her home. Know when to leave what you've planned to talk about and discuss the more urgent felt need of the group. Know when to leave a dead issue and when to dig deeper on a hot issue. The most important goal is to follow what God is doing in the midst of your small group and get out of the way.

Nine: Thou Shalt Always Listen Twice As Much As You Speak

We've heard it said, "God gave us two ears and one mouth–figure it out!" Great advice! Listen twice as much as you talk. Those who give kids their ears will capture their hearts and minds. Listen to what students are saying. Listen to how they talk and what they talk about. Ask them to clarify their thoughts and opinions, so you can be sure of what they really mean. Listen also to the things that aren't said–those are just as real as their words. Listen for attitudes, emotions, hurts and disappointments. Listening truly is an open doorway to ministering to the heart.

Ten: Thou Shalt Be Their Pastor

Remember that your role as a small group leader is one of a pastor and a shepherd. Know what's going on in students' lives. Pray for your group regularly. Offer encouragement and accountability. Be an agent of spiritual challenge in the lives of your small group members.

CHAPTER 9

Discipleship: Getting Kids Involved

Jon and Michelle are cousins. Their families had similar involvement in the church. Both were active in their high school, received good grades and had lots of friends. Jon and Michelle both made commitments to Christ at the same age and attended the same church.

Jon is now an active leader in the church, but Michelle dropped out of church after high school. Why? What happened? Of course there are theological reasons, but there's a greater, less complicated answer: *involvement.* While Jon was involved in the ministry, Michelle was just a spectator.

Moving to Involvement

The question facing anyone who is serious about discipleship is how to get students to move from being spectators to being participators, involved in their faith. The bottom line in youth work is not how many kids are coming to your youth ministry right now. The bottom line is where your kids will be five to ten years from now. How are you preparing them to be lifelong followers of Jesus Christ? How are you preparing them to be Christian leaders?

Contrary to some prevalent philosophies of youth ministry, mature discipleship does not come by memorizing a discipleship manual or graduating from a discipleship program. Discipleship is not a program; it's not "just go through these five books on discipleship and then you'll be a disciple." Discipleship is not about knowledge transfer; it's about life transformation. It is a long-term, character-building relationship that challenges people to take what they have been given by our Lord and share it with others. Discipleship is about living the Christian life in the context of relationship with another person so as to help that person be all God dreams for him or her to be.

How can you develop a stronger sense of involvement and discipleship in students? You must be a discipler, equipper and model.

Being a Discipler

If you see your role as that of a teacher, a dispenser of knowledge and truth, you don't have high enough goals. To nurture student involvement, use the method that Paul suggested in 2 Timothy 2:2: "The things you have heard me say in the presence of many witnesses entrust to reliable men who will also be qualified to teach others." Teach first, but teach for the purpose of helping people transfer what they have learned—and who they are becoming—to other people.

One of the questions you must ask as you disciple is, *Am I preparing my students to be hearers of the Word or doers of the Word?* A discipler is constantly motivating others to live out their faith in their actions. Two verses sum it up best: "Dear children, let us not love with words or tongue but with actions and in truth" (1 John 3:18) and "Do not merely listen to the word, and so deceive yourselves. Do what it says" (James 1:22). As disciplers, our calling is to be mentors to this generation of young people, helping them live out their Christianity.

Being an Equipper

Youth workers who desire to see long-lasting results must be equippers. The "I-need-to-do-it-all" mentality might be great for the smoothness of the program, but it can be detrimental for growth within the lives of your students. Always look for ways to train and equip young people. Ephesians 4:12-13 reminds us that our job is "to prepare God's people for works of service, so that the body of Christ may be built up until we all reach unity in the faith and in the knowledge of the Son of God and become mature, attaining to the whole measure of the fullness of Christ."

Our calling is to equip students to do the work of the ministry so that they (and others) will mature into the fullness and the likeness of Jesus Christ. For us to do it all alone is to disobey our calling and to develop spectators, rather than fully functioning followers of Jesus.

One of the most difficult areas of ministry for many youth workers is the area of delegation. It's not that we lack the desire, we just sometimes lack the forethought to develop others. When it comes to delegating, Dave Stone's "Four Phases of Leadership" is extremely helpful.[1]

1. I do it, and you watch.
2. I do it, and you do it.
3. You do it, and I assist.
4. You do it, and I do something else.

The first time I (Jim) asked Doug to help me with a retreat, he was nervous about being in a leadership position, and I was nervous that he would not do as good a job as I would. I took responsibility for most of the retreat preparation, but he was by my side observing (I do it and you watch). During the next retreat I gave him more responsibilities and we led the retreat together. He gained both confidence and enthusiasm (I do it and you do it). On our third retreat I handed the leadership to Doug. I became his assistant. My job was to watch, observe and make helpful comments. I remember helping him when he needed a Plan B, because the snow retreat had become a mud bowl. The retreat didn't run as smoothly as if I had been the leader. After all, I had put on scores of retreats. This was only the third retreat in which Doug had taken over my leadership (you do it and I assist).

The fourth time Doug and I tried this process was a very memorable experience for me. He was totally in charge. In fact, he had a new assistant. I was in charge of a cabin of rowdy senior guys in our youth ministry (you do it and I do something else). Doug's leadership ability was excellent. His talent in administration far exceeded mine. At first I felt awkward about not being in on the decisions of the camp; however, it gave me the opportunity to pour my life into the guys in my cabin and it gave Doug the opportunity to see that he was capable of doing a great job of leading a retreat. Now there were two people in the church who could lead a youth retreat, with more on the way.

As you equip students to do the actual work of the ministry, the results will be evident in their enthusiasm about their faith and what God can do through them.

Being a Model

One of the most memorable experiences in my Christian life happened while I (Jim) sat in what I thought would be a dull chapel service at the Christian university I attended. A thin, short bald-headed missionary stood up to speak. As he looked out at the crowded auditorium, he pointed his finger and shouted, "You are the only Jesus somebody knows!" He kept repeating the same phrase over and over. Finally on the tenth go-round, he looked straight at me, pointed his index finger and again shouted, "You are the only Jesus somebody knows!" It was as if God turned on a light inside my brain and heart. It dawned on me as never before that I represented Jesus Christ to those around me who knew very little about Him—to those who seldom, if ever, read the Bible or attended church. Through my life, actions and lifestyle I was modeling Jesus Christ to them. *You* are modeling Jesus Christ to the students in *your* youth ministry.

Kids find heroes among musicians, celebrities, actors/actresses, or athletes whose lifestyles are contrary to Scripture. When it comes to the Christian life, kids also imitate their leaders. That's why ministry that emphasizes relationships is so important. The best way to model the Christian lifestyle is through a consistently open and honest life. When students see in you a person who loves God but isn't perfect and still has problems, they will want to identify with your Christian faith. Our students need to see us as people who are in process, just like them, of being transformed and changed into the likeness of Jesus.

My (Jim's) life verse for youth ministry summarizes the call to discipleship and modeling the Christian life. It was Paul's philosophy of ministry, as well as his heartbeat for the people of Thessalonica: "We loved you so much that we were delighted to share with you not only the gospel of God but our lives as well, because you had become so dear to us" (1 Thessalonians 2:8).

Yes, we are called to give our young people the gospel of God, but we are also challenged to give them our very lives. Your actions, your lifestyle, your openness and your vulnerability will teach your students more than any curriculum lesson you ever will. And it will be those things that they will remember long past the lessons you teach and the programs you plan.

Since role modeling is the most important aspect of Christian education and discipleship, we believe we need positive male and female role models in leadership. One of the most powerful ingredients of discipleship is to have positive role models of both sexes in front of students. The question is, What are we modeling?

The typical American Christian church still gives students the impression that in most churches men are the leaders and women bake the cookies. The girls in our ministry need to see women in leadership. They need to see other women exercising their gifts to minister to the Body of Christ. One of the most exciting trends of youth ministry in the past five years has been an increase in the number of women in youth ministry. For far too long I've heard teenage girls say, "I want to marry someone like Scott, my youth worker" rather than, "I want to have a ministry like Megan has had with me."

When girls see women leading and ministering (particularly in youth ministry), it gives them hope that God can use them to do tremendous things for the Kingdom. Students need to see men and women working together in partnership. It gives girls a vision to minister to others; it gives guys a better perspective on women.

Person-Centered Ministry

Throughout the life and ministry of Jesus we see a person-centered discipleship ministry. Jesus spoke to large numbers, but the majority of His time and energy was focused on a few people. We've found that the single greatest success in a ministry is when we get our eyes off the big numbers and focus on individuals. Helping students become lifelong followers of Jesus isn't about programs; it's about relationship. Programs are the framework within which ministry takes place. The key to seeing students' lives transformed into followers of Jesus is found in shepherding, one life at a time—but what does it take?

Be a Friend

We can't shepherd from a distance. We need to be involved in the lives of students if we are to see any lasting ministry happen. By spending time with students, you communicate value and concern for their lives. Shepherding means that we are willing to take the time to enter into students' lives, to build relationships with them and to be there at the critical moments of their lives.

Arrange times with students in your group to just get to know each other. This is not a time to bring out your Bible and preach; instead, use this time to find out as much as you can about the student, and let him or her get to know you better. You might end up talking about school, sports or whatever else the student happens to be into. Even in a one-hour conversation you can learn a lot about a student, and you've probably made a friend for the rest of the year. Sometimes the student may share about his or her family struggles, dating problems or other concerns. The key is to build a relationship and be genuinely interested in their lives.

Be a Pastor

We can sometimes forget that we as youth workers are also pastors to our groups. Shepherding students—being their pastor—is a role that every youth worker, whether paid or volunteer, is called to play. It is important to periodically assume our pastoral role, finding out where students are spiritually and helping them grow.

Spiritual growth is both a journey and a process. We need to be proactive in helping students walk along that process. Our calling as youth workers is to take students from where they are now and to lead them where they need to be. A good shepherd is always thinking, *Where is this student on his or her journey with Christ? Where does God desire for him or her to be? What resources are available to get him or her there?*

Students need follow-through and ongoing nurturing. Take the initiative to periodically get together with students individually just to talk. Many times you'll see the conversations turn to some very valuable dialogue. Even if you feel the conversation is getting nowhere, the fact that you initiated a meeting with that student may be a very significant event for him or her and lead to more influential discussions in the future.

Be a Counselor

Like it or not, every youth worker is a counselor. You may not be a *professional* counselor, but the fact remains that you *will* counsel kids in your ministry and you *will* have a great effect on them. It's not a matter of *if* but *when* you will encounter students in crisis. Research indicates that peers or adults, not certified counselors, do most counseling. Also, many professional counselors contend that the *best* counseling takes place in a nonclinical setting.

Counseling requires listening, and listening is the language of love. A good counselor is a good listener. Let young people talk. They need to verbalize their problems before they can understand your input. Don't jump to conclusions; many kids will not tell you their real problem until the very end. When listening to a student's tale of woe about his or her tyrannical parents, also keep in mind that there are two sides to every story.

There will be many times when you'll be called upon to be a counselor. After an event someone might ask to talk with you, or a family might ask for your input concerning their problems. One-on-one counseling will play an important part in your overall effectiveness in ministry.

If you haven't already, become educated in basic counseling skills. Many community colleges and seminaries offer basic counseling courses. Read books on counseling. Talk with a professional counselor or your pastor for helpful ideas. But by all means, become educated in basic counseling skills.

When counseling, it is crucial to know your limits. Some situations are too complicated for an amateur. Develop relationships with a few good counselors in your area whom you can utilize for referral. Find out about their philosophies and approaches. Most counselors will welcome calls from you with questions about situations you are involved in. If a counselor isn't willing or able to give you some time and attention, find someone who will.

Even after you have referred someone to a counselor, stick with your shepherding role. Don't just dump the young person on the counselor. Your support and encouragement will complete his or her counseling experience.

Be a Mentor

Take the time to get to know your students. This is how you'll find where they are and where they need to be. One of the more effective discipleship methods is a one-on-one study program. Select a growth book or workbook together with your discipleship group or an individual person. Choose something that is of both legitimate value and genuine interest to your student; then commit to one hour of study per week for a fixed period of time (such as six weeks).

As you work through the material, try to avoid a teacher/student relationship. Instead, approach the material as two learners. When the two of you study together, the atmosphere is much more conducive for learning. Leave time in your hour together for sharing and prayer. After you have completed the predetermined length of time, evaluate your progress and decide whether or not to continue with another study. More often than not, you'll find that this is such a great experience for both of you that you will want to continue.

Making It Happen

For years I (Jim) have asked my adult volunteers to commit to an extra hour and a half of ministry each week. I've always felt that the more ministry involvement adults have, the longer they will stay as volunteers. I ask the volunteers to spend one hour a week meeting with a student to study a growth book together. During this time they will study the Word of God, but they will also talk and build a relationship. I then ask the adults to spend 15 minutes making phone calls to students each week. One week they may only talk to one student; the next week they may reach five students. I figure they will average around three calls a week. Lastly, I challenged them to take 15 minutes a week and write a positive, affirming note or e-mail to three students. Within 90 minutes each week, those volunteers will have had a significant influence in the lives of seven students.

90 Minutes of Influence

60 minutes in growth book	1 student
15 minutes for phone calls	3 students
15 minutes for notes/e-mail	3 students
	7 students total

Small Is Good

My (Jim) wife, Cathy, loves small groups. Over the years she has led several support groups and has always had the same successful results. In a small group atmosphere there is more open sharing, vulnerability, encouragement and community. The group becomes the high point of each person's week. It's a time of intimacy and acceptance. Small groups go deeper and often have a greater impact than any other ministry program. Cathy's expertise is not in front of a large crowd, yet her small-group ministry has had a greater impact on kids' lives throughout the years than any of our large group activities.

In a world that shouts "bigger is better," small is more effective when it comes to seeing lasting impact in the life of a young person. In a small group atmosphere students can be known, and they can be real. True accountability can only take place when we know each other. The ingredients of an effective small group ministry are

- Three to six kids meeting regularly for a set period of time
- A time of heartfelt sharing, encouragement and support
- A time of prayer

Other options may be a Bible study or worship time. However, if these needs are being met in another area of your ministry, you may want to focus more on the personal sharing as the main part of the small group.

Although we're not for a totally homogenous youth ministry, sometimes the more the students have in common, the easier it is to start a small group. You'll want to take into consideration age, sex, spiritual maturity and location. You'll want to start with a commitment to meet regularly for perhaps only six weeks and then reevaluate. The longer you meet together, the deeper the sharing will tend to be. Some small groups end up taking on a ministry project together; other groups dissolve after only a few meetings. Some groups meet specifically for prayer, others for Bible study, and still others for a set purpose (such as meeting the needs of the children of alcoholics or of kids from divorced homes). Small groups can be one of the most effective discipleship vehicles in your ministry. They can be time consuming, but the results are definitely worth it.

> Chapter 8 describes this method of ministry in detail, with the emphasis on the staff putting one-on-one ministry into practice.

CHAPTER 10

Worship: Encountering the Living God

One of the most exciting trends in youth ministry today is the desire and hunger on the part of young people for worship. In fact, there is a worldwide wave of the Holy Spirit that is moving and breaking into the lives and hearts of students. Like never before, they desire to connect with the living God through passionate and intimate worship experiences.

Many people are asking what the next model or strategy of youth ministry is going to look like. Whatever it looks like, the basis for the next generation for youth ministry must focus on helping students encounter the living God of Scripture in a personal and dynamic way. Worship is one of the greatest tools we have for doing this. The result will be students who are passionate seekers and followers of God, desiring nothing less than to serve and follow Christ with their whole lives. When the groundwork has been effectively laid and students have developed the skills to worship, they can have a regular and meaningful worship experience, even in the confines of a more traditional church.

The Importance of Worship

God is worthy of our worship, because of who He is and what He has done. As we are reminded in Revelation 4:11 and 5:12:

> You are worthy, our Lord and God, to receive glory and honor

> and power, for you created all things, and by your will they were created and have their being. Worthy is the Lamb, who was slain, to receive power and wealth and wisdom and strength and honor and glory and praise!

To live the Christian life is to be a worshiper of God. Worship plays a vital role in the life of a believer. It is not an option but a foundational action and discipline in maturing as a Christian. It needs to be an important part of our ministry to students—for good reason. Scripture places the worship of God as the highest priority of a Christian. Just consider some of the words from the book of Psalms:

> Praise the LORD, O my soul; all my inmost being, praise his holy name. Praise the LORD, O my soul, and forget not all his benefits—who forgives all your sins and heals all your diseases, who redeems your life from the pit and crowns you with love and compassion, who satisfies your desires with good things so that your youth is renewed like the eagle's (Psalm 103:1-5).
>
> Give thanks to the LORD, call on his name; make known among the nations what he has done. Sing to him, sing praise to him; tell of all his wonderful acts. Glory in his holy name; let the hearts of those who seek the LORD rejoice. Look to the LORD and his strength; seek his face always (Psalm 105:1-4).
>
> Let everything that has breath praise the LORD (Psalm 150:6).

Worship Helps Us Understand God's Character

As we worship God, we gain a better understanding of who He is and what He has done for us. Many of the psalms call us through worship to remember the acts of God and to make them known to the nations and future generations. Worship is a way to keep His character and acts fresh in the minds of our students. As they sing about His mercy and love, they can recall how God has been faithful in mercy and love in their lives.

As they sing Scripture-based songs focusing on the character and nature of God, the Holy Spirit is released to bring about personal and dynamic heart change.

Praise and worship are vehicles to help students understand the fullness of who God is—His character and His attributes. Love, mercy, forgiveness, holiness, providence and redemptive acts—all become more of a reality to students as they have time to reflect and respond to God in worship. Good worship can teach good theology, as well as help us touch the heart of God.

God is enthroned in our praises; He is surrounded by them (see Psalm 22:3, *NLT*). God, through the person of the Holy Spirit, dwells in the midst of worship. When we, whether individually or corporately, actively worship our God, we invite His presence to be a part of our gathering. We invite His healing, convicting and forgiving presence to be a part of our ministries—releasing Him to move and change lives. God is living and active; through worship He can individually minister to lives and hearts, helping us to understand Him in a fresh way and to walk in the newness of knowing Him.

Worship Is an Active Response to God

Søren Kierkegaard is said to have challenged Christians not to ask about a worship service "How was it?" but instead "How did I do?" Worship is a main avenue to be able to reflect back to God our feelings and desire to follow Him. Not just the duty of the Christian, worship is a lifeline to share our hearts with the heart of God—where we can commune with Him, sharing our thoughts and desires. Much like the Christian life itself, worship is not a spectator sport but an active response. It demands involvement and participation. The main reason our young people get so little out of worship is because they put very little into it. Involvement in the worship experience is key.

When we view worship as an *active* response, we can understand that we are actually participating in the celebration through our own personal worship as well as in corporate worship, which includes praise, music, prayer, confession, forgiveness, thanksgiving, sharing of gifts, Scripture reading, proclamation and communion. When kids say the worship service is boring, we shouldn't apologize. Rather, we must help them understand for themselves if in fact the worship really wasn't relevant or if they simply came with low expectations. Since worship is an active response, we must help students understand why and how they should actively participate in worshiping God.

Worship is a stimulated response to the unconditional love that God has shown to humankind (see Romans 5:8). We must help Christians understand that they are to love God out of a response for what He has done for us and not merely out of responsibility. Genuine worship moves from an inward response to an outward response, beginning in the heart before it can be truth expressed from the lips.

Worship Builds Community

Worship fulfills a major need of adolescents; it gives them a corporate identity. Worship provides a sense of family within the church. It helps students move their focus from themselves, giving them a sense of greater community that is responding to the love of God. It gives meaning through collective association with other believers and the elements of tradition. All forms of worship, whether highly traditional or relaxed and contemporary, have ritual and tradition. It is that sense of ritual and tradition that gives students a sense of community and belonging to something greater than themselves.

The unfortunate fact today is that statistically, a sense of community is something students rarely encounter. From broken families to busy lives, students are starved for a sense of community and belonging. As they encounter a community that is seeking the face of God, they will naturally be drawn to it. They desire connectedness—not only to others but also to something (or someone) greater than themselves. Although worship can be intensely personal, students best express worship in the midst of community. Worship is their chance to engage the living God in a personal way, in the midst of a community of others seeking His face.

Worship Is Transformational

Worship has a transforming power. When we encounter God for who

He is and see ourselves for who we are, we are truly changed and transformed. Isaiah 6:1,5 states:

> I saw the Lord. . . . "Woe to me!" I cried. "I am ruined! For I am a man of unclean lips, and I live among a people of unclean lips, and my eyes have seen the King, the LORD Almighty."

Just as Isaiah was brought face-to-face with his own sinfulness, so too will our students see theirs when they encounter God. Yet just as Isaiah's sin was wiped away and he was commissioned to change his world, so are we and our students. As they encounter God and see their own lives in contrast to His glory, they will see their sin, repent, and receive forgiveness and restoration. Then they can be called to impact their world. Worship is a time to interact with God and listen to His call. It is a time to put our priorities in order. It is a place to reflect on our journey with Him. In worship we know that God will speak. We need to teach students how to listen to His personal and corporate Word through the many aspects of worship.

Worship is not based on performance. It is not based on mere entertainment—or godly entertainment. Meaningful and transformational worship means taking the opportunity to encounter the living God and having the space to respond to Him in creativity. It is examining the depths of God and the depths of our hearts and responding to what we find there.

A Call to Worship

Given the reality of the need for worship, what can youth workers do to cultivate meaningful worship experiences?

1. **Teach what worship is and how to worship God.** Many Christians assume that when you enter into a relationship with Christ, you automatically know what it means to worship God. This is just not the case. God deserves our worship and honor; we need to learn what it means to worship Him "in spirit and truth"

(John 4:23). That is why transformational ministry with students must include solid, biblical teaching on the magnitude of worship in every believer's life.

2. **Help young people understand the characteristics and nature of God.** You might want to teach a series on the attributes of God. As you look at His qualities of unconditional and sacrificial love, patience, steadfastness, holiness and creation—to name only a few—it becomes very apparent that God is worthy to be worshiped. Far too often young people view the Lord as a God of works and not of grace and wonder. No wonder they are not excited about worship!
3. **Take the lead as a worshiper.** If you are a person with a passion for worship, that passion will infect your ministry. We need to take the lead in valuing and practicing meaningful worship. Our students need to see us worship. They need to see and hear about the impact it has made on our lives—how we view God and live in light of that knowledge. We've noticed that in youth ministries where worship is a priority, the entire group will be more excited about worship. If you personally do not participate in worship, don't expect your group to be passionate about it.
4. **Let students plan and lead worship.** When we allow students to lead, plan and implement worship experiences, they will find worship more meaningful. As students are allowed to be a part of the creative process, they will participate more and more. From planning worship events to leading a worship team, students are more than capable and more motivated to make worship meaningful. Let students put together the order of worship: the songs, the sharing and the creative response to the worship time. Allow them to have a hand in the overall worship experience; you'll never regret it!
5. **Provide students opportunities to respond.** We do a great disservice to students when we lead them to encounter the living God and don't give them time and space to respond to Him. Whether through a simple opening prayer time or some other creative response, we need to give students time alone or corporately to

reflect and respond to God's voice in their lives. Encourage them to respond to God creatively.

6. **Let students come as they are.** We need to make young people aware that they are always welcome to worship God. Students need to feel the freedom to worship God as *He* leads them to and where and when He leads. Whether kneeling, sitting or standing, hands raised, down at their sides or hands clasped together, we need to give students the freedom to come as they are. After all, what matters most is not the outward appearance or posture but the state of the heart—the inward devotion to the holy and righteous God.
7. **Help students encounter the awesomeness of God.** Often the problem in motivating students to worship lies in the fact that we don't paint a picture of a God that inspires or moves them to worship Him. We need to intentionally teach in awe of who God is. His Word is filled with passages that speak of the fear of the Lord. We need to help students understand the bigness of God and to fear Him (literally to stand in awe, honoring and respecting Him). We cannot truly worship God's mercy and forgiveness until we understand the awesomeness of His character and how undeserving we are of His grace and mercy.

The Length of a Little Creativity

Unfortunately, when it comes to worship, many have placed worship into a very small box. Our times of worship can seem very mechanical and predictable. Since many students have never been exposed to more creative styles of worship, they are unaware of possibilities that may make their worship of the living God a more vital and positive experience.

One of the people often overlooked by the church is the artistic, innovative person. Creative worship tends to relate well to this type of person. By using a more varied approach to worship, you will see that some of the possibilities that you personally might not choose can be highly meaningful to someone else. In fact, the beauty of worshiping God is that He is bigger than our particular style or preference of worship.

For creative worship ideas, visit YouthBuilders at www.youthbuilders.com. Also check out *Fresh Ideas: Worship Experiences* (Ventura, CA: Gospel Light, 1999) by Jim Burns and Robin Dugall.

CHAPTER 11

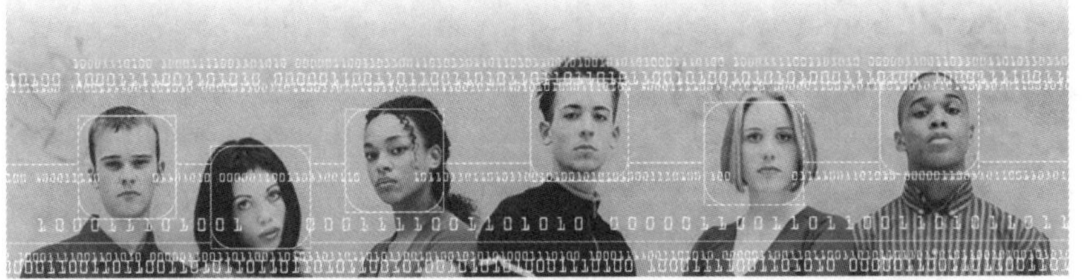

Camps and Retreats

All of us have experienced the feeling. You know the one: that feeling all youth workers get right before leaving for a camp or retreat. It's a mix of emotions that can be summed up in the words "why" and "what." *Why on earth do we do these things? What did we forget? Why do I stay up late, later than I have ever before, doing things I would never do any other time? What is God going to do this weekend?* The answer to those questions must be the driving force for continuing to do camps and retreats. Why *do* we do them? The answer is simple: We are involved in camps and retreats because of the incredible spiritual impact they can have on our students.

Spiritual Impact

It was Christian educator John Westerhoff who said,

> If we really wanted to be effective in Christian education, we would eliminate Sunday schools and use the money that we spent on them for camps and retreats. If you could get everyone in your church away for two weekend retreats a year, you would have more and better Christian education than a whole year's worth of one-hour Sunday school classes.[1]

The value of retreat experiences is incalculable in the lives of students. More often than not, it is at camps and retreats that major life decisions are made. The time, effort and energy expended in preparing for camps and retreats are time, effort and energy well used for the kingdom of God. Consider these thoughts. Camps and retreats

- **Have a Sense of Excitement**—They are high-water marks in most every youth ministry. There's a sense of excitement as you pull away from the church parking lot. There's a sense of excitement as we drive into the facility. It's a chance to get away, to be refreshed.
- **Get Us Out of the Ordinary**—They get us out of our usual surroundings and our usual schedule. They place us into a more relaxed environment, away from normal distractions that clamor for our attention. It is within this relaxed, unordinary and sometimes even quiet environment that students can hear the voice of God more clearly.
- **Are More Casual**— In camp and retreat settings, it is much easier to relax, open up and have fun together. There is a sense that we are away from home and that it's okay to be ourselves.
- **Are Highly Relational**—They can be key in developing new relationships, as well as in deepening existing relationships. Time can be spent away from distractions—no television, no phones, no Internet, no work schedules, no appointments, no meetings—just time to be together to interract and connect with one another. Because we are away from the busyness of life for a time, our focus can be on connecting with our students in deeper ways.
- **Make Us More Spiritually Open**—It is within the environment of camps and retreats that students can be brought face-to-face with God Almighty. Campus Crusade for Christ says that 75 percent of their 10,000-plus personnel made a first-time commitment to Jesus Christ at a camp or retreat. How many times have we seen students do the same? Many times in our ministry, the times spent on camps or retreats were hallmarks for our students in their spiritual lives. We've all seen students make life-altering decisions—to surrender their lives to Christ, to get out of bad relationships, to turn over areas of their lives that they have been holding onto, and more. It's not that God speaks louder at our camps or on our retreats; it's that we place ourselves in a position to hear His voice more clearly.
- **Build Lifelong Memories**—Whether it is life-altering decisions

that are made, significant conversations that take place or a certain activity that we do—rich memories are developed as we do camps and retreats with students. They may be deeply spiritual memories; they may be creative, out of the ordinary or even simple, yet all the memories that we carry away from camps and retreats have a profound impact on our lives.

- **Build Tradition**—In an ever-changing world, our camps and retreats can have a tradition-forming influence. As memories are developed and relationships fostered, students begin to look forward to a particular trip or a particular location. Those times and locations stir in us a sense of who God is and what He has done in our lives. They become markers—almost like altars in the Old Testament—identifying a specific place and time that God met us and changed our lives.

A 27-year-old man came up to me (Jim) at a restaurant and said, "Years ago, we went on a weeklong houseboat trip together. It was the greatest week of my entire life. Seldom does a day go by without me thinking about that significant week. Until recently I've strayed from God, but the memory of that single week on the houseboat with our church group has drawn me back to God." To be honest, I had almost forgotten the trip and barely recognized the man. Yet that one-week trip had built a foundation for him, a moment in time where God met him and changed his life. That is the power of doing camps and retreats.

Recently, I (Mike) was speaking at a winter camp and experienced what can happen spiritually in the lives of students. It was a Sunday night, and after encountering God in worship and through His Word, we had a response time when students came forward with 3x5-inch index cards on which they had written an area of sin that was plaguing them. One by one, they came forward to stand before the cross, pick up the hammer and a nail, and literally nail their sins to the cross of Christ. Student after student hammered their nails into the cross, experiencing the freedom and forgiveness that come from surrendering at the foot of the Cross. As the band led us in worship, it took almost an hour to get the students through the lines. Tears were shed and freedom was found. Some stayed at the altar, kneeling and worshiping God. We were on holy ground. Few people left unchanged by that encounter.

Camps and retreats are powerful times, where we can be open to what God wants to say. They are times where memories are forged and relationships are built or strengthened. Camps and retreats are opportunities for us to get away from our normal cluttered surroundings and enter another environment where we can encounter God. Never underestimate the power of creating healthy life-altering memories and traditions through camps and retreats.

GUIDELINES

Set Goals

A camp or retreat can be an extremely valuable experience, yet many times because of the lack of proper planning or established goals for the experience, it doesn't meet our expectations. No matter what camp or retreat you are planning, be sure to have a clearly stated purpose for the event. Know what you're trying to accomplish; it will make all the difference. Your planning, your activities, your program, your spiritual emphasis—everything should revolve around your stated purpose.

Each leader involved in the event should have in mind a clear picture of the purpose of the camp or retreat. If it is an evangelistic camp, let the leaders know that and then discuss how you plan to carry out the task of accomplishing this goal. If the camp is designed to develop a stronger community within the group, it will more likely happen with established goals.

Prepare a Flow Chart

A flow chart is an organizational tool to help you plan an event, carry out the responsibilities and keep accountability of jobs in order to make it easier to carry out your goals. The purpose of the flow chart is to let nothing slip by you. Once you've created the chart, you won't have to re-engineer the responsibilities for the next retreat; instead, simply adapt some of the tasks to new areas added for the following year.

Using a flow chart will assist you in your preparation and delegation.

When people have clear-cut responsibilities spelled out on paper, they will generally follow through better than with unexpressed expectations. When you put together a flow chart for each camp or retreat, place realistic dates for completion of the tasks. This will give other people a better understanding of their responsibilities and will let you get a better feel for the overall picture and timing needed for pulling off the event.

Provide Excellence in Your Promotion

When it comes to promoting the camp or retreat, honor your students with excellence. You may or may not be a graphic artist, but most likely there is someone in your church that would be willing to use his or her giftedness to make your promotional piece stand out. Usually a little more time and money make a drastic difference in promotional material. Whether it is a printed piece or a video, a mailer or a brochure—be sure to go the extra mile in creating promotion that is aesthetically attractive and informationally accurate. And remember, one of the most effective forms of promotion is the personal invitation of another student or leader. The words "I want you to go with me" carry a lot or weight in the eyes of students.

Check the Facilities

I'll (Jim) never forget the first year I chose the lake for our waterskiing trip. We were going to camp for two nights in the public campgrounds. We figured we would be right at the beach and transportation wouldn't be a problem. Because I thought there would be covered facilities, we didn't think we would need big canopies for shade. Two days before we left for our trip, with all the information already in the hands of the students and their parents, I decided to call a friend of mine who lived near the lake to ask a couple of questions. I found that the campground facilities were four miles from the lake. There were no showers or changing rooms—nothing but a few outhouses. I learned that I needed a special license to launch the boats on this lake and that there were no fire pits for our evening times of worship. I was in a panic. We ended up going to another lake with only mediocre facilities. The retreat would have run much more smoothly if only I had checked out the facility ahead of time.

Take the time to check the facility—in person, if possible. Take a few students with you to get their reactions. You'll find that this is a great way to spend some great relational time with those students too.

Be Aware of Insurance Liabilities

If parents knew the gambles churches often take when it comes to insurance, they would shudder at the thought of allowing their children to be a part of some of our events. Many youth workers think someone else in the church has taken care of the insurance for camps and retreats. Before you ever go on a camp or retreat, familiarize yourself with the entire insurance package of your church. Does your insurance cover snow accidents or winter sports? Does your church insurance cover other people's cars? What is the insurance policy of the facility to which you're going? Many times churches are inadequately covered when it comes to camps and retreats. Know what your church's insurance covers. Know what your destination's insurance covers. Know what parents' insurance will need to cover. Insurance policies vary from facility to facility and church to church, so know what you are dealing with before ever leaving the church parking lot.

Provide Adequate Leadership

Your camp will only be as successful as the quality of its leadership. Prepare your leaders; let them know what you expect from them before they go on the trip. Challenge them to have a significant conversation with each student for whom they are responsible on the camp or retreat. Be sure that every leader has the tools and the information to effectively lead; this includes providing every leader with a copy of the schedule, group discussion questions, directions and maps, appropriate finances and financial information, and the flow chart and guidelines for the trip.

Camps and retreats can also be a successful method of recruiting future leaders. For some reason the open atmosphere of a camp or retreat gives adults the confidence they need to work with students. When adults have a significant camp or retreat experience with students and begin to develop relationships, they become much more likely to join the youth staff. A camp or retreat may also show adults that youth ministry is not their calling. Either way, be sure to keep your eyes open to the leaders of your camp or retreat. Be looking for people who have significant experiences and those who don't.

While on the trip, there are a few simple rules to follow.

1. **Be flexible.** More often than not, plans will not go quite as intended. Something unexpected *will* happen; just expect it. Have a Plan B prepared. When things do not go according to plan (the snow melts, boats break down, etc.), you will need a back-up plan. Remember to go with the flow. Sometimes when plans don't work out and we need to be creative and spontaneous, God does the most amazing things. Memories are built and traditions are formed not only with the things we plan but also with the unexpected and the spontaneous.
2. **Program activities for 17 hours a day.** In other words, be over prepared. It is much easier to cut the program than to have the kids bored because they have nothing to do. Know what you are going to do and be sure that you have everything you need to do it. Print out the schedule for the time at camp, but don't let the students see it. The element of surprise will create an exciting atmosphere. Don't be predictable; be as flexible as you possibly can.
3. **Go easy on the rules.** Even though there are certain rules that must be shared, try to do it in a creative manner. Call them traditions and share them with creativity and humor. Your students will remember them much longer. A few of the common traditions can be summed up as follows:
    - Attend all meals and meetings.
    - No messing around and being where you shouldn't be (girls in guys' rooms and vice versa).
    - No making out.

Evaluate and Debrief

We believe that at the end of every retreat or camp, debriefing and evaluating the experience is a *must*—with both students and leaders.

Giving students the opportunity to evaluate their experience will help you see the good aspects of the event and what areas might need improvement. It is also an opportunity for them to sit quietly for a moment and reflect upon what actually did happen in their lives. A time of evaluation and debriefing with leaders will help them to digest the experience, decide what ministry action steps are needed and set in motion plans for the event the following year.

After a camp or retreat we usually feel too exhausted to spend much time in evaluation, but the time spent will save hours of preparation for the next experience. Have a special dinner when you get home from the event or have a thank-you party with a time of evaluation soon after the event. The information you gather will be priceless for future events.

Have a Time of Reunion

Some time after coming home from a camp or retreat, host a reunion, either at the church or in someone's home. This is a great time to relive some of those memories from the trip, look at a video or photos from the retreat, as well as hear from students about the impact that was made in their lives. A reunion can be a great encouragement for students to continue to live out the decisions they made at camp. It also brings together some of the students that went to camp but have still not quite connected with the rest of the ministry.

> For over 50 ideas for camps and retreats, a sample camping flow chart and a sample evaluation sheet, visit YouthBuilders at www.youthbuilders.com. Also check out *Fresh Ideas: Incredible Retreats* (Ventura, CA: Gospel Light, 1999) by Jim Burns and Mike DeVries.

CHAPTER 12

DEVELOPING STUDENT LEADERS

As I (Jim) look back over my years in youth ministry, I realize that I've helped produce apathetic kids! No, I didn't develop a plan for apathy in the Church or plan on developing lukewarm Christians. My goal was to get young people to fall in love with Jesus, to want to grow in their relationship with Him and to be passionate about their faith. But as I look back and evaluate, not just my philosophy of youth ministry, but what we did practically, I see that sometimes we were the biggest barriers in helping motivate students to be lifelong followers of Jesus.

MISCONCEPTIONS

We say that we are about the business of helping students encounter God, grow in their relationship with Him and become lifelong followers of Jesus—but in practice we do just the opposite. In fact, there are a number of misconceptions we can have about how to get kids excited about their faith and involved in leadership.

One: Youth Ministries Should Be Entertaining

We live in a society that demands entertainment, so in youth ministry we sometimes believe that to have a successful program, we must keep the kids entertained. The more energy, the more exciting the program, the bigger the show, etc., the more successful we will be in ministry. *Wrong.* If our young people are to grow in their passion for Jesus, our first priority must be for them to experience the work of Christ firsthand.

For example, we can never just talk about missions and expect students to understand. They need to *do* missions. Experiential learning is always the best learning. If we must choose between entertaining students with a great speaker on missions or having them *experience* ministry by visiting a rest home or doing some other hands-on ministry, then we must choose the real experience every time. We have not been called to entertain students; we are called to help them encounter and experience Jesus firsthand.

We have to be honest and ask ourselves, *Are we creating spectators of the Kingdom or participators and servants for the Kingdom?* This is not an excuse for a boring youth ministry, but when students are involved in and experience the Kingdom firsthand, they'll tend to be less apathetic and more excited about their relationship with Jesus. Are we about entertainment, or are we about equipping students to be lifelong followers of Jesus?

Two: Bigger Is Better

Whenever we're with a group of youth workers one topic invariably comes up: numbers. Although it may be cloaked in spiritual terms, the underlying question is the same: "So, how many students do you have in your group?" At one point I (Mike) became so frustrated with the question that I started replying, "Enough." Sometimes I'd reply, "I don't really know; they're not there all at the same time."

The question implies that the larger the group, the more successful the ministry. Even many church boards measure the success of the youth worker by the number of students he or she attracts. But that couldn't be further from the truth. Some of the most unhealthy ministries we've ever seen have been large youth ministries. It's easy for students in a large youth ministry to slip in and out unchanged—still spectators. Large youth ministries seem to struggle more to develop servants and leaders. This is not to say that having large groups isn't good; rather, we're saying that bigger isn't always *better*.

No youth worker can develop a large youth ministry with integrity unless it is broken into smaller units. It's impossible for students to feel cared for in a personal manner in a large group unless they're somehow connected to a smaller group within it. If we desire to work in the structure of a large youth group, we must constantly break down that structure into more personal units to keep students from becoming apathetic, overwhelmed or simply neglected.

I've (Jim) challenged youth workers to look instead at the *percentage* of members in a church. Which is more impressive—100 students in a 2,000-member church or 15 students in a 150-member church? From that perspective, many large youth ministries might be considered failures. The bottom line of ministry is not how many kids are coming to our youth ministry but where these students will be five to 10 years from now and how we are preparing them to be lifelong followers of Jesus.

Three: Adult Leadership Should Take on the Major Responsibilities

Adults are usually more dependable than young people, but students need to have genuine responsibilities. Although a youth ministry with complete adult leadership might run more smoothly, the kids will sit back and expect to be catered to rather than to serve. Once students become spectators in a youth ministry, they'll quickly grow apathetic.

I (Jim) remember how one of our students, Brian, came to most of our activities, yet he never seemed to fit in with the rest of the group. At his previous church, Brian told me that he was active and growing—but he was certainly not that way with us. Finally, one day I called his previous youth worker and asked him about Brian. He gave me a great insight that Brian was really gifted on the computer and had done a lot with their group on the technical side of the ministry.

The next Sunday at church, I took Brian aside and told him I heard he was gifted with computers and that our ministry needed a person to help out with the tech team, running all of our PowerPoint and other programs. His face lit up. Immediately Brian's passion returned; he now felt needed. As Brian became involved, his apathy not only faded, but it was also replaced with a passion for God and ministry.

Students need to take on responsibility. As long as they are spectators, they will never fully grow into lifelong servants of Christ. The adult leaders with the most charisma often produce followers, not other leaders. We need to be developing and equipping our students "for works of service, so that the body of Christ may be built up" (Ephesians 4:12). That's our calling.

Four: Students Are Not Ready for Service in the Church

The call to the Christian life is the call to selflessness and to service. Most students are ready to go further and deeper in their Christian life; they just need a challenge. A young person on one of the leadership boards of the church, for example, can be a great source of new ideas, enthusiasm and a refreshing perspective.

Veteran youth pastor Ridge Burns took a group of teenagers who were mostly apathetic about their faith and set spiritual fires in their hearts by allowing them to create what he calls Sidewalk Sunday School. His youth group took on the responsibility of ministering to a group of latchkey kids in a poverty-stricken housing development a few miles from their church. Every weekday the youth group was at the development. They played games, made crafts and told Bible stories. As the students got to know the people, they became a miniature social welfare agency, helping people with shopping, electric bills and many other important details of life. These students ended up renting one of the apartments as their headquarters and paid for the entire ministry out of their own pockets and with fund-raisers. Needless to say, the incredibly renewed, positive spiritual life of the students came out of their excitement from being vessels of ministry used by their Lord.

Students need to see that they're not the church of tomorrow; rather, their gifts, abilities and services are needed *today*. We must do everything we can to assimilate students into the life of the church. Looking back, youth ministry in the past has been far too isolated from the big church. Our ministry will never be finished with students until they become integrated into the life of the church, carrying out the mission of the entire church and not just the youth ministry.

Five: "For Something to Be Done Right, I Need to Do It!"

Because we can be the biggest roadblock in developing our students, we need to ask ourselves a few questions:

- *What are students currently doing within this ministry?*
- *What am I currently doing that could be done by a student?*
- *What absolutely, positively needs to be done by me as the leader? (What would cause the ministry to die if I didn't do it?)*

If we were honest in answering these questions, we'd find that we aren't using students as well as we could and that we are involved in more than we need to be. In fact, by taking on most of the responsibility, we are actually hindering what God wants to do in the lives of our students. God has given students ability, talents and giftedness. Are we helping to develop those gifts, or are we hindering them and actually encouraging our students to be spectators of *our* ministry?

Positive Peer Ministry

The best way to overcome these misconceptions and move students from being spectators to followers of Jesus is through student involvement, or peer ministry. We must constantly be asking questions such as, "How can the students in our ministry feel ownership?" "What areas of our ministry can best be done by students?" "Are the students in our ministry getting trained and empowered to do significant Kingdom ministry?"

The goal, or the calling, of ministry is not to build an empire in our own honor. Our youth ministries should never be focused on our charisma or personality as leader. Too often we have seen what seemed to be thriving ministries crumble when the head leader left. Such ministries were built on the personality and giftedness of that one person, focusing on who that person was, instead of who Jesus is. When we base our ministry on the previously mentioned misconceptions, we focus the ministry on ourselves (and maybe a few other key adults). When ministry becomes focused on entertainment, a program or a few ministry superstars, the result is students who spectate, rarely feeling ownership or involvement. Our calling in youth ministry is to help students move from dependence on us to dependence on Christ. The only way that happens is when we involve students in the ministry, letting them minister and lead their peers. It's ministry to students by students. Not only is it an antidote for apathy, but it is also an effective vehicle for ministry. Students will listen to their peers perhaps more than they will ever listen to us.

Peers have a profound impact that you or I will never have. Each year in May, our group (Mike's) has what's called Senior Month. It's a month set aside to honor our senior class. Each weekend is focused on and planned by the senior class. A few years back, as we were putting together the month, I met with the students who were going to share on those particular Sundays. We worked and worked, going over and over their messages. When their day came, some were, well, less than perfect. Actually, some were almost embarrassing. But what a response from the group! After each message, students lined up to talk to their peers. It wasn't the creativity behind the message. It wasn't that their delivery was flawless. It was communication and ministry with peers. We can share the same message and share similar experiences, and students will be more impacted by their peers every time. It's the feeling of *Hey, I'm going through that right now, and if they can follow Jesus, so can I!* Our students were motivated because they saw their peers involved in the ministry.

The cure for apathy is *involvement.* The road to involvement is often slow—and even painful—but it's worth the price. When students feel cared for, have meaningful responsibilities and begin to use their gifts of service in the church and the community, then they're more likely to remain in the church permanently. When students have the opportunity to minister to their peers, lives are changed—not only the lives of the students in the group but also the lives of the students doing the ministering. Give them a chance to dream and be a part of ministry, and it will become a lifestyle for them.

Developing a Peer Ministry Program

In some churches, the emergence of a peer ministry program can cause fear in some students. Some students will jump at the chance to be involved in some form of ministry; others won't. Some students may fear that they don't have the giftedness or the ability to be involved in ministry. The key for us is to help them see their own potential in the eyes of God, and there are several truths we need to keep in mind.

Students Are Already Ministers

All Christians are ministers. One of our goals as youth workers is to help students develop and experience a lifestyle of ministry.

One morning I (Jim) couldn't attend a Bible study. At the last minute I called Alex, a high school senior, and asked him to lead the Bible study. He wanted to cancel it instead. His philosophy was "No youth pastor, no Bible study." He replied to my question, "We need a minister." I told him, "*You* are a minister." I finally convinced him to lead it. He fumbled through the Bible study his first time, but I never returned to that early-morning group because Alex was capable of leading the group. In fact, the group grew in my absence. Young people are called to be ministers, not merely for the future, but for the here and now!

We're in the Equipping Business

The best youth ministry happens when you give students ownership. The only way for them to grow in ministry and leadership is to let them lead with you. Some youth workers have made the mistake of believing that releasing ownership means handing over the reins with no development. That's simply not true. Our job is to equip and empower our students for ministry. The only way to do that is to give them responsibilities that matter and to empower them to carry out those tasks.

This is also where spiritual gifts comes into our ministry. Depending on our theological slant, we often fall into the trap of emphasizing only a select few of the spiritual gifts that appear in Scripture. We need to expose students to spiritual gifts and afford them the opportunity to explore what their particular gifts might be. The New Testament reveals that the purpose of spiritual gifts is to equip Christians for ministry (see Ephesians 4:11-12). In order to equip our youth for ministry, we need to help them explore their spiritual gifts and find where those gifts and abilities fit into the kingdom of God.[1] As the Body of Christ is built up through the ministry of students, their spiritual gifts will naturally emerge.

Young People Have Something to Offer

In a news special that I (Jim) saw about the rise of teenage murders, the news reporter said, "The kids put a lot of blame on TV and drugs. But I think those are just excuses. I believe the major thing is that these kids just don't have any stake in our society. From infancy on, they are told that they are not worth very much." Students need to know that they are significant. They need to know that they can offer an alternative to what the world has to offer. They need to know beyond a shadow of a doubt that they do matter—that even in this world of the media and technology their lives *count*. They need to know that they are not alone and powerless and that they can make a difference in this world for all eternity. They need to know that they have a profound impact by how they live their lives, what they stand for and what they choose to do for the kingdom of God. This generation, more than any other, needs to hear this message loud and clear.

Students Need a Specific Ministry Role

As mentioned before, students need to have roles and responsibilities that are meaningful, gift-appropriate, timely and challenging. They need tasks, roles and responsibilities that are clearly defined and measurable. They need to know what role they are playing in the ministry and in the importance to the Kingdom. As students gain a handle on a specific ministry that is meaningful, gift-appropriate, timely and challenging, they will begin to see God use them in incredible ways to impact His kingdom. When they experience the victories—and even the frustrations—of ministry, they will grow deeper in their knowledge and experience of who God is. The problem is that sometimes we give our students roles and responsibilities that are unclear or, worse yet, unimportant. Instead, we need to give specific ministries and challenges.

Students Need to Be Released to Do the Work of the Ministry

An effective peer ministry is one in which students are released to do ministry. We release students when we allow them to dream. We need to frequently ask our students, "If you could do anything for the kingdom of God and knew that you'd never fail, what would you want to do?" The answer to that question can be the starting point for many ministry opportunities. It allows God to place within our students a dream and a vision for ministry. When they have a chance to dream and the freedom to develop and pursue their vision, life-changing ministry is developed.

We also release students when we allow them to fail. They need to experience the responsibility and consequences of leadership. Too often we keep a Plan B ready to bail students out of their difficulties. What we are communicating is that we don't believe that they will pull through with their responsibilities. It also communicates that their effort is really not that important and if they don't have the time to fulfill that responsibility, we'll be there with Plan B. We need to communicate that there is no Plan B—if they don't fulfill their responsibilities, then what they're responsible for just won't happen. Too often, youth workers and parents rescue students from the consequences of their failures. Students need to be released in ministry in order to know that what they do matters and that we are looking to them to follow through.

Building a Peer Ministry

There are a number of ways in which to develop a peer ministry. Whatever model or strategy you use, every effective peer ministry must have three components.

1. **Spiritual Accountability**—Every person involved in peer ministry, or student leadership, needs to be in a mentoring

relationship. Spiritual accountability is a necessity. Be sure to provide spiritual nurture and accountability to students who are involved in ministry. This can be through studying a workbook one-on-one with a leader, small-group accountability or a mentoring relationship with a leader.

2. **Ministry Skills**—Every student needs to be equipped with the skills to fulfill his or her role, regardless of what that particular role is. We cannot just give students responsibilities and walk away. We need to walk beside them, equipping them with the tools they need, whether those tools are administrative, relational or teaching skills. For every role that students take on, we should ask ourselves, *What tools and skills does this student need to be successful in his or her specific ministry?*
3. **Hands-On Ministry**—Every student needs to be involved in hands-on ministry opportunities. Peer ministry and student leadership is not a club, nor is it another discipleship group. Students need to get their hands dirty in the work of the ministry. They need to learn the servant aspect of leadership. No matter what a student's ministry role, make sure it is an active one.

The one pitfall of many student-leadership, or peer-ministry, models is that they focus on a select few—those that have either volunteered or been hand selected as leaders by the youth pastor. Developing lifelong servants and leaders for the Kingdom needs to have a broader focus. What about the students who don't volunteer or are not selected? Ministry and leadership are not just for the all-stars. Our calling is to help *every* student have an opportunity in which he or she can serve and experience the joy of ministry.

The model of peer ministry that we prefer is based on getting students involved in meaningful, gift-appropriate, timely and challenging ministry roles. It's a model that focuses on the truth that every Christian is called to serve and be involved in some form of ministry. As students serve within specific ministry teams, natural student leaders will emerge from within each team. This gives the ministry a farm system for developing student leaders.

Ministry Team Development

With Ephesians 4:12 in mind, our overall goal in ministry is not to merely develop a small group of leadership students but to provide avenues for every student to be obedient to the call to serve and contribute to building up the Body of Christ. In order to accomplish this we must move more toward developing a ministry-team mind-set, giving every student an opportunity to serve on a specific ministry team that captures their individual giftedness and passions. Each ministry team can be centered on meeting the needs inside and outside the youth group. Each ministry team should be lead by a specific leadership core that consists of a smaller team of adult and student leaders. The following list is a sampling of ideas for ministry teams in which students can be involved:

- Outreach
- Visitor Follow-Up
- In Reach (Care and Community)
- Worship
- Drama
- Message Preparation
- Promotion
- Technical Ministries
- Prayer
- Small Group Leader
- Photography
- Website
- Office Support
- Campus Ministries
- Hospitality

The options are limitless.

As a wide variety of students begin to serve on a ministry team, naturally gifted leaders will begin to rise. Some of those leaders might be predictable; others might surprise you. As the student leadership core begins to recognize and develop new leaders within the team, those students should be brought into the leadership core.

For a student leader commitment form, visit YouthBuilders at www.youthbuilders.com.

CHAPTER 13

Missions and Service

Some years ago, Cathy and I (Jim) took a trip with eight high school students. We all piled into a van and traveled over 1,500 miles to counsel at a camp, hold Bible studies and do a service project. It was a three-week drama of loving, service, tension, rowdiness and sainthood all wrapped up in one experience. Today all eight of those students are in some form of Christian ministry. I believe they chose to be in ministry as adults because they had a chance to have their hearts broken with what breaks the heart of God when they were in the impressionable years of adolescence. Getting young people involved in missions and service is a key necessity for Christian growth and maturity.

The True Call

The Indian leader Mahatma Gandhi challenged Christians when he said,

> In my judgment the Christian faith does not lend itself to much preaching or talking. It is best propagated by living it and applying it. When will you Christians really crown Jesus Christ as Prince of Peace and proclaim Him through your deeds as the champion of the poor and oppressed?[1]

One does not need to be a Bible scholar to observe that throughout the Gospels, Christ challenged us to become servants with hearts for mission. Christ's call is a call to serve.

Christianity is not about what Jesus can do for me and my life; Christianity is about what we can do for Jesus, surrendering our lives to Him and serving others in His name and for His glory. Take Jesus' parable in Matthew 25:31-46 for example. In the parable, Jesus contrasts two sets of people: the sheep (those who met the needs of others) and the goats (those who, for whatever reason, moved right past those in need). The sheep were ultimately ushered into the presence of God, while the goats were cursed and sent away. The key is found in how each group reacted to the needs of others.

This parable is a clear mandate to meet the needs of others. In addition, Jesus gives His followers a glimpse into what meeting the needs of others entails.

Be Sensitive to the Needs Around Us

We live in a world of desperate need—all we have to do is open our eyes and ears to recognize it. The sheep and the goats from Matthew 25 encountered similar needs: people who were hungry or thirsty, strangers, people who were sick or needy and people imprisoned. Their world was, as ours is, filled with people in need. Our calling is to open the eyes of our students to see the needs right outside their doors. Our hearts need to break with the things that break the heart of God. That happens as our eyes are opened to see the world through God's eyes.

See the Face of Jesus on Those in Need

Beyond just seeing the need, the great truth of Matthew 25 is found in verse 40: "I tell you the truth, whatever you did for one of the least of these brothers of mine, you did for me." Notice the phrase "brothers of mine." Jesus is intimately concerned for those in need; He calls us to no less.

Psalm 34:18 states: "The LORD is close to the brokenhearted and saves those who are crushed in spirit." When we look into the eyes of those in need, do we see the face of Jesus? When Mother Teresa received the Nobel Peace Prize, she was asked by an interviewer, "Why is it that you've committed your life to the sick and dying in the streets of

Calcutta?" Her reply was staggering: "I haven't committed my life to the sick and dying of Calcutta. I've committed my life to Jesus, and it just so happens that I see His face on the sick and dying of Calcutta." When we tangibly reach out to minister to those in need, we are ministering to Jesus Himself.

Use the *Whatever* to Impact Others

"*Whatever* you did for one of the least of these brothers of mine, you did for me" (Matthew 25:40, emphasis added). Jesus is looking for us to do the small things—to literally do *whatever* we can to meet the needs of those around us. More often than not, it's not in the large things that lives are changed; it's in the small things. It is ordinary people doing ordinary things through the power of an extraordinary God. We in youth ministry need to help our students see the amazing things God can do through them as they surrender and are obedient to do the small things to meet needs around us. We need not only to help our students see their potential to change lives, but we also need to provide them with concrete opportunities to do just that.

We firmly believe we are not giving students a true understanding of what it means to be a follower of Jesus Christ if we do not help them understand that being a follower means a lifestyle of servanthood and a heart for missions.

Build a Global Vision

As our students grow in their relationship with God, we must help them develop a global vision. Most American adolescents are not aware that the Body and work of Christ extends past the boundaries of our own country. As youth workers, we must educate our students to the fact that it is our responsibility as Christians to meet the needs of the less fortunate. After all, it was Jesus who said: "From everyone who has been given much, much will be demanded; and from the one who has been entrusted with much, much more will be asked" (Luke 12:48).

One of our goals as youth workers must be to expose students to opportunities to see beyond American Christianity. Our students are infected by a disease called "afluenza." Its symptoms are the mixing of true needs with wants. Mission and service projects give students a different perspective on their own needs versus wants, bringing them face-to-face with their own selfishness and self-centeredness. After a mission trip to a Mexican orphanage, one of my (Jim's) students exclaimed to her parents, "We aren't middle class; we're rich!"

Beyond Split-Level Theology

We believe that one of the grave sins of the Church in years past was to separate the ministries of evangelism and social action. Nelson Bell, the great Christian statesman and missionary doctor to China, put it best: "If you separate evangelism and social action, you only have half a gospel."[2]

In past generations, the theologically conservative Church became uneasy with the liberals' desire for social action, so it backed away completely from social action and social justice. On the other hand, the liberal Church became so caught up in not wanting to look like fundamentalists that it walked away from evangelism. Students today must come to terms with the fact that social action and evangelism are inseparable. Renowned theologian Dietrich Bonhoeffer put it this way:

> To allow the hungry man to remain hungry would be blasphemy against God and one's neighbor, for what is nearest to God is precisely the need of man's neighbor. It is the love of Christ, which belongs as much to the hungry man as to myself, and that I share my dwelling with the homeless. If the hungry man does not attain to faith, then the fault falls on those who refused him bread. To provide the hungry man with bread is to prepare the way for the coming of grace.[3]

Creating Awareness

For many students, the idea of mission and service brings a mental picture of men and women walking through the jungles of Africa preaching to naked natives. Creating awareness is the first step toward helping students understand the need for mission. We must create curiosity, desire and interest. Today's young people need to hear and see the amazing things God is doing throughout the world through people who are committed to seeing lives changed globally. There are several ways of creating a greater interest, desire and awareness in missions.

- Invite a dynamic speaker to share about their experience with missions.
- Invite some students from another youth ministry who have experienced firsthand what God can do on a mission trip.
- Use some of the great resources from various mission agencies that will expose students to the needs around the world.
- Teach on mission and service. The Bible itself is the story of the mission of the Church; teaching on the book of Acts will help your students to see that we are *still* a part of writing the history of what God is doing in the world.
- On your way to a youth ministry event, drive through some local poverty areas to show students the needs of those right around the corner.

Taking One Step at a Time

One of the common mistakes that youth workers make is to go on a two-week trip immediately after one mission presentation. Actually, for long-term results it is better to first sensitize the students to the needs of the world. Not very far from home are desperate needs with easy access for a youth group to experience missions firsthand. A trip to a rest home, convalescent hospital or cancer ward at a children's hospital will help students become immediately aware of the needs in their area. A trip to the inner-city, a rescue mission or a soup kitchen will remind your students of the desperate hunger of people in their own county. By sensitizing the students to the need, you are preparing them to have their hearts broken. Look for those opportunities right around the corner. Plan to take advantage of them and schedule them into your event calendar, whether as a large group event or by encouraging small groups to adopt a mission or service project.

Dirtying Hands and Opening Eyes

You can share all about missions and service, but until people actually experience them for themselves, they are only spectators. It's important to provide hands-on experiences for students—knowing Christ comes best from experiencing His work firsthand.

In order for students to experience missions and service firsthand, we must create an awareness, sensitize them to the need, help them develop viable and hands-on options for ministry and then prepare them for leadership. After they have been sensitized to the needs of others, you need to help them explore various avenues to meet those needs. They need hands-on experiences in coming up with genuine and realistic ideas for missions and service. Here are a couple of ideas for starters:

- Go through Compassion International's Compassion Project and challenge your students to have the youth ministry sponsor a child in a developing nation.
- Before visiting a rest home or a rescue mission, read Matthew 25:31-46 and let students dream up ideas for involvement.

Preparing Students for Ministry

Student preparation and training is an important (and sometimes overlooked) aspect of youth mission experiences. We need to prepare students in every way possible. If they are going to do construction, give them a basic course in the construction you'll be doing before you have them do the work. If they will be running a Vacation Bible School, rehearse the stories, crafts and games beforehand. Good preparation involves teaching students all you possibly can before the project begins.

Get into the Word

Preparing students spiritually is as important as preparing them for their physical tasks. If they are going to work among the poor, read biblical passages on ministry to the poor before you leave. Help students to see the spiritual foundation and calling we have to reach out and minister to others. Have students keep a journal prior to, during and after the experience so that they can see the hand of God on their trip and in their personal lives.

Pray

Make sure that prayer is number one on your priority list. Pray for finances, direction and flexibility needed on the project, for sensitive hearts to what God wants to do and for lives to be changed for His glory. As a part of the training, spend a significant amount of time in God's Word and in prayer. That time alone will greatly impact your students.

Two weeks before leaving for Poland with a group of students, we (Mike) were several thousand dollars short of our financial goal. After spending an entire training session praying for our financial need, one of our girls shared the need with her mom. In passing, her mother shared the need with her boss, a Jewish man from Poland. When he found out that as a part of our trip we were going to be taking students through Auschwitz, he pulled out his checkbook and wrote us a check for the entire amount. Before we ever got on the plane, God met us and changed our lives.

Unite as a Ministry Team

Do everything you can to develop team unity. For extended time in training and community building, plan an overnight retreat with your group. Go to a camp that has a ropes course (or some other extreme activity) and do it together. Take your group rock climbing. Whatever you can do to foster team unity, trust and community within the group will reap incredible results on your trip.

Know the Culture You're Ministering In

Because a mission and service project can be one of the most life-changing faith experiences in the lives of young people, we must take the preparation seriously. The more prepared the students are for their experience, the greater the impact will be during the actual ministry.

- If you are going to a foreign country, be sure to help students understand the culture. Help them learn as much of the language and the cultural norms of the country as they can. It's important that they know what to do and what not to do.
- Have them study the people groups they will encounter.
- Study the history of the country or the region in which you'll be ministering.

All of these ideas will help students better understand where they are going, how they can be culturally respectful, what the people are like and what some of their needs might be.

A Game Plan for Mission and Service Projects

Teach on Mission and Service Regularly

Give students the biblical foundation for the call to service and the mission of the Church. Students need to know how important mission is to the heart of God.

Start Small

Mission experiences are so significant that small is usually better—the smaller the group, the greater the spiritual impact. The more people we bring, the more it can revert to a youth ministry outing or camp.

Get Your Key Staff and Church Leadership Behind You

Be sure to include key church leadership in the planning and implementation of the trip. Have the finance person help with the budget; have the children's ministry director help with the Vacation Bible School training; and communicate with the elders, senior pastor and finance board about the vision and purpose of the trip. The more support you have from church leadership, the better the experience will be.

Have Adequate Finances for the Trip

If your mission trip takes you to unfamiliar territory (this applies especially to cross-cultural and foreign mission trips), make sure you have adequate financial resources. Prepare for unexpected expenses such as needing to spend the night in a hotel, higher transportation costs, etc. The greater the budget need, the more you will need the backing and support of the church leadership and the church as a whole. Financial support is a great way for the church to be involved and get behind the vision. Be sure to reach out to as many people for financial support as possible—remember, a little from a lot goes a long way!

Build a Tradition

Building a long-term ministry relationship is essential to helping students see that ministry itself is a long-term commitment. Find a mission experience that doesn't end with the first trip. Your students will look forward to building a relationship and a history based on a certain mission experience. A long-term commitment will also help students see the fruit of their labor. If you are in one location one year and then another location the next year, your students will miss out on the blessing of seeing long-term ministry results.

Encourage Adult Participation

You will need a higher adult-to-student ratio on a missions trip than for most other youth ministry events. The more adults you have, the smoother the trip will run; and practically speaking, adults make great public-relations people when the trip is over. Time and time again we've heard from leaders about the impact trips have had on them personally; many have even gone into ministry full-time after volunteering for missions trips.

Make a Pretrip Visit to the Ministry Site

Whenever possible, be sure that you've seen where you're going and done what you're planning for your missions trip before you ever take your students. Ask the questions that parents, church leadership and an adult leader on the trip would ask. Find out as much information as possible ahead of time and hand out that information to everyone concerned, including parents, church leaders, adult leaders and students.

Debrief Each Day's Experience

Many of the students will be experiencing life on a new level when they embark on missions trips. You will need a regular time to review each day's new adventures; spend time in worship, encouragement and sharing. Allow students to share what God is doing in their lives and new insights they may have about ministry and about God.

Debrief after the Trip

When you return from the missions trip, be sure to take the time to debrief the entire experience. Have a written evaluation for each team member, student and adult to fill out. The information will prove an invaluable resource for planning future trips.

Provide Opportunities for Students to Share Their Experiences

It's essential for students' spiritual growth to share their experiences when they return home from a missions trip. If at all possible, allow time in the worship service at church to have the students share. Many of your church's small groups and Bible studies would welcome the opportunity to listen to what the students have to share. You can also share with youth programs from other churches.

> For ideas on mission experiences, visit YouthBuilders at www.youthbuilders.com. Also check out *Fresh Ideas: Missions and Service Projects* (Ventura, CA: Gospel Light, 1999) by Jim Burns and Mike DeVries.

CHAPTER 14

Developing a Dynamic Volunteer Team

One Sunday morning, I (Jim) was confronted by a youth worker who was observing our Sunday morning program. The morning was not quite up to par; it was a dismal attempt at programming, my talk was mediocre at best, and the worship leader didn't show up. To top it all off, some of the students in the back of the room actually got into a fight during my talk! After the meeting this confident young youth worker said to me, "I don't understand how you could have a few hundred kids here this morning, while the most I've ever had is 18. I'm a better communicator than you are—and I can definitely put on a more interesting program."

I replied, "You're probably right. But did you notice all the adult volunteers sitting with the kids? I believe that God will give us only the amount of kids we can actually handle. You are the only adult youth worker at your church; it's a one-man show. How many more students can you handle by yourself? If I were you, I'd recruit adults to help you and then watch the numbers increase!"

Perhaps the most important (and often most overlooked) aspect of youth ministry is building a dynamic youth ministry team. In fact, we would go so far as to say that beyond your programs—and even beyond the students themselves—your most precious commodity is your volunteer team. The writer of Proverbs reminds us that "for lack of guidance a nation falls, but many advisers make victory sure" (Proverbs 11:14). The point is clear: the quality and quantity of your youth ministry directly depends on the quality and quantity of your volunteer leadership team.

More often than not, leaders are the biggest roadblocks in developing a dynamic ministry team of volunteers. Sometimes it's the guru mentality that thinks, *But I'm the youth leader. I need to do everything. If the students need to be ministered to, I'll be the one*. Other times it's the Lone Ranger mentality that believes, *I'm too busy ministering to students to develop others. I'm the only one there is. I guess if you want to do something, I'll get to you when I need you*. We can also fall into the trap of telling ourselves, *Well, when I look around at my church, there just isn't anybody who can help*. The issue may not be that there truly isn't anybody; instead, the issue is that we're looking for the wrong type of person.

No matter what our state of mind, we need to remember one fact: to minister to a wide variety of students effectively, we must minister in the context of a team. To have an effective youth ministry today requires a team-oriented mind-set. It takes time and energy to build a team, but the long-term results are well worth the investment.

We cannot do ministry all on our own. There is no way we can impact the lives of students from up front or through a program. If we are to see long-term impact, we need to develop a ministry team who can enter into students' lives and nurture their growth in Christ. That can only come through a team of adults who are willing to enter into the lives of students and develop relationships that foster personal spiritual growth and accountability.

Bringing a group of adults together to develop a team ministry is no easy task. Unfortunately, there are no simple formulas or methods that insure instant success. If you want to develop a team ministry, it will take your time and attention—not to mention your energy. Just as students need attention, so does your volunteer team. It needs to be more than just one more thing to add to our To Do list; it needs to be a foundational vision for ministry.

If we truly want to see students become life-long servants and followers of Jesus, we need to gather a team of caring adults that have the same passion to see student's lives transformed—a team that can shoulder the load, carry the vision and walk together through the good and bad times in ministry.

As long as we focus on keeping students attracted to the ministry and keeping them entertained, we can get away with having just a few volunteers run programs. These programs may draw numbers, but they will lack depth. We firmly believe that on the day we stand before God, He won't be asking us how many kids came to our ministries. He won't be delving into our programming. He'll want to know what we did with the students He entrusted to us. Are we faithful with the students He has entrusted to our care?

Diversity—Underestimated Power

One of my (Jim) past volunteers, Carl, taught me an incredible lesson in youth ministry. Carl was working at a bank when he volunteered to help with the youth group. My initial reaction was that it wouldn't work. Carl was brilliant but shy. One Sunday morning he asked me if he could give an announcement at youth group—he wanted to take the kids bowling. I replied, "Carl, our students don't really like to bowl; they're too sophisticated for that." But he persevered, so I let him give the announcement after all. It was a horrible display of communication. There he stood, complete with polyester pants and a shirt pocket full of writing utensils, telling the kids he would take them bowling next week. To my surprise and joy, 25 students went bowling with Carl! We even started a bowling league. Carl was an incredible volunteer who had a huge heart for students.

Here's what I've learned: students need a variety of role models. A good team ministry has a mixture of adults, from singles to married couples, college age to grandparents, from athletic types to computer programmers. A diverse staff will relate to a diversity of kids. If you have only one type of personality or interest group on your volunteer team, you will generally miss the opportunity to minister to kids who can't relate or feel that they don't fit in.

A Vision and a Plan

Just as we need to have a vision and a picture of where we are going as a ministry, we also need to have a vision and purpose for building a dynamic ministry team. Developing a volunteer team is a purposeful, proactive venture. It is not something that just happens all on its own. We need to have a clearly defined goal and plan for what we are trying to accomplish in and through our adult volunteer team. We've implemented a purpose statement, which is much like a mission statement for the overall direction of the ministry, to give us a picture of where we were going and some ideas of how to get there.

> In the lives of our volunteers: We exist to *enlist* God's people to be released into ministry through *encouragement* and *equipping* so that they are *empowered* to fulfill their calling to minister.

Purpose statements can give us handles on what to do with adult leaders, as well as an evaluation tool for where we stand in the process.

Recruitment

It's almost impossible to find a youth worker who has enough help! Recruiting volunteers to help in youth ministry is seldom easy and can seem impossible—but it is absolutely necessary. Enlisting people to serve in the ministry is not a once-a-year venture; it's a never-ending cycle of recruiting, equipping and releasing others into ministry. The key to successful recruitment is to have a plan and keep your eyes and ears open—to actively search for potential team members.

Know Your Needs—List the Roles and Responsibilities

When you recruit, know what kind of job you need done and the kind of person you are looking for to do it. For example, if you are looking for a small-group leader for high school, list the responsibilities, time commitments, curriculum possibilities and accountability structure, and indicate how you will support them. When people have a better understanding of what's involved, they will tend to volunteer more readily. Be sure that the roles you give to volunteers are more than just crowd control and clean up. One of the major reasons volunteers leave the ministry is because they feel no meaningful purpose in their roles. We need to craft roles and responsibilities that place people into ministry experiences that will stretch them, change them, change others and utilize their giftedness to impact the kingdom of God.

Ask for a List of Potential Volunteers

Sometimes the church leadership can be your greatest help in enlisting volunteers. Most often they are in touch with potential leaders in the congregation. Ask for 10 minutes in one of their meetings to brainstorm possible names together; then contact those people and tell them that at the last board meeting their names came up as people who might make great youth leaders. Potential volunteers will be blessed and honored that the church leadership sees them in that light.

Have Students Enlist Adult Volunteers

One of the greatest fears of any adult asked to help with the youth group is, *Can I relate? Will the kids like me?* A way to alleviate that fear is to ask your students who they'd like to have working with them. After gathering some names, approach the adults by telling them that the students mentioned their names when asked who they'd like to have as a part of the youth ministry. Knowing that the students want them, potential volunteers will have greater confidence in being a part of the ministry.

Use Existing Volunteers to Enlist Others

I (Mike) can't remember the last volunteer I ever recruited. Why? Because by the time I talked with them, they were already interested. Perhaps the best recruiters of volunteers are other volunteers. Existing volunteers are wonderful recruiters because they move in different circles than we do. They can represent the ministry as a volunteer, answering any questions a potential volunteer may want to ask but might hesitate to ask you. Challenge your volunteers to enlist one person every year that they serve. Most of them will do even better than that.

Look at Existing Programs or Events

Every summer we go on a high school waterskiing trip. It happens to be one of the more effective enlisting tools we have. Every year we have people from our congregation who come along with us on that trip–and come home changed by it. Invariably all they needed was to be a part of a short-term commitment, to see the results and be touched. Camps and retreats are incredible places to invite people who are interested in getting a taste of what the youth ministry is.

Look Outside Your Church

Many Christian universities and colleges have internship programs. We've had great success with students who are ministry majors or psychology majors who would love to do an internship for school credit or simply for experience. It can be worth the effort and energy to contact a local Christian college or university to see what avenue is open to your ministry on campus. Some options might include running an ad in the university newspaper, posting an ad in the student center or listing opportunities on a bulletin board for ministry positions.

Develop a Process for Smoothly Integrating Volunteers

Too often, when we meet people who are vaguely interested in being volunteers, we jump right in, get them to sign on the dotted line and then throw them to the wolves! New volunteers need to go through some form of an orientation/training before starting ministry–to see the overall vision, where they fit in and what their role really looks like. They need to be able to ask questions and be given some of the guidelines and expectations we have for people involved in the lives of students. A clearly defined process is necessary and should include the submission of an application (with references) and an interview, sufficient time for the applicant to consider and pray about what God wants him or her to do, the opportunity to observe a program and, finally, a written commitment.

Be Able to Handle Rejection

Too many youth workers get bitter and frustrated when no one is knocking the door down to volunteer. One of my (Jim's) good friends is an insurance sales executive. I was telling him of my feelings of rejection when someone I ask to volunteer turns me down. His advice was brilliant:

> We expect to make a sale 2 out of 10 times. We never know who will buy, but the odds are in our favor that for every 10 contacts we make, 2 will respond favorably to our offer. The secret is to not feel personal rejection but to expect the odds to finally work in your favor.

If you ask enough people in a thorough manner, you will get positive and long-lasting results.

Spiritual and Personal Development of Your Team

Just as we desire that our volunteer team minister to and shepherd our students, so do we need to shepherd our volunteer team. Our teams need to know that the head youth leader genuinely cares for them beyond what they do for the ministry. For our teams to reach their full ministry potential, they must feel shepherded and nurtured.

Foster Spiritual Growth

Great youth ministry skills without a passionate, intimate relationship with God result in adult volunteers who know a lot about youth ministry but rarely lead students to places of intimacy with Christ. We cannot solely focus on the development of ministry skills. The question we need to be asking ourselves is, *How are we fostering an environment where adult leaders are growing themselves in the knowledge and grace of God?*

True ministry comes from the overflow of our passion and love relationship with Jesus, not from the overflow of our knowledge of youth ministry. Too often we rush right past the spiritual development of volunteer leaders in a rush to develop their ministry skills. We assume that they are experiencing dynamic and impacting growth in their personal spiritual lives and that all we need to do is teach them the right skills. The spiritual growth and health of each adult leader needs to be the number one priority of the team.

Develop Community

Youth leaders need to make it a priority to develop a sense of community in their volunteer team. This sense of community is the by-product of intentional team-building and the communication of value. As our team gets to know and value one another and builds the bonds of community, our students will catch a glimpse of what the Body of Christ is all about. John 13:34-35 states:

> A new command I give you: Love one another. As I have loved you, so you must love one another. By this all men will know that you are my disciples, if you love one another.

It is this mutual care, support and encouragement that builds community and fosters a sense of being a valued part of something bigger than ourselves.

Spend Time Together

We need to be proactive in developing relationships; your investment of time with adult leaders is a sign of your caring about and valuing them. The adult leadership team needs to know that you genuinely care for them beyond the mere fact that they are the people who will drive students on an outing or lead a small group.

Consider it time well spent when you meet your adult leaders on their territory. If Ryan likes to play basketball, play basketball with him. If David and Teresa take their family to a local park most Saturday mornings, offer to bring the picnic lunch one Saturday. Take dinner over to their house one night. Visit them at work and go out to lunch. Run errands together. Play together as a large group. Here's just a sampling of things to do: miniature golfing, bowling, deep-sea fishing, paint balling—the list is endless. The point is this: playing together is a way of building relationship, as well as community.

Offer Accountability and Mentoring

Students aren't the only ones who need godly mentors; adult leaders do too. They need people who will walk with them in their ministry and in their personal lives. This isn't a role to be filled by us alone, though; we need to care enough to enlist other adults who will pour into the lives of the volunteers, just as we want them to pour into the lives of our students.

A number of years ago, I (Mike) was challenged in this area. I made it my mission to find others who would come alongside our volunteers as mentors and coaches. We found parents, former youth pastors and others who had a heart to minister to the ministers. Their role was one of support, mentoring, cheerleading, pastoring, prayer-partnering and acting as the sounding board for our adult leaders. Potential volunteers were amazed that we would provide this development team to give to them as they gave to students. It is not odd to hear from our adult leaders, "I seem to receive more than I could ever give."

Provide Growth Experiences

One of the most powerful avenues we have to shepherd our leaders is by providing opportunities and experiences by which they can grow. Whether through books, tapes, CDs, videos or conferences—we need to be searching for experiences that will help our adult leaders journey closer to the heart of God. The results will be amazing. Adult leaders who will work with students need to journey to places of growth and intimacy with Christ.

Yearly leadership retreats can play a vital role in inviting our adult leaders to encounter God. Through worship, fellowship, prayer and times alone with God, a retreat can be effectively used to bring us back to God-focused ministry and lives. For years, we've been utilizing our yearly retreat as a spiritual renewal time for volunteers. Year after year, the focus has been the Saturday morning solo time. We send our leaders away for two to three hours to be alone with God. We don't give them anything in particular to read or an assignment outside of being with God in His creation and letting Him speak to their hearts. Most read God's Word, journal, pray or worship. After gathering back together, we spend time sharing what God is doing in our lives and in the life of the ministry. This tradition has been a cornerstone in the life of our ministry and the highlight of the year for our adult team.

Equipping for the Task of Ministry

Most people in youth ministry today have great hearts but little training or knowledge. They desire to be used by God to affect life change in students but are nervous about the how-tos of ministry. We can greatly increase the effectiveness of our staff by training and equipping them for the task of ministry. Recently I (Mike) asked our volunteer team, "What are some areas and issues you feel you need to be better equipped in in order to minister to your students?" Here were some of their responses:

- Building relationships with students
- Leading a Bible study or small group
- Counseling teenagers
- Sharing Christianity more effectively
- Balancing time, life and ministry (while still having a life!)
- Helping students grow in their faith
- Understanding current youth culture issues
- Helping students' families
- Helping students face the issues of teenage sexuality and drug and alcohol use
- Helping students build a healthy self-image
- Dealing with a student who may be feeling suicidal[1]

Take time to ask your volunteers this same question (even if you have only a few) and then develop a year-long training program to equip them for the work of youth ministry. In ministry environments where volunteers feel nurtured, valued and equipped, the turnover rate for adult leaders decreases considerably.

Be Ahead of Your Team

The mark of a great leader is to be a learner. In other words, keep ahead of the staff in your own growth and equipping. There is not *one* person in ministry who has it all together and doesn't need to learn and grow. Read, listen to tapes/CDs and attend seminars. Take the information you are being impacted by and learning from and pass it on to your adult leadership team.

Use Resource People

No doubt there are men and women in your church and community who could spend an hour or two sharing with your leaders about their particular areas of expertise. Use a licensed private counselor, school counselor, nurse, doctor, college professor, other church pastors, parents or even a youth worker from another church in your area to share their knowledge. Don't be intimidated or afraid to ask, "Who can help equip our staff in this area?" The power of utilizing resource people is that they can say the exact same thing you would say, but your team will receive it from them as the absolute truth!

Use Resource Material

From books and videos to audiocassettes, CDs and the Internet—there are many resources to equip leaders for the task of youth ministry. Some teams will read a book together every month and then spend an evening discussing it; others will hand out monthly audiocassette tapes or CDs; still others will forward articles and devotions from websites. The investment of time and finances to equip and shepherd your team is an investment you must make.

Attend Conferences and Seminars

There are a variety of conferences and seminars all across the country, ranging from one-day seminars to multiple-day conferences, from Web casting to satellite simulcasts. As technology progresses, access to great training resources and events increases. Visit various websites to find out what seminars and conferences will be in your area.[2] Again, the time and effort of the investment will reap huge dividends, in training and equipping and in time spent together building community.

Make Meetings Meaningful

Some of the greatest frustrations in youth ministry are volunteer meetings. Some of us may need to rethink our meetings. Rather than business meetings focused on information, we need to use meetings to our benefit as well as the benefit and encouragement of our team.

Most of our business can be done using handouts, newsletters or e-mail. When you're together, make it count. We need to have a specific purpose for every meeting. If it is for equipping and training, make sure that what you do focuses on those areas—likewise for building community and relationship. As for the length of each meeting, remember: It's better to have your team asking for more, rather than begging for less.

Most adult leadership teams meet at least monthly. Staff meetings should be well planned and purposeful. Utilize them for *connection* (building community); *celebration* (sharing victories and struggles of what God is doing in the lives of students); *shepherding* (worship and spiritual encouragement) and *information* (keeping everyone up to date on preparation, goals, dreams and vision). Include a mealtime, where informal sharing and relationship can occur. Pray as an adult leadership team, seeking God's heart and direction for the ministry, as well as for particular students who have needs.

Whatever avenues you choose, be sure to equip your staff on a regular basis in the skills they need to confidently minister students. The greatest investment you can make in the lives of your students is to invest time in the lives of the adult leaders.

Empowerment

If it is true that we can only effectively minister 8 to 10 students on our own, we need to develop and empower others. Empowerment is about releasing control and influence. Empowering adult leaders in youth ministry is about letting *them* have the influence in the lives of students. It means allowing them to be the pastors and shepherds of the students. It means that our phones will ring less, and theirs will ring more. It means that after speaking at a youth ministry event, students will go to talk their adult leader, instead of you. It can be a humbling experience but one that will increase the influence of the ministry.

Styles of Leadership: Management or Sales?

A number of years ago, I (Jim) came to a personal crossroads in my youth ministry. As our youth ministry grew, my personal time with the kids began to diminish. The larger and more involved the ministry became, the less time I had available to do what I loved to do—spend time with students. I felt overwhelmed with administrative responsibilities and out of touch with the kids I was supposedly influencing for the kingdom of God.

Then one day during lunch with a college friend, things came together for me. Tom sold insurance and was such a great salesman that his company wanted him to go into management. It was an incredible opportunity, but he couldn't decide what to do because the part of his job he loved most was spending time with his clients. The management job was a positive step forward in his career, but he had to ask himself, *Am I sacrificing what I enjoy and what I'm good at in order to build my career?* We never really came to a decision that day about his situation, but his dilemma helped me come to some conclusions about mine.

I had to ask myself the same type of question, translated into youth ministry terms: *As the head of our youth ministry team, should I be in management or sales? Should I supervise our ministry by training and equipping leaders, or should I devote my time to the students themselves?* For the first time in my life, I realized that I was kidding myself to think that I could do both effectively in a large youth ministry setting.

One of the most freeing experiences for any youth worker is to make the choice between management or sales, and to feel okay about that choice. This doesn't mean that if we choose management, we'll never talk with a student. It does mean that we must *define our roles* as youth workers. I eventually realized that I could be most effective over the long haul if I shifted to equipping and empowering a team of adult and student leaders to do the work of the ministry.

The time I have invested in leadership has been time invested in more students' lives, with better long-term results, than I could have achieved on my own. My choice was clear: I had to equip adult leaders to do the relational work of the ministry, empowering and releasing them to have the greater influence in the lives of students. If you're in the same situation, consider these insights from someone who has been down that same road.

- **Be realistic in evaluating your gifts and passions.** What is it that you love to do in ministry? What don't you like? Where is your giftedness? The answers to these questions should help you formulate a picture of what you should be doing in ministry.
- **Analyze your current setting.** Ask yourself, *Am I operating in my area of giftedness?* Often we find ourselves ministering in areas that are outside of our giftedness, or we may have been promoted beyond our giftedness. Do some serious evaluation to see where you are in ministry.
- **Do what you do best and find someone to do the rest.** Be involved in what you do best: your areas of passion and giftedness. As for the other areas—it is vitally important not to let them fall by the wayside but to find people to fill in the gaps. If your passion and giftedness is in building relationships but not administration, find someone to handle the administration and you focus on relationships.

Whichever direction you go, whether in sales (working directly with kids) or in management (equipping others to minister), take enjoyment in the knowledge that youth ministry in any role is a high calling and a high privilege. You're playing an invaluable part in the future of some of God's most treasured creations. No matter what the role, ministry is about the eternal. Regardless of the role you play, it's about seeing lives changed for Christ–it's still ministry.

For beneficial volunteer forms such as student ministry team applications, expectations, a commitment form and a reference form, visit YouthBuilders at www.youthbuilders.com.

CHAPTER 15

Developing an Internship Program

For most of my (Jim) youth ministry years, one of the primary focuses of our ministry has been developing and working with an intern program. Many churches today are using interns as a way to minister more effectively to students and provide interns with practical on-the-job training. A properly managed intern program can positively impact and change the face of a church.

My (Jim) first experience with interns was negative. Most of the interns in college or seminary had a very difficult time. They were usually given the entire youth program at the church. They were responsible for all the teaching, recruitment, retreats and whatever else they could get dumped on them. They often had very little support or encouragement from the pastor or other church leaders. Students were deeply hurt because they had seen four or five interns go through their program within a very short time. Just when they were getting to know and trust the intern, he or she would move on to bigger and better things.

Many intern programs are not really intern programs at all. More often than not they become cheap labor. For some churches, an intern program is simply a chance to get the problem of finding youth workers off the backs of the leadership and parents.

An intern program done correctly can greatly benefit both the church and the intern. However, we must always remember that an intern is *in training*. A good working definition of an intern is "a person who assists an experienced youth worker and learns how to properly minister and serve the needs of youth." An internship program should not be a system of cheap labor or a way to meet a need; it is a thoughtful, proactive ministry for the purpose of developing future youth ministry leaders.

The Supervisor Is the Key

The key ingredient to a successful internship program is the *supervisor*. Almost anyone can be fairly successful in youth ministry if he or she has a supervisor who is willing to invest time and energy in the intern's life. If the supervisor looks at acquiring interns primarily as a way to decrease workload, he or she is mistaken—the time and input are simply rearranged.

Two very important questions for a supervisor to ask him- or herself before getting involved in an internship program are, *Am I willing to invest the amount of time it takes to do an internship program right?* and *Am I willing to take possibly less time with the kids and put more time into the lives of the interns?* The time commitment is costly and the price is high, but the rewards and dividends are Kingdom altering.

Measuring Effectiveness

A good internship program has accountability built in. Since training and equipping is vitally important, we must find ways to build accountability for the interns. Over the years, one of the most effective ways we've seen of keeping interns accountable is through a weekly update form.[1] Honestly, most interns will not enjoy taking the 20 minutes or so that it takes to fill out the form at first. Eventually, however, they will see it as a useful measurement tool and discussion starter. They will be incredibly appreciative of the feedback they get by using the form.

The weekly update form is divided into 10 areas and can be used as a launchpad for interaction.

1. **Highlights of the Week**—This section gives interns a chance to evaluate the week's highlights, and it gives the supervisor a better understanding of what is going on in the intern's life. Focusing on

the highlights gives us a chance to celebrate together and look for teachable moments in the experiences of the week.

2. **Areas of Ministry**—In this section, interns share the areas of ministry responsibility they are currently working on. It helps keep them accountable for their roles and responsibilities and can offer some topics for training discussions. For example, an intern might share that he or she is struggling with the administration of an event. This would give you, as the supervisor, an opportunity to talk through some administration skills that might help.
3. **Relational Ministry with Students**—This section gives interns and supervisors valuable insight as to who the intern is spending time with and how much time they are putting into building relationships with students. This area can especially be helpful if you have more than one intern. For example, you might discover that most interns are spending the majority of their time with the same kids and that other kids are not getting much-needed relational contact.
4. **Relational Ministry with Adult Leaders**—The purpose of this section is to encourage interns and adult leaders to spend time working on building relationships with one another. It is also a tool for discussing the needs of your volunteer team, helping formulate the direction you may need to be going in the spiritual and ministry development of your leaders.
5. **Personal Time with God**—This section of the weekly update form is specifically designed for sharing what God is doing in the lives of the interns and what areas He is working on to make them more like Him. It would be easy to gloss over this section in a hurry, but it is essential that interns have time to focus their own spiritual growth in the midst of ministry. This section helps interns see the importance of caring for their own souls—that it must be a daily choice and priority—and that authentic ministry comes out of the overflow of what Jesus is doing in their lives.
6. **Life Balance (Ministry, Personal, Spiritual, Physical, Mental and Emotional)**—At the beginning of the year, ask interns to set personal goals for the upcoming year. This section allows you to

hold them accountable for balancing their lives and meeting their goals.

7. **Insights on Ministry**—This section is designed for interns to write their own thoughts and insights on ministry; this could include venting frustrations, sharing personal struggles or presenting suggestions. What they might not tell you in person they may write on paper, providing a springboard for great discussion.
8. **Prayer Requests**—Prayer is powerful. We know it's true, yet often its importance is overlooked. This section gives you the opportunity to pastor your interns, letting them know that you care for them as individuals, rather than simply as your staff. As supervisor, set aside time each day to pray for your interns, and use this section to help you to be specific in your prayer focus. Interns will appreciate the care, especially when you follow up with them on those areas of their lives you've been praying about.
9. **Miscellaneous Items**—Sometimes there are areas that don't fit into the other categories on this form. Our interns have used this section to share everything from fears and dreams to frustrations with other staff and adult leaders—and a host of other issues and topics. Interns aren't required to fill in this section; just knowing that they have the forum to share anything they want to can give them a sense of partnership and openness.
10. **Work-Related Hours**—This section is for interns to list how they spend their work hours. Help them understand that this is *not* a means of checking up them, but it is a way of holding them accountable to take a day off, take time away from the church to be refreshed, etc. If you see a weekly update form with too many hours listed or no day off, ask why. It's too easy to allow interns to burn out before they really get started, if we don't help them establish good boundaries and a discipline of rest and relaxation.

Meeting with Interns

As we've highlighted, too many internship programs fail from a lack of input into the interns' lives. Interns need to meet with their supervisor on a regular basis—*at least* once every week. These are times to go through the intern's weekly update form and give support, encouragement, training and input. Be sure to collect the forms a few days in advance of the meeting so that you have time to look them over and comment where needed. This allows you to come with insight, help and training to bear on an issue that arises out of an intern's response on the form.

Evaluation

Interns need to be observed and critiqued regarding how and what they are doing. It is extremely important to remember, however, that critiquing entails positive comments, not just negative ones! Take the time to observe and mentor. You must be willing to sit with the kids and get a feel for how the intern is doing. You might also consider taking notes to remind you of areas—positive and negative—that you observed and would like to discuss with the intern later.

Training

Some supervisors think they can stop preparing for meetings when an intern comes along; in actuality, an intern needs someone to come alongside and offer training. *You* are the one to help them in all aspects of youth ministry. After one of my (Jim's) interns took a youth ministry position on his own, he soon called me up to say he had no idea how to prepare a budget. That was actually *my* mistake; I failed to work through all areas of youth ministry with him when he was on my staff. Rather than dumping on interns, we need to learn the art of development and delegation. The difference between dumping and development is the time spent in support and equipping.

Shepherding

As supervisors and mentors, we need to realize that we can greatly minister to the spiritual needs of our interns. For many, this is the first time they have ever worked in a church. They usually have a sense of awe, wonder and fear that asks, *How could God use a person like me?* As mentors, our role is to help shepherd them, developing a caring and transparent relationship with them. I (Jim) find that much of my pastoral ministry centers on my intern staff. If we can keep our interns spiritually healthy, they in turn will be able to help students grow in faith.

Sales Is the First Step

If you've reviewed all of the commitments required of a supervisor/mentor and still feel that both you and your church are ready for an internship program, then the next step is *sales*! Huh?! Allow us to explain: The most important person you must sell the idea to is the senior pastor. When he or she is on your side and has caught the vision, the next step is presenting the idea to the elder board.

Before you ever present anything to the church leadership, put the idea on paper. Make sure that your proposal is well thought out and professionally presented, geared toward the mind-set of your church's elders. Also, ask the senior pastor and a board member to help you work on the formal presentation. Here are some items to include:

- A thorough job description
- A list of the positives and the negatives associated with an internship program (this will enable board members to see that you have put thought into the proposal)
- The financial cost to the church (including a small stipend for the interns will enable them to afford more time in the ministry and will help hold them accountable)
- The benefits of the program to the church (stress the fact that the program will provide more individual attention to the youth and a greater overall capability for outreach)
- The benefits of the program to interns

On-Going Support Is Important

Once you have the internship program put in place, the best way to keep it going is to build steady support. Let the congregation see the interns in the worship service; give reports to the elder board on the progress of the program; allow the interns to meet with the elder board to talk about their experience; and encourage the interns to meet and spend time with the elders and staff outside of the church office or meetings. The congregation and the church leadership will see the payoff of the investment they have made in the internship program, and the result will be support for the program in the future, as well as a win for you.

Working with interns can be a great joy—or it can be an administrative nightmare. Before you take on the responsibility, make sure you look at all the consequences thoroughly and ask yourself, *Am I willing to watch my ministry and time commitment change in order to develop interns?* The answer to that question will let you know whether or not you are truly ready. If you are ready for the responsibility, then the change is almost always for the better—and it will benefit not only your church but also the Church as a whole and the interns themselves.

For beneficial internship program forms such as the internship application, job description, evaluation and personal goals, weekly form update and a sample proposal, visit YouthBuilders at www.youthbuilders.com.

CHAPTER 16

Building Support Within the Staff and Church Leadership

I (Jim) remember complaining late one Monday evening to my wife, Cathy, about an explosive board meeting where both of my proposals were denied. "I feel no support from the staff or the elder board. They have no idea what great things are happening in our group. They have no vision for what can take place in our youth ministry," I told her.

My philosophical (and at times blunt) wife questioned me, "Have you ever told them what's happening? Have you ever taken the time to build relationships with the adults of the church? Jim, do you communicate your desires and dreams with these leaders?"

Did she ever burst my self-absorbed bubble! I was still angry, but her point had come across loud and clear—if you want to build support with the leadership of the church, you must be willing to invest the time necessary to build reputation and relationships. We are the ones who live with our youth ministry programs, not the board members; we have no right to expect them to join our team and buy into our vision without an established relationship and proper communication.

Battleground or Launching Pad?

Too many youth workers look at their relationship with the leadership in the church with a them-versus-me attitude. For some, it is an almost paranoid feeling that the rest of the church is out to get the youth ministry and that our relationship with church leadership is a battleground where we fight, claw and scratch with those who are ignorant of what youth ministry is all about. What we truly need is to change our attitude, not theirs.

We need to approach our relationship with church leadership as a launching pad—a place where great ministry can be supported, nurtured and moved to a new level. Is your relationship with your church leadership more a battleground than a launching pad? There are necessary proactive steps to developing better relationships with the leadership of your church.

Look in the Mirror

Anyone who works in the church will eventually come to the realization that there will always be church politics. It's as if Matthew 18:20 would be better written: "Where two or three come together in my name, there [will church politics be]." Wherever there are people who are flawed and sinful (even church members), you'll find decisions and motives that are not always pure and right. However, God is much bigger than church politics—and the antidote is found in building support within your church leadership.

A good look in the mirror and some honest evaluation may reveal that your attitude and actions need to change. Rather than join in the church politics game, we should take a different approach—one of building support and mutual sacrifice for the good of the entire church, not just our ministry. Do you look at every decision made by church leadership through the lens of how it will have a negative impact on *your* ministry? Or do you take a team approach to the overall mission of the church, living out Philippians 2:3: "Do nothing out of selfish ambition or vain conceit, but in humility consider others better than yourselves."

Take the Initiative

We youth workers must be willing to initiate communication and relationships with church leadership. As you look at your priorities and time commitments, a very important part of your ministry as a whole should be taking time to develop relationships with the leadership of your church. Make it a habit to share a meal with each elder in your church at least once a year. During the meetings, share your dreams and desires, but also get to know the elders as people. Ask about their families, ask about their dreams and desires for the church, and seek advice in their fields of expertise.

I (Jim) remember a breakfast that Cathy and I had with an elder and his wife. We had a wonderful time sharing about life. Toward the end of the breakfast he asked, "Jim, what did you want to meet about this morning?"

I said, "We have no agenda. We just wanted to get better acquainted."

He smiled and said, "Oh, I was waiting for you to ask for some extra funding for some youth project."

I was sorry he thought the only reason for the youth pastor to get together with a leader was to ask for something. When you take the initiative to meet with the leadership, you are building a foundation of relationships. The leadership will tend to be more supportive because they have a relationship with you. They know your heart, your passions and your dreams. Those deepening relationships will result in reputation.

The same philosophy should go for the staff at your church, including the janitors and administrative assistants. Regular times together either as an entire staff or with particular staff people will help you understand the total needs of the church and will help staff members understand the unique world of youth ministry. Many youth leaders have a habit of distancing themselves and their ministry from other areas of the church. The unfortunate result of this habit is suspicion and generalizations: "You know those youth workers—they just play with the kids all the time." Comments like this are borne out of a lack of understanding. We need to be the ones to bridge the gap and reach out to others in relationship. There is no better witness of the Body of Christ than a group of diverse ministries striving together in unity.

If you wait for the leadership of the church to develop a relationship with you, it will probably be a long, quiet wait. Youth workers should initiate personal relationship with senior pastors or supervisors. A regular time together away from the confines of the church office is best. Time spent together with the senior pastor or your immediate supervisor outside the walls of the church opens up incredible opportunities for interaction. If the senior pastor likes sports, go to a game together. During these times you can share dreams, ministry goals or just find out a little more about each other. Some of the loneliest people we've ever met in ministry have been senior pastors. Remember that although most senior pastors can be left alone relationally, all of them are subject to hurts, frustrations and joys—the same as we are.

People in church leadership are basically too busy and overcommitted. They will seldom take the initiative to develop a relationship with you—however, if you take the initiative to get on their calendar, in the long run it will be a blessing and an encouragement to everyone involved.

Clarify Unexpressed Expectations

After graduating from college, Todd went directly into youth ministry. He was an incredibly gifted youth worker. Although he had never talked about it with the senior pastor, when Todd applied for the job, he expected that they would meet regularly to discuss his job as well as to share their personal lives. He expected the same relational experience as an intern as he had had in college. It never happened. Although the pastor liked Todd and enjoyed the time they spent together at staff meetings, he was simply overcommitted. His philosophy of how their relationship should work was entirely different than Todd's. He wanted to hire someone who could do the job and didn't need his input.

The only time Todd had significant contact with the pastor was when there was a problem. Todd was deeply hurt and angry, reacting to an apparent lack of interest in him and the youth ministry, yet the pastor never knew how Todd felt until the day Todd resigned. As he walked away from the church, Todd didn't know his senior pastor and his senior pastor didn't know him. Who was to blame? They both were.

From the beginning, both assumed the other had the same expectations. Before he ever took the job, Todd should have had in writing his expectations for supervision, and the pastor should have been prepared to share his. Even at the end, Todd should have communicated his feelings more clearly, rather than just resigning his position and leaving the senior pastor wondering why.

As in any working environment, conflict on church staffs is normal. Yet in the Church we tend to believe that it is not Christlike to have a difference of opinion, so we repress our conflict until anger takes over our logical thought process.

Unexpressed expectations are one of the major hindrances in church work. If you want to save a great deal of future misunderstanding, learn to express your thoughts and expectations—and put your expectations in writing. This will save many hurt feelings in the future. If you're in a position currently and feel frustrated, *please* take the initiative to talk with someone and get those expectations out in the open before further damage is done.

Have Written Job Descriptions and Regular Evaluations

Not long ago I (Jim) heard that one of this country's finest youth workers had been fired. A slip of morality? No. A theological difference? No. Under qualified for the job? No.

Dave (not his real name) was a veteran youth worker in a growing church in suburban San Francisco. He had been employed by the church for five years. He was a phenomenal youth worker with a heart for students. A week after he was told that he was being let go, he took almost 200 high school students to winter camp. At a training session a year before this incident I had spoken to over 70 adult leaders who were involved in his youth ministry.

When I heard that Dave had been fired, I was stunned. Needless to say, Dave, his wife and their two children were also stunned. They had absolutely no idea why his job would be terminated. The day before the elder board's six-month review of staff, the senior pastor told Dave that he was excited about their youth ministry and that he looked forward to a long relationship of ministering together. A day later, armed with the full support of the elder in charge of youth ministry, the senior pastor told Dave that he needed to find a new job because the elders had fired him.

Here are the facts I could discern: Neither the pastor nor any elder had interviewed the students, adult volunteers, two paid interns or Dave himself. Furthermore, the firing was a complete surprise. Finally, no one ever conducted a review of his work, unless casual pastoral discussions of the youth ministry count as evaluative reviews.

The church, of course, was up in arms over the situation and even called in denominational representatives to examine what appeared to be blatant irresponsibility on the part of the elders and the senior pastor. Sadly, this is not an isolated case. I had heard of two other such firings in the same year. What can you do to prevent this from happening to you?

First, ask for a job description. Be sure to have in writing what the church expects from you as the youth pastor. Make sure that the job description is clearly defined and explains roles, responsibilities, time commitments and line of authority. Don't forget to get the salary and benefits package in writing, as well. A clearly defined and thorough job description can clear up a lot of misunderstandings and unexpressed expectations.

Ask the church leadership to articulate their expectations. Dave's case was definitely a case of unexpressed expectations. Periodically look at your own job description (hopefully you have one!) and evaluate your duties and responsibilities in relation to the description. Church leadership can easily forget exactly what you were hired to do, and some pastors might forget that they hired you for youth work and not a host of other jobs. If you don't know your church leaders' specific expectations, then you're gambling because you may not be spending your days (and nights) how they would expect. If you don't have a job description, be sure to get one as soon as possible!

Second, ask for a performance review every six months. A monthly review is common in many businesses, yet most churches conduct no reviews at all. If you take the initiative to sit down with your staff supervisor and an elder every six months (assuming they aren't taking the initiative themselves), you'll be able to better determine what they expect from you. You'll also open up communication lines. Don't expect it to just happen; you'll probably have to set up the performance reviews yourself, months in advance.

Third, ask for your performance review in writing. If there's ever a question about your ministerial performance, you'll have hard evidence of whatever criticism and compliments you've received. As ugly as it seems, church employees are often fired because of hearsay and uninformed assumptions. Even though this may sound too formal for your taste, guard yourself by having it in writing. Use your written evaluations as a benchmark for growth and future planning for professional development. Be sure to ask more than "How am I doing?" type questions. Find out what you're doing well, where you can improve and where the church would like to see the youth ministry grow in the future.

Get the Church Leadership Involved

Invite the senior pastor, your immediate supervisor and even the members of the board to youth events. Since board members and pastors often react prematurely and without deliberation on a seeming problem in the youth department, let them see the youth ministry firsthand. In fact, having them participate in some of the group's events will allow them to see what God is doing in the midst of the youth ministry. Let them experience what you deal with day in and day out. It will give them a better understanding and appreciation for the youth ministry and your role in it.

After a board member and his spouse spoke to our group about marriage, he was ecstatic in his report back to the board about his time in our ministry and what God was doing. Actually, I (Jim) thought the evening was mediocre at best, but I sure appreciated the compliment. Sometimes all that is needed is for our church leadership to have a little hands-on experience with our youth ministries to gain a better appreciation for what God is doing.

Communicate Clearly

An easy way to gain support and build relationship with church leadership is to choose to communicate clearly with them. Go the extra mile and be sure that church leadership—especially your senior pastor and board members—are kept up-to-date and informed. Richard Felix, former president of Azusa Pacific University, expressed the following three key expectations regularly to his cabinet: "Bad news first, no surprises and full disclosure." That's great advice. Make sure that your leadership knows about everything. There's nothing worse for church leadership than to be questioned about something of which they have no knowledge. It can signal the death of support. We need to find opportunities to communicate the things that mean the most: our vision, dreams, victories, needs and, of course, upcoming events!

At a board meeting, have students and adult volunteers share their experiences at retreats, camps, mission trips, etc. Invite the board members to pray over students and adult leaders. Have students serve at board member retreats, as a way to be near church leadership and build relationship.

You can keep church leadership informed by simply adding members to the mailing list for your youth ministry. Don't assume they know what's going on with the ministry—they're busy people with their own priorities. Send monthly e-mail updates to anyone who wants to be a part of the youth ministry family. Include the following in the e-mail:

- A calendar of events
- Stories of what God is doing in the life of the ministry
- A section describing the needs of the youth ministry
- A prayer request section
- A vision section (written by you), explaining what the ministry is all about and where it is going in the future

Work Through Criticism

If you've been in youth ministry more than an hour, criticism is bound to come. There is no way to live up to everyone's expectations of who you should be as a leader and what the youth ministry should look like. The question is, How will you deal with it? Some of us want to run and hide, ignoring the criticism. Others will become defensive, immediately writing off the person and the criticism as unfounded and misinformed.

Some of the best advice I (Mike) ever received about criticism went something like this: "There's always a kernel of truth in every piece of criticism—can you find it?" We need to look at every piece of criticism the same and find the truth in it. It may be 100 percent accurate or 99 percent false, but there's always something to take away from criticism. Our job is to find it and apply it to our lives while asking God to help us grow and develop into the leaders He wants us to be.

Another great piece of advice I received in dealing with criticism was to ask myself, *Is this the hill on which I care to die?* In other words, is this the issue that I'm willing to fight to the death over? We need to choose our battles wisely.

Considerations Before You Take the Job

A few years out of seminary, my (Jim's) old seminary support group got together for a weekend retreat. We were spread out all across the country in churches of various denominations and sizes. The common thread was that we were all somehow connected to youth ministry, and we all worked in the Church. We spent the majority of the weekend complaining and griping about senior pastors, the leadership board and the politics of the Church. A couple of the members were extremely disillusioned with Church work and were contemplating major career changes. Only a few years earlier, we were in school with idealistic thoughts that we would change the world, never giving a thought to the types of conflicts that we were now facing in the Church.

No one had helped us prepare for the trauma that sometimes takes place within the politics of the Church. To avoid such trauma (or at least lessen its effects) there are several items that need to be discussed before you ever take a youth ministry position at a church.

Job Description

1. What will my job description be and what are your expectations for me?
2. Who is my immediate supervisor?
3. What are the hours expected? (Note days off, nights out, etc.)
4. Are there any other pastoral responsibilities?

Benefits

1. What is the financial package?
2. What is the vacation policy?
3. What are the insurance benefits?
4. Are there any other benefits?

Support and Development

1. What is my immediate supervisor's role in my development?
2. Will I receive time off and financial support for continuing education?
3. What is the personnel review process?

Other Items

1. What is the overall church budget? What is the youth budget?
2. What is the history of the church? Of the youth ministry?
3. What is the purpose, or mission, of the church as a whole?
4. What are the ministry values that propel the ministries of the church?
5. What are the dreams and vision of the future for the church?
6. Where does youth ministry fit into the overall plan for the future of the church?
7. What would an effective youth ministry look like?
8. Who has the final say in church leadership decisions?
9. What are the nonnegotiables in being a part of the church staff?

Suggestions

1. Be aware of the differences in staff members' personalities.
2. Discuss philosophical and theological differences before you take the job.
3. Ask to meet with all the staff members, including assistants and janitors.
4. Meet with the students, parents and any existing youth leaders and be sure to ask questions.
5. Attend a worship service.
6. Sit in on a weekly youth ministry gathering.

C H A P T E R 1 7

Your Budget and You

No one ever told me (Jim) when I went into the ministry that I would be spending so much time dealing with money. Between budget proposals, costs of supplies, event budgets, camp registration fees, facility rentals—in addition to my own financial pressures from choosing a ministry career—there are times when I feel a business and finance course would have been more helpful than the church history classes I had to take. Just try collecting the right amount of money from students for pizza—what an ordeal that is! Or maybe you've collected camp registrations and money by putting them in your pocket, only to realize—after it all went through the wash—that your new wad of paper might have been important in a previous life. Despite our experiences, we need to realize how important the area of finances really is. Regardless of your personal view of money or your training, the fact remains that if you choose to be involved with youth ministry, you will need to learn how to handle finances.

What on Earth Am I Doing Here?!?

When dealing with budgets, it's important to prepare them the same way as the board members and church leadership prepare their own budgets. This means research and documentation—people are much more open with finances if the person requesting funds has done his or her homework. The extra time you take to make sure that your budget package is accurate, thoughtful and professional will make a huge difference. Before jumping in to prepare your youth ministry budget, there are several things that must be considered.

Learn the Budget History

It is important to see past church budgets and find out who makes the final decisions. It helps to examine what the church has valued in the past, as well as the history of increases within the overall church. Seeing these in black and white will give you a sense of how the church budget operates, as well as showing you what the church truly values. Matthew 6:21 rings true: "For where your treasure is, there your heart will be also."

Plan in Advance

When you plan the program ahead of time, you will have a much better idea of your financial need. The people making the financial decisions in the church are very accustomed to making plans two or three years ahead of time. It takes time, effort and energy to think in advance, but the financial dividends are well worth it.

Investigate Alternative Means of Financing

The church should not be stuck paying for everything. The students and/or their parents can pay for some youth ministry events themselves. Paul Borthwick, a senior consultant with Development Associates and a veteran youth worker, makes a good point: "Good budget planning does not require that we make the students pay for everything, but students must be allowed to 'own' their own program by being involved financially."[1]

Pass along much of the expense of events to students in the form of registration fees. However, be sure that you don't do so many large-ticket events that you financially exclude some students from being able to be involved. Look at your year in macroperspective and see what the cost would be for each student, and consider families who have more than one student involved in your ministry. What kind of financial impact are we placing upon families just for the sake of bigger and better events? The more low-cost events that you can run, the better. Think through the option of scholarships for students for larger events and write those costs into the event budget. You may also want to think about finding a few people who will catch the vision and help with donations to offset the cost of an event.

Set Priorities for This Year and the Future

A simple glance at your youth ministry budget will reveal what you value in ministry as well as your priorities for the future. In our ministry, we valued the development of adult leaders—paid and volunteer—above everything else. Therefore, the single largest line item in our budget was for the development and training of paid and volunteer leadership. If you want to see an area of your ministry expand in the future, make sure that you are allotting funds toward that area.

Be Realistic and Responsible

A budget must be prepared with the utmost thought and integrity. One of the mistakes that youth workers often make is that they either budget much lower than their real need or propose a budget that looks like a page from the federal government's budget. We should never lose sight of the fact that the budget represents stewardship of God's money. People sitting in the pew are giving, and part of that money goes to help fund your budget. We are accountable to our congregation, and ultimately to God, for the way we spend His money.

Communicate Your Vision and Your Budget

It's one thing to do your homework concerning the budget; it's another thing to be able to communicate it clearly and concisely. Make sure that you explain, in writing, your vision for the year as well as any fiscal impact it may have. You may want to add to your budget report the prior year's budget and expenditures as a comparison. Explain any variances: those areas where you didn't spend what had you thought you would and those where you spent more than you had planned. Relate how those areas will (or won't) change for the following year. Also, if you are including new areas into the budget, be prepared to explain why those areas were added and provide a detailed description of what the fiscal impact will be.

Keep Expenditures Updated

You should receive monthly updates on your budget. If you do not, ask for them. Once you have those in hand, look them over and write down notes pertaining to different accounts: why there are variances or unexpected changes. Make a copy of the financial statement and give it to the financial decision makers. This will communicate that your budget matters to you and that you value keeping the decision makers informed about the budget on a regular basis.

What About Fund-Raising?

A few years ago, I (Jim) was asked to address a denominational youth worker convention. After my speech, I was asked if I would do a workshop on fund-raising. I agreed to it, expecting only a few people to attend the workshop. When I finished my general session, the person in charge told me I would be doing my workshop where we were—in the ballroom.

"Why?" I asked.

She replied, "You'll have the biggest workshop."

As I looked at the printed agenda, I noted that all of the other workshops appeared more interesting and important than mine.

As I opened my workshop on fund-raising, I was intrigued by the number of people who came, so I asked, "Why are you all here?" The resounding answer was that fund-raising was a part of everyone's youth ministry in one way or another and that while most youth groups are forced to raise funds for some areas of their budget, most youth workers have a dislike for it.

Have a Plan

Imagine this scenario: One of your adult leaders reminds you, "It's getting close to Valentine's Day, and we *always* have our winter fund-raiser." This is your first year on the job, and you've never heard of the winter fund-raiser. Even your senior pastor brings up the subject, so you go ahead and make the arrangements, not wanting to break tradition.

Unfortunately, this is the case for too many youth ministries across the country. There is no plan—just a tradition. One youth worker for a large church told me (Jim) that he had a very healthy budget; his only problem was that all of it had to be raised through fund-raisers. I asked him if any other department in his church had the same budget arrangement, and he quietly shook his head no. The only reason to do a fund-raiser is if there is a specific plan for which you need funds and there is no better way to get the necessary funding.

Have a Purpose

Most fund-raisers are self-centered and self-propagating. What are we teaching our kids when we ask them to raise funds for *their* annual Valentine's Day party? Many youth ministries are moving away from raising money for themselves and toward raising money for worthy mission or service projects. Not only are they raising money for others, but even their fund-raising event serves a purpose.

One youth group in Illinois raises thousands of dollars a year for the needy of their community by having the city of Chicago hire them to pick up trash in certain sections of the city every two months. In turn, they donate the money to shelters for the homeless in the city. The students in my (Jim's) group put together a 10K Run for Hungry Children that has become an annual community event. All of the money we raise goes to meet the needs of hungry children in the world. I've witnessed firsthand that raising funds for a selfless purpose will help our kids become more motivated.

Get Others Involved

If people in your church are willing to donate to the students or a mission trip, then make sure your donors get an update before you leave on the trip, while you are on the trip and after the trip. This keeps them involved and lets them see that their money was spent on a very worthwhile project. Here are some ideas to accomplish this goal:

- Within a week after you receive a donation, have one of the students write a thank-you note to the church family.

- The week before you leave on the trip, write a one-page update and a list of prayer requests.
- Reserve one night of your trip for students to write postcards to all the donors. Every donor should receive at least one postcard.
- After your trip, invite donors for a celebration meal and program. This will give students an opportunity to share their special experiences and to give donors another word of thanks. Incidentally, these same donors will be the prime candidates for next year's fund-raiser.

WHAT ABOUT PERSONAL FINANCES?

Neither of us (Jim and Mike) are financial planners. In fact, both our wives handle our checkbooks at home because they do a better job at it than we do. However, there are a few principles we've chosen to live by that we'd would like to pass on to you.

Develop a Personal Budget

No one chooses youth ministry as a career because of the exceptionally high salary. Write out a budget and live within that budget. One of the greatest areas of stress in ministry centers is money—or lack of it. A well-planned budget will help you make wise decisions about your finances.

Stay Out of Debt

Credit-card debt is a killer. Make it your goal to live within your budget and to pay off your credit cards every month, rather than carrying over balances. It's too easy to accumulate a large debt and pay more than you've ever imagined in annual percentage rates. That item you thought you couldn't live without can cost *much* more than you bargained for if you talk yourself into thinking it's OK to pay it off in the upcoming months.

Express Expectations and Frustrations

Eric came to me (Jim) filled with rage because he just realized that three months after taking his intern position he was making less than the minimum wage. It was a bad financial situation, but Eric knew what he was getting into before he took the position. He was paid for 15 hours a week, but he seldom worked under 40 hours. The extra time was his choice. As his supervisor, I continually challenged him to put less time in at the church. Eric's bitterness and resentment got in the way of his ministry.

Be sure to express expectations and frustrations when they arise. Don't let them simmer and become a boiling mess of anger and bitterness. If you are married, make sure your spouse understands exactly what your financial situation will be, and do not take the position if you believe that either one of you will be bitter about it in the future.

Talk About Your Needs with the Church Leadership

For some reason, many of us believe that because the Church is a Christian institution it is inappropriate to bring up our financial needs there. As a result we don't insist our churches give us the financial support we need and deserve. We've learned that if we don't bring up the subject, usually no one else in our church will look out for our financial needs. Be proactive in sharing your needs and even your budget if necessary.

My (Jim's) friend Judy was a candidate for a position at a church in Denver. After two visits and a really good feeling about her new potential position, she was offered the job. She called the church back and said, "I have some good news and some bad news. The good news is that I feel God wants me to be at Central Presbyterian Church."

They asked hesitantly, "What's the bad news?"

She replied, "I don't feel that God is calling me to the salary you offered."

They renegotiated the salary, and Judy moved to Denver.

Have the Church Pay for Legitimate Expenses

I (Jim) once shared the idea with my senior pastor that Cathy and I wanted to start having five students come over every other week to our home for dinner. He thought it was a great ministry idea. He clearly saw it as a ministry and part of my job. I then asked for the funds to pay for those ministry meals and found quite a different response. It took him a lot longer to agree to that request.

The church you work for is responsible for your legitimate expenses. Make sure that you get prior approval *before* spending the money.

Make Your Own Giving a Priority

How you handle your finances is a role model to the students and adults you work with in the church. This may sound overly simplistic, but most of the people I know who make Christian giving a high priority in their lives have a much better handle on their finances than others do. How you handle your finances and your financial stewardship plays an important role in how you carry out your Christian commitment as a whole. Just as we call people to honor God by being good stewards, so should we follow our own advice.

Seek a Wise Tax Consultant

You will want to find an accountant knowledgeable in church work to help you with your taxes. Many youth workers have found out much too late about the tax benefits of working for a church. There are specific benefits and tax deductions that you may be entitled to. Be sure to find someone who knows all the options and is able to help you sort through them.[2]

Save and Invest Wisely

Savings and investments are two often overlooked areas of personal finance. Most of us know we need to save and invest, but too often it is something that is put off for the future. A good rule of thumb is to save or invest a total of 10 percent of your income (or more, if possible). Another financial goal we should strive for is to have three months' worth of salary either in savings or in easily liquidated assets. Unfortunately, the vast majority of people in the United States have less than $1,000 in their savings account and have no real plan for the future. It is well worth the time and expense to sit with a financial planner and have him or her help you get on track with debt, savings, investments and insurance policies.

S E C T I O N I I I

Programming—The Creative Spark of Ministry

CHAPTER 18

PRINCIPLES FOR STRATEGIC PROGRAMMING

I (Jim) have been in way too many youth ministry seminars where a successful youth worker shares his or her new idea or programming technique to bring hundreds of kids to youth ministry, and I go home and try it, expecting incredible results. The results, however, are usually the same: it bombs. I can't help but think, *Did I miss something here? Was I out of the room when the essential key was shared? Maybe I didn't take good enough notes.*

We often seem to be looking for the quick fix—a technique or program that will deliver to us the perfect youth ministry. If you read this chapter looking for such a program, I'm afraid you will be disappointed. Programs that are used in one church don't necessarily work in another. What works with students in San Diego, California, may not work with students in Atlanta, Georgia, or Boise, Idaho. Needs may be similar in the lives of students, but how we go about meeting those needs should vary.

I (Mike) once heard it said that "our mission and message should never change, but our methods should always change." What worked even a few years back may not work in meeting the needs of today's student. While we need to be rock solid in our mission and purpose as a youth ministry, our methods and programming should constantly be reevaluated regarding their effectiveness. Our focus in this chapter is to look at principles for strategic programming that help us attain our mission.

Develop Programs to Fulfill a Purpose

Most youth ministries have very few goals and true purposes for their programming. The average youth worker plans programs anywhere from three days to one hour before any youth ministry event and pays alarmingly little attention to purpose or content. This style of programming produces programs that are often repetitive and done out of tradition, with few measurable results worthy of support by church leadership. The long-term result of such maintenance-oriented youth ministry is a lack of continuity and purpose.

The main goal of strategic programming is to develop programs and ministries that fulfill a purpose. More often than not, we work in reverse. We come up with a great idea or something that someone else has tried (often with better results because it was born out of a vision or purpose) and we force it into our calendar with little thought as to how it will fit into the overall picture.

The key questions we need to be asking ourselves before we ever start programming are, *What are we trying to accomplish with this program?* and *How does it fit in to the overall purpose and mission of the youth ministry?* Mike Yaconelli of Youth Specialties once told a group of youth workers, "One of the common characteristics in youth work is no continuity of program. I find too many youth ministries with no plan, no sense of direction. They have no long-term or short-term goals. There is no method of evaluation or concern for the whole."

Lasting and impacting ministry is ministry done on purpose, not by accident. We in youth ministry have been guilty for too long of not knowing why we're doing what we're doing. Having a clear–and biblical–purpose leads to a ministry with direction. A key foundation of effective youth ministry is developing a picture of what we are trying to accomplish and how we are planning to get there. In short, we must have a clear picture of purpose. Rather than rushing ahead with great programming ideas, we would do well to stop and ask ourselves, *Why should we do this?* Answering this question will give us several things.

- **Direction**–When we have a clear picture of where the ministry is heading (or should be heading), we will have a basis for what we should be striving for and investing in. We will be able to define a purpose and end goal.

- **Focus**—Having a clear picture of where we're going and what we value gives us a better grasp of what it will take in order to get there. The picture of how our students should be when they exit our ministries will provide focus and passion for our programming.
- **Support**—A clear picture of purpose is attractive to both church leadership and parents and will give them something to support. Having a clear picture will show that we've put thought and effort into what we're trying to accomplish in the lives of our students.
- **An Evaluation Tool**—If we approach our programming through the lens of purpose, we will have a benchmark with which to evaluate the growth and effectiveness of our program. We can ask ourselves, *Are the things we are doing as a ministry accomplishing what we have set out to accomplish?*

Know Your Audience

After navigating questions of purpose, the next layer of questioning needs to focus on the audience—the students we are trying to minister to through the program.

- Who is it that we are trying reach?
- What are they like?
- What are their needs?
- How will this program or ministry be designed to meet that need?

If the purpose of the event is outreach, answering these questions will give you an idea of how to develop the program in order to reach out to students in your area. Your answers should drive everything from content to promotion to evaluation. We need to keep a watchful eye on our audience and understand who they are, what they are going through and what they are truly searching for, if we want to program events that will truly have an impact.

If the purpose of the event is for Christian students to encounter God through worship and prayer, then you might ask the following audience-related questions to help you craft the event to the personality and individual needs of your group:

- What have students experienced before in worship?
- What do we want them to experience about worship?
- What are some worship experiences that will stretch students and help them focus on who God is?
- How do the students feel about worship and prayer?
- What are some possible roadblocks that this group may have that we may need to prepare for?

Before you plan the details of the event, take a few moments to formulate some more specific questions that will make it more relevant to your group. The answers will give you a picture of what the program or ministry needs to look like to fulfill the vision.

Know Your Resources

There comes that moment in all planning when we need to ask ourselves the question, *Can we really do this?* It is at this point that we need to analyze our resources, which are more than just finances and facilities. We also need to look at the resources of time, energy and leadership. Do we have the time and energy to put into this? Do we have the leadership in place or could we develop the leadership needed to make this dream a reality? Do we have what we need? Can we get what we need to make this happen?

You may have an incredible idea for meeting a need in your community or in the life of your youth ministry, but to make it a reality you need to look at your resources. If the resources are not available, you may need to set the idea aside until resources can be obtained or you may need to enlist other churches in implementing and making the idea a reality.

Plan in Advance

Youth workers have a reputation for doing things at the last minute; unfortunately, the reputation stems more from truth than fiction.

When we fail to do advance planning, we lose the time necessary for creativity and working on the finer details. We are rushed to a final product that might be less than effective.

Program Planning

Programming strategically takes time. Remember to count the cost of your time as a resource. Do you have the time to do the program right? We have a saying in our ministry whenever we enter a time of programming; we remind ourselves, "Go big, or go home." Roughly translated, this means that if we don't have what it takes to do it right, then let's not do it. Our students and our God deserve our best. Now that doesn't mean you need to wait until everything is perfect before launching a ministry or program. It means a commitment to not do anything unless it can be done with your whole heart. The pieces may not all be in place completely, but you should have a handle on what you are trying to accomplish.

Years ago, I (Jim) learned a valuable lesson about advance planning. I had gathered together two students, my wife, a volunteer leader and an elder from our congregation to brainstorm what we wanted to teach in the youth ministry over the upcoming season. We asked the question, "What do we want a freshman to know when he or she graduates from high school?" We came up with ideas and subjects that I would have never thought about myself, ranging from love, sex and dating to doctrine. When we finished brainstorming, we took these topics and put them into our four-year plan. Many of the important topics were repeated each year. None of the topics went for longer than six weeks. I can't tell you that after this one evening we followed our four-year outline perfectly. However, our students received a broader topic presentation because we chose to look into the future and plan in advance.

A number of positive results happened because of this one evening of planning. We planned our content far enough in advance to give us the time to research and really think through the creative side of the program. For example, because we knew in September that we would be emphasizing missions in March, we could put together a higher-quality program. In September we asked a psychologist in our church to speak on sexuality in May. He would have been unavailable had we waited until

April before asking him. Planning in advance helps you not only see the long-term plan but also affords you the time to be creative and think through the elements that you would otherwise have no time to think about or research.

Event Planning

The same idea of advance planning for programs applies to youth ministry events. If you plan events a year in advance, you will have the opportunity to plan better events with a broader base of help. There is no reason why the snowboarding/ski trip can't have a date on the calendar a year ahead of time. If the retreat is planned at the last minute, you'll have to take most of the responsibility—but given enough time a lot of the dreaming and preparation can include students and adults, especially those who normally do not get as involved.

We're not saying that every element of each event must be planned out in detail months ahead of time; our suggestion is to have the date and someone in charge of the event far enough in advance to give ample time to do strategic planning. Someone once said, "When you fail to plan, you plan to fail." Planning in advance frees you to be more involved in the relational aspect of the event than in the logistical aspect.

An often forgotten aspect of advance event planning is to think through all the aspects of planning: beginning, middle and end. We are often great at thinking about the beginning of an event, but as time wears on, we forget all of the details of the middle of an event, or we lose sight of the end result and don't finish well.

This became apparent when I (Mike) had one of our interns plan an all-night event. We began far enough in advance that I thought the intern would have a great handle on all the details. The afternoon of the event, I came into the office, ready for a great night, and found the intern sitting in his chair, resting his head on the desk. Oblivious to the situation, I thought he was praying for God to do great things through the evening. He was praying all right—praying for the transportation that he forgot to secure weeks in advance. Within the next hour, I came to find out that there were a whole host of things that were in limbo for the evening.

After that event, we developed an event planning form to help guide us through the beginning, middle and end of an event. The form is a work in progress. We've added to it over the years; we've had other youth ministers add to it over the years. It's a tool for thinking through all the aspects of planning. When we think through and plan for all the little details, it actually frees us up to be more spontaneous for those last-minute changes.

Realize That Environment Is Essential

Programs can rise and fall depending on the environment. Most youth ministry events take place in sterile church rooms with uncomfortable chairs lined in a row, giving the feel of a school classroom.

When you are planning a program, take into consideration the location of the meeting, including the size of the room and the seating arrangements. If the room is too large, it could seem cold and cavernous. Seating—and the style of seating—can set up an environment that is conducive to what you are trying to accomplish. If you are looking for a relaxed environment for small groups, don't use the church—instead use someone's house for the evening.

Another environmental truth for youth ministry programming is that it is always better to have students asking for more, rather than begging for less. The attention span of the average teenager is approximately 10 minutes. This means that we need to keep the pace moving, change experiences regularly and keep the meetings short and purposeful.

Probably the most important part of the youth group meeting is the interaction that takes place before and after the program. It may be necessary to remind adult leaders that the program includes not only the meeting itself but also the interaction time before and after the meeting. Whenever possible, foster an environment that will keep the students around and available for discussion and interaction. If you stop the meeting a little early, this will provide more time for interaction before they need to leave. This informal time truly is where some of the best ministry takes place. Don't discount those times; they're when appointments are made, hugs are given and connections or reconnections are made.

Take Time to Evaluate

An event does not end when the last student goes home, when the room is put back together or even after the receipts have been tallied. It is not over until you and your planning team (hopefully comprised of students and adult leaders) have taken time to evaluate the event or meeting.

Pull out all the planning paperwork. Look over each and every aspect of the planning, from the inception of the event to the final receipt turned in. Ask yourself and your team the following questions:

- Did we accomplish our stated purpose or goals for the event?
- What helped us achieve the purpose? What hindered it?
- Did our audience receive what we intended from the event?
- As you look back, what stands out in your mind? What went well?
- What can be improved?
- What needed more time devoted to it?
- What needed less time devoted to it?
- What was the environment like for the event?
- Should we do this event again? What should we do differently next time?
- What could we do next time to develop the next generation of leaders?
- What future plans, dates, etc. do we want to make as a result of this event?

> For a beneficial sample student ministries event planning form, visit YouthBuilders at www.youthbuilders.com.

CHAPTER 19

Creative Teaching—So They'll Never Forget

Teaching and speaking are two of youth ministries' constants. No matter whether you're paid or volunteer and no matter to which denomination you belong, the great equalizer is that we all have to stand in front of our students weekly (or more often) and communicate information and at the same time sound interesting. Some see it as a necessary evil; others thrive on the opportunity. Either way you look at it, presenting the Word of God is one of our main callings as youth workers. We have the awesome opportunity to plant His Word into the lives of students and watch it sprout over their lifetime.

Open the Road Map

In Colossians 1:28-29, Paul states:

> We proclaim him, admonishing and teaching everyone with all wisdom, so that we may present everyone perfect in Christ. To this end I labor, struggling with all his energy, which so powerfully works in me.

That is the reason we teach the Word of God—to lead others toward maturity in Christ. I (Mike) can especially relate to verse 29; it is a struggle. I don't know anyone who can dynamically and authentically speak to students without laboring through and crafting their message. Although it is a labor, God does provide His "energy, which so powerfully works" in us. He wants His Word to impact our students' lives even more than we do.

Ecclesiastes 12:9-11 (*NLT*) gives us further insight into what makes for dynamic teaching and communication:

> Because the Teacher was wise, he taught the people everything he knew. He collected proverbs and classified them. Indeed, the Teacher taught the plain truth, and he did so in an interesting way. A wise teacher's words spur students to actions and emphasize important truths. The collected sayings of the wise are like guidance from a shepherd.

Wise and insightful teaching focuses on the plain truth. If we really think about it, we'd realize that that is exactly what students want today. They want the truth. They want to know what's real and what God has to say about life. We also see that the Teacher taught in an interesting way, or literally taught in a way that captured hearts and minds. That's our call as communicators—to present the life-altering Word of God through the power of the Holy Spirit to our students so that the truth of God captures their hearts and minds. Lastly, we are told that His words spurred action in their lives. Our communication should always be for challenge, for action and for change in the lives of our listeners.

God has given us quite a mandate: we are to take His eternal Word and share the life-changing truth of it with our students. Much like worship, when God is truly encountered within the pages of His Word (and not just the words), our students will be forever changed.

Know the Essentials for Effective Communication

Regardless of where you are and who you are, you can become more creative and effective in presenting spiritual truth to your students.

Effective, powerful communication starts before we ever begin to move our lips and before we ever put pen to paper or words on a computer screen. We need to believe that God's Word is living and active—and then act as if we believe that. For dynamic and lasting communication, there are five essential things we need to keep in mind and practice.

Stay Connected with Jesus

Whether we want to admit it or not, our personal spiritual life is the foundation of our communication. What the Lord is doing in your life personally is the most precious resource you have as a communicator. Matthew 12:34 reminds us of an important truth: "For out of the overflow of the heart the mouth speaks." What comes out of your mouth—and the eternal impact it will have—is directly related to the state of your heart. If our souls are shallow, our communication will be shallow. If we are seeking to know God and growing more and more in love with Him, our communication will have a Spirit-filled vibrancy and passion.

It is therefore of the utmost importance that we immerse ourselves in God first—through His Word, worship and prayer. As we seek to know and follow Him, God will open the door to truth and conviction that will revolutionize our communication with students. It will be like Peter and John in the book of Acts; when they spoke, there was power and conviction—so much so that when those around them "realized that they were unschooled, ordinary men, they were astonished and they took note that these men had been with Jesus" (Acts 4:13). There is something about staying connected with Jesus that brings dynamic power and conviction to our teaching.

Make It Interesting

Jim Rayburn, founder of Young Life, said "It's a sin to bore kids with the gospel of Jesus Christ." One of the greatest hurdles we encounter in communicating with students is boredom. Unfortunately, that is a reflection of our preparation and delivery. It's not that we need to be flashy, entertaining or humorous in our style; what we need is to deliver the Word of God with passion and enthusiasm. There should be a passion and excitement about what God has to say. When our students see us excited and changed by God's truth, they will more openly investigate it for themselves.

Make It Relevant

One of the biggest complaints from students is that God's Word doesn't make any sense to them. That should be a motivation for us to strive to make the Word of God come alive with application and relevancy. Help students encounter God and His truth in a vital and relevant way. A goal for us in our communication should be that our listeners would walk away saying, "Wow, I never saw that story quite like that!" If we can help students see the relevance of God's truth in their everyday lives, they will develop a sense that God truly does speak today through His Word. The result will be that as they graduate from your ministry, they will see God's Word as a source of direction and authority wherever they may go.

Know Your Audience

Students attending Sunday morning services and weekly Bible studies come with a variety of needs and from a variety of settings. One student just had a fight with her mom in the car on the way to church and that was left unresolved. Another just found out that the girl that he has been interested in for a while is also interested in him, and there is love in the air! Both of these students are sitting in the same room as you begin your teaching time, but their attention span and openness to hearing from God is radically different. We need to take into account the drastically different situations each student faces, and realize that our communication time begins hours before we ever move our lips. When we craft our messages, we need to take into account who our students are: what they are like, where they come from and how our message communicates to the needs in their lives at the current moment.

Consider Different Learning Styles

Most people have a dominant learning style that affects their communication in more ways than they may realize. There are four main learning styles, according to educational research; and because your style of teaching greatly determines your impact on the students to whom you are communicating, you need to understand each of these learning styles and which style you tend to reflect the most.

- **Innovative/Feeling**—Innovative learners like to learn from specific experiences. They relate to people easily. They love small groups and the opportunity to share ideas. Innovative people tend to be sensitive to the feelings of other people. They can be extremely imaginative and usually function best in social settings. They need to feel a part of the group, and unless they are accepted among friends, their learning may be inhibited.
- **Analytic/Watching and Listening**—Analytic learners are listeners. They make careful observations before making a judgment. These people like to view things from different perspectives and are always looking for the deeper meaning of things. They seek facts and ask what the experts think, and their strength is in creating concepts and models.
- **Common Sense/Thinking**—Commonsense learners look for logical analyses of ideas. They are excited about systematic planning and act only upon an intellectual understanding of the situation. They are very practical minded; usually they want to know how things work and how they relate to real life. They are the kids who ask questions such as, "Is this story practical?" and "How does that work?"
- **Dynamic/Doing**—Dynamic learners do not lead a dull life; they influence people and events through *action*. Dynamic learners have the ability to get things done and are not afraid to take a risk. You'll find that they prefer the trial-and-error method, which sometimes can come across as being pushy. Their favorite question is "What can this become?" I (Jim) once asked a dynamic learner on my staff, "What are the theological implications of

the project you want to do?" His answer: "Who cares? It needs to get done!"[1]

Although most people tend to have a dominant learning style, no one learning style is better than any other. As far as educators can tell, each style has the same number of geniuses and the same number of people in general. So what are the implications for teaching? We tend to teach in a style that reflects our own dominant learning style. If we are not careful, we will risk losing kids who are least like us in learning styles. Therefore, we must vary our methods of teaching; we must constantly ask the ourselves the question, *Is my teaching and communication style meeting the needs of all the kids in my group?*

Count the Cost of Being Creative

As Colossians 1:28-29 reminds us, preparing to communicate the Word of God can be a costly task. It requires labor and struggle, which is good news for people like us because all too often that's what message preparation feels like. There is a cost to wanting to be more effective and creative in how we present spiritual truth.

Creativity Requires Time Alone

We know of very few people who are so incredibly creative that it flows out of them on command. Unfortunately, many people seldom come up with creative ideas because they never take time just to let their thoughts flow. Our fast-paced society has led us to believe that solitude is wasted time. Nothing can be further from the truth. The most creative people we know take time to be alone. Time alone is the cornerstone of creativity. It is in those times alone that we can refuel our spiritual tanks, seek His direction in what we need to be teaching and how best to present those things.

Creativity Requires Exposure

We need to be exposed to others who are creative. Being with others can ignite our passion and creativity. As we focus on a series or a subject, gaining insight and perspective from others can be invaluable. The final product has more of a synergistic flavor than if we were to do all our brainstorming in a vacuum.

I (Mike) can remember sitting in a room full of youth workers at an area youth pastors' lunch where we asked the question, "What have you done to teach the issue of God's view on sexuality to your youth ministry?" The answers were amazing. Our collective creativity came out, ideas flowed, and by being with other creative people, we ourselves felt more empowered in our own creativity. I think we all walked away with at least a dozen great ideas—from object lessons to guest speakers, from illustrations to insights from God's Word and from video clips to movies and television shows—all of which could be used. Sometimes being creative takes less time than you have already been devoting to plan a Bible study, since you can use someone else's ideas. We were more creative in those 15 to 20 minutes than we would have been on our own.

Wayne Rice, one of the founders of Youth Specialties, once told me (Jim): "The essence of creativity is the ability to copy." I laughed at first, but then I realized the profound truth of his statement. He wasn't talking about plagiarism; he was simply saying that we learn best from others who have tried things before us. We have had coaches, mentors, teachers and disciplers who have helped us travel the same road they have traveled. My first sermon was a *copy* of composition structure, gestures and even much of the content from that of my pastor. To be creative does not mean that we can't use other people's ideas. In a real sense, there really is nothing new under the sun. Creativity means that we take what others have learned and adapt, change and apply that wisdom to our situation, making it new for us.

Creativity Requires Risk

Risk is hard for some of us. We avoid trying something new or different for fear of failure. The man with the highest lifetime batting average is Ty Cobb, with a .367. He is considered one of the most consistent, successful hitters the game has ever known. However, look a little closer—behind the batting average is a truth: Every time Ty Cobb stepped into the batter's box, there was a two-thirds chance that he was going to fail at his attempt to get on base. Only one-third of the time was he successful in what he set out to do. Thomas Edison was perhaps the greatest inventor of all time, yet it took him over 900 attempts before he created a working lightbulb. According to Edison, every time he experienced failure, he merely "found out one more way not to make a lightbulb."[2]

Creativity Requires Excellence

The bottom line in creativity is this: Honor God and your students with excellence. This means going the extra mile in brainstorming, preparation and delivery of your messages and other times of communication. Youth workers need not be perfect; we must, however, choose not to cut corners in our preparation. This means spending time in prayer before and during the preparation period and then crafting and recrafting the message content. It means practicing illustrations, previewing video clips, actually doing the object lessons in advance and making sure that all the audiovisual equipment really does work!

Excellence requires time spent in advance preparation and planning. The further in advance, the more time you can let a message or a series percolate in your mind and heart. Finding illustrations, case studies, video clips, stories or object lessons can occur much more easily when you have the time to keep your eyes and ears open. This can't happen when you're only preparing a day (or hours) in advance. Go the extra mile to honor God and your students by spending time in preparation.

Creativity Can Be Dangerous

With all the discussion on the issue of creativity, a warning needs to be given here. We cannot allow creative ideas to overshadow the message and the truth that we are trying to communicate. I've (Mike) used what I thought were incredibly creative object lessons in the past, only to find out that my students remembered what I did but can't seem to remember the point behind it. Equally, there have been too many times in the past where I found an idea and crafted a message around it, rather than starting with the truth that I wanted to communicate and then finding creative ideas that illustrated and supported the truth. Our preparation needs to begin with the question, *Lord, what do You want to say?* rather than, *What's the latest creative object lesson or video clip I have and how can I (artificially) craft a message around it?*

Put the Pieces Together

When any of us stand before a group of students and talk for any length of time, we have the rare privilege of having students actually listen to what we have to say. If our presentation has not been well thought out and put together, then we are robbing our listeners of an encounter with God and His truth that could have been transformational in their growth and knowledge of Him. Therefore, we must have the confidence that we have adequately prepared mixed with the realization that we need to fully rely on God's Holy Spirit for leading and direction. This is the platform we need as we speak to impact the lives of our listeners.

Fix Your Attitude

There are three Greek words that help us understand the importance of our attitude in communicating to students, and every message to your students should have all of these elements present.

1. ***Ethos*, the Credibility Factor**—Students will ask us, "Can I trust you?" Credibility with students doesn't come through a title or achievements; it comes when we connect with our listeners with transparency, vulnerability and integrity. It is communicated in the words that we say and how we present them. Share openly and honestly from your life: your fears, dreams, struggles—even your doubts. The more transparent we become, the greater our credibility. Rather than using the word "you," use the word "we." Perhaps the greatest compliment I (Mike) have received lately was from a sophomore girl who said, "You don't talk at us, you talk with us—you're one of us." Credibility was being fostered.
2. ***Pathos*, Empathy**—Teens will ask, "Do you really care for me? Do you understand me?" In order to speak effectively, we need to seek to understand where our students are coming from. We need to

ask ourselves a few all-important questions: *What are the needs of my listeners? God, what do you want to communicate to these students on this issue? How can I present this so that it will really connect with these students?*

The more we build relationship with students, the more we will understand their world. The more we understand their world, the more we can speak into it the truth of God. When we speak to students, they must know that we understand them, love them and *feel* with them.

3. ***Logos*, the Word**—If our students know that we are being real and that we care, then we can speak the truth. The proclamation of the Word is essential, but remember that people don't care how much you know until they know how much you care. Make sure that as you present the Word, you do so on a level that students can relate to. Don't shy away from speaking on tough issues like sin, repentance and holiness. Students today are looking for the truth. They want to truly know who God is and what it means to be a follower of Jesus. As was said a long time ago, "We need to share the whole counsel of God"—not just what we think students want to hear.

These three concepts can be summed up in one sentence: Always be yourself, always love your audience, and always do your homework.

Organize Your Message

When you prepare a message, you need to know exactly what you want to get across to your audience. Many people give messages to students with only a vague idea of what their message really is. Write down in as few words as possible what we like to call the Big Idea. If you can't capture what you want to say in one sentence without using the words "but," "and," "in addition to" and "also," you're trying to say too much. Rather than presenting your message by spraying out all kinds of information in the hope that something will hit, state your Big Idea to make the message clear and concise. Only after you've developed your Big Idea should you move onto the body of your talk. An organized message will have three components.

1. **Introduction**—The introduction of any talk is the most important. Why? Because it's how you will capture the attention of your audience. Your introduction should serve as a way to connect with your listeners, building credibility and empathy. It establishes openness, transparency and relationship. It should grab your audience with the need to listen to what the rest of the message is all about.
2. **Body of the Message**—The body of the message is where you present the main points of the Big Idea. Main points might include a Scripture, an illustration and an explanation. A couple of words of caution here: First, the more points you have, the more confusing the message may become; and second, we need to be careful not to formulize our Christianity (five steps to a dynamic prayer life, three ingredients to have joy in your life or eight keys to successful evangelism, etc.). The days of three points and a poem are dead. What students are looking for today is a story—teaching through narrative. Students connect with stories of people's lives and the truth that is illustrated in the stories.
3. **Application**—Every message should have an application or actions steps. This is the "So what?" of the message: *What should I do with what we've talked about? How does this, or should this, impact my life with God and others this week?* We must give our listeners an opportunity to respond. If you are talking about the issue of prayer, give students some issues to pray over or some way to put prayer into action that week. Truly effective communication brings about results and action.

Find Fresh Material

The challenge of continually giving our students fresh material is extremely difficult. One of the mistakes that many youth workers make is in not developing a good resource system. There are numerous ways to find material, and we've included only a few here.

Draw from Your Life Experiences

Every day, each of us experiences situations and events that can give meaning to a future message. Make a habit of writing down potential ideas, situations, illustrations or thoughts. They can come from conversations, reading, watching people, TV, newspapers and a host of other sources. Keep your eyes and ears open.

Draw from Your Time in God's Word

Both of us (Jim and Mike) have a goal to read the entire Bible in a devotional manner once a year. As we read the stories in the pages of Scripture, insights and thoughts jump off the page. It may be a story, a verse or even a word. Sometimes it is what is said or done—sometimes it is what isn't said or done. Keep a pencil with you as you read Scripture. Don't merely read God's Word for message material, however. Read God's Word as a follower of Jesus, first and foremost. Allow the words and truth of Scripture to impact your heart and life first, and then speak from that place! Your communication will grow in power and passion.

Use Reference Materials

If you know a particular passage or theme that you'll be speaking on, be sure to read any commentaries, word studies or other reference materials you can find that may shed light on the subject or passage. Before you ever pick up a reference work, however, be sure that you read and reread your passage, even in different versions. Allow the Word of God and the passage to become your own. This will keep you on track and keep you from simply restating what someone else thinks about the passage.

Listen to Students

As we spend time with students in building relationship, we can gain valuable insight that will impact our teaching. We can hear their hopes, dreams, fears, struggles and frustrations. This information can lead us not only to the subject to teach on but also how to present it effectively. Perhaps one of the most impacting messages I (Mike) have ever given came about because I asked my discipleship group a few questions on the issue of loneliness. What came out was a month's worth of material on the issue–its causes and impact and how to deal with it in our lives.

Read Books Written for Students

One of the greatest sources of material is books written for students. The authors are usually outstanding youth communicators. They have spent years developing their material. Be careful not to plagiarize, but use their insights to guide you. Learn from them about communicating truth to students today.

Learn from Good Communicators

If you want to be a good communicator, listen to/watch cassettes, CDs or videos–or if possible, attend live presentations–of some of the best communicators you know. Not only will you be inspired, but they'll also be a source of thoughts that may lead you to materials for the future. Be careful to develop your own style and not imitate the speaking style of some other communicator, but you can learn a lot from these experts.

For a list of sample teaching topics, visit YouthBuilders at www.youthbuilders.com.

CHAPTER 20

Ideas for Creative Communication

Now that we've established that creativity is a key ingredient for communicating God's Word effectively, the goal of this chapter is to provide practical tools for how we can be creative in our communication. This is not meant to be an exhaustive list of creative components. We're hopeful, though, that this chapter will serve to ignite some of your own creative ideas and tools in communicating the Word of God to your students. As we venture to look at ideas for creative communication, there are a few truths that we need to keep in mind.

Students Learn Best When Learning Is Experiential

Everyone learns best by experience. Edgar Dale's Cone of Experiential Learning shows how important it is to get people to experience the work of Christ rather than to simply listen to it. Most people only retain 5 to 10 percent of what they are taught through verbal or written methods, but when people actually experience something as they learn it, they retain over 80 percent of the content.

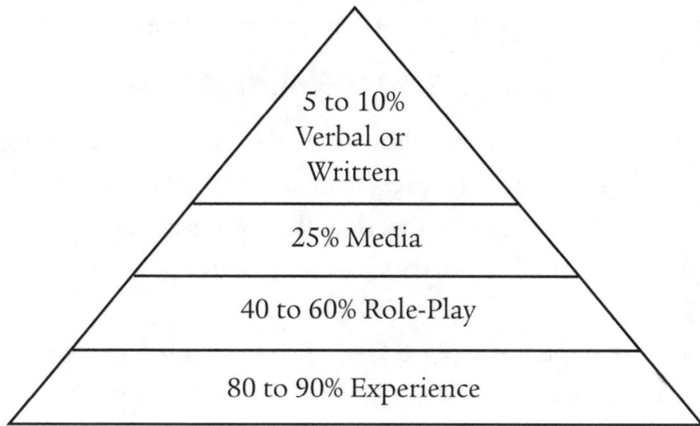

Students Learn Best When Learning Involves Self-Discovery

Rather than spoon-feeding truth to students, we need to lead them on the journey of self-discovery. Once they discover the truth for themselves, they are much more apt to apply it and own it. We must continually evaluate our learning experiences by asking ourselves, *Am I motivating my students to want to know the truth?* One of the main goals of a youth worker should be to create a desire for spiritual growth and knowledge.

Students Learn Best When Learning Involves Response

It is imperative to provide students an opportunity to respond and act upon what they are learning. We need to give students time to apply tangible action steps. It may be a guided challenge, where we outline some avenues for application of the message, or a self-guided discovery, where students reflect on the following three statements:

- React (I felt . . .)
- Fact (I learned . . .)
- Act (I will . . .)

Whatever we do, we cannot walk away from any message and leave the listeners without a clear and practical idea of how to live out what they've just heard.

You Need Strategies for Creative Communication

Keeping in mind the different learning styles students have as well as the need for experience, self-discovery and response, there are a number of communication strategies that work well. As you read through the various possibilities, take the risk and try something new in your teaching ministry.

Experiences—Life's Teachable Moments

Despite what some Christian educators say, we firmly believe that the mountaintop experience, or significant memorable event, is an excellent learning experience. The campfire on the last night of camp is usually what we best remember years later. In the Old Testament, when the parents of our faith experienced significant events with God, they would build an altar and continue to remember their encounter with Him for the rest of their lives.

Significant Events

It's important to periodically create significant memorable experiences. I (Jim) know of a youth worker who invited a prostitute to speak to his group—not a reformed prostitute but a practicing one. She was not an exceptional speaker, but her story of sexual abuse, drug addiction and running away motivated the kids to begin a ministry to runaways and prostitutes in their city.

Sometimes a significant experience can be a guest speaker sharing an area of expertise with students. Whether it's a doctor speaking about sexuality or AIDS, the senior pastor speaking about the church, a director of a funeral home speaking about death and dying, a professor of apologetics posing as an atheist, or a panel of parents—keep your eyes and ears open for people who have expertise in a particular area; their sharing can lend to a great time of communication.

On-Site Experiences

Taking students on a field trip can be one of the most memorable learning experiences. I (Jim) asked a group of youth workers if they had ever been on a field trip when in elementary school; most had. As they shared their experiences, I asked them what else they remembered learning that school year. Most could remember the smallest details of that field trip, but they had trouble remembering even the major details of the school year.

On-site learning can be something as simple as a trip to a hospital, a rescue mission or a cemetery. Instead of just reading about the temptation of Christ in Matthew 4, go to the tallest building in your city or the highest mountain in your area. Let students sense the temptation when Satan said to Jesus, "All this I will give you . . . if you will bow down and worship me" (Matthew 4:9). It gives students a chance to see, hear, feel and touch what you're talking about.

Ask yourself, *Where can I teach this so that it would have more of an impact?* Go to a funeral home and talk about death and dying. Go to a bus stop or airport and talk about the busyness of life. Go to a crisis pregnancy center and talk about the issue of teen pregnancy and abortion. Go to your local schools and talk about them being a local mission field for your students. Go to the janitor's storage room and talk about what it means to be a servant. The options are limitless.

Current Events

Keep your eyes and ears open to current events. As you watch the news or read the newspaper, make notes about what is going on in the world. Use those as illustrations, as well as teachable moments. Tragic events such as the Oklahoma City bombing and the shooting at Columbine High School in Littleton, Colorado, both lend themselves to the discussion of several questions: "Where was a loving God when all this happened? Is He still in control? Why does He allow evil in the world?"

Creating Tension—Walking the Talk

Creating tension can force students to make decisions that reflect what they truly believe, not just what they *say* they believe.

Case Studies

A case study is a real-life story that places students in tension, bringing them face-to-face with real issues and choices. Universities and graduate schools, psychology projects and the business world all use case studies. When you study a real-life situation, it brings out incredible discussion. It forces students to think and decide what they would do.

There are books with case studies already written, or you can write your own. When you write your own case study, keep in mind that students should never be able to figure out who the person is (in case it is an embarrassing story). When you have finished writing a case study, write out important discussion questions and relevant Scripture to help students work through the case study.

Activities

There are activities that will do a wonderful job of creating tension as well. One of the games is called Agree/Disagree. On one side of the room, place a sign on the wall that reads "Agree"; on the other side of the room, place another sign that reads "Disagree." Develop statements that you will read to your students. These statements need to be appropriately vague, so there is a little room for personal interpretation. Read the statement and instruct students to move to one side of the room or the other but not in the middle—they have to vote one way or the other! Here are some statement ideas:

- There are certain situations in which it is okay to lie.
- Social drinking is okay as long as you don't get drunk.
- All we need to do is ask Jesus into our hearts to be saved.
- People are basically good.
- God guides Christians in everything they do.
- Christians are just as messed up as anyone else.

A decision-making activity can also lead to stirring discussions. You can vary the activity by having students stand up if they agree and remain seated if they disagree.

Stories and Illustrations— A Lost Art Form

Jesus used parables more often than any other teaching method. The great preachers of our time are also great storytellers. Students today especially connect with stories. They connect with narrative-style preaching and teaching that use stories to communicate truth. Therefore, utilizing stories from Scripture that capture a particular truth will have more impact than just dealing with propositional truth. Instead of talking about temptation, sin and consequences from a theoretical viewpoint, use the story of David and Bathsheba. Students are swept up by a story; use this to your advantage.

Personal Illustrations

Personal illustrations are by far the most powerful form of storytelling. Tell how you experienced a particular truth. Share your personal thoughts and insights on how God is working in your life in the area you are speaking on. This will not only capture students, but it will also show them that God is indeed living and active today. When you are sharing personal illustrations and stories, be sure to remember the following points:

- The best illustrations are born out of your real life, so be honest and accurate—don't lie about a situation for effect or claim a story that didn't happen to you.
- Be sure to share stories of failure and struggle, not just personal victory.
- Share your thoughts and feelings—not just facts.
- Don't tell a story just to tell a story. Know how the illustration applies to what you're trying to communicate.
- Think about your audience. Be sure to share your illustration in such a way that your audience can relate to it.
- Make sure that your illustrations have a universal feel but, at the same time, don't disconnect you from your listeners.
- If you can use humor effectively, do it. If not—please don't!
- If you are going to use humor, use it at your own expense, *never* at the expense of a student.

Student Stories/Testimonies

Testimonies and personal illustrations shared by peers can be incredibly powerful, bringing together the power of personal story and peer influence. When one of their peers has an opportunity to share, students listen. *Which of my students can share a life story about this issue or truth?* is a question we should ask ourselves with frequency.

Nonpersonal Illustrations and Stories

There are wonderful resources out today that can help with stories and illustrations. Much like using personal illustrations, be sure that there is a point to be made with them and make sure that you make that point loud and clear. Make the illustration a tool, not the driving force, of the message. Don't find yourself preparing or crafting a message around an illustration. Once you know what your message is about and what point you need to make with an illustration, then begin to do some research. Look in book resources, check online at various Internet sites, and even check out children's books.[1]

Object Lessons—Seeing Is Believing

Object lessons use a physical object to represent, explain or display a spiritual truth, helping to create a visual memory or learning experience with meaning. These may be a bit harder to develop, but if you can pull them off, they are amazingly powerful. Object lessons have a way of staying with our listeners.

There are still students in our youth ministry who will never look at a blender, a nail, an apple, a bar of soap or a sliver of rag the same way. To this day I (Mike) still talk with students who have kept their rusty nail from a message I gave over a year ago on the Cross and the cost of our sin. Coming up with an object lesson takes time and sometimes comes with an element of risk, but again, it is well worth the time and effort you put into it.

Creative Expression—Lights, Camera, Action!

Rarely do we in the Church give students the opportunity and the forum to use their artistic expression. In almost every youth ministry, there are students who need the opportunity to be creative and the avenue to express their ideas by learning through the arts. Poetry, creative dance, art, drama and music are all very important ingredients for many students to express their faith. We need to always be looking for opportunities to allow our students to express creatively who God is and what He is doing in their lives.

Drama

In any youth ministry there are students who are excited about drama. Some of the students may not only want to perform dramatic productions, but they might want to write them as well. Encourage students to write and perform dramas to introduce or enhance your messages.

- **Spontaneous Melodrama**—On-the-spot, unrehearsed, humorous adaptations of biblical stories can well be used in conjunction with messages. This gives students an opportunity to be involved, laugh a little and see the biblical narrative from a different point of view.
- **Role-Playing**—This is a useful form of drama that places students in someone else's position in which they must solve a problem or act out a scenario. In so doing they begin to understand a little more about what it is like to be that person. You can role-play stories from Scripture or modern issues of the Christian faith. This strategy helps students get into the subject in an enjoyable and nonthreatening way.

  Biblical narratives come alive when role-played. We've used everything from the David and Bathsheba story, to Abraham and Isaac, to the disciples on the boat in the storm on the Sea of Galilee, to the feeding of the 5,000. Once we used the story of Mary telling Joseph that she was with child (see Matthew 1:18-25). The beauty, sacredness and humanity of the situation became so much more clear as students read between the lines, and ad-libbed an argument between Mary and Joseph. At first I (Jim) was offended, but then I remembered that Joseph was going to quietly divorce Mary until he was paid a visit by an angel of the Lord. We will never look at that story the same way again.

Music

With the explosion of worship sweeping across the world, the avenue of musical expression is an obvious place to allow students to express themselves. Have a student worship team formulate their worship set around the theme you'll be teaching on. Have them write music for it. If you have musically gifted students, have them perform a special music number (before or after you speak) that deals with the message content. Send out a crew of students armed with a video camera and have them make a music video for a song that you want to use for your message. There are many ways to use music to enhance your message.

Other Forms of Expression

Look for creative writers who would write poetry or articles for your newsletter. Many students who take creative dance at school may want to perform for the group with an interpretive dance to a Christian song. Have students draw a picture of what they think God looks like or how they picture a certain Biblical character or story. Have students respond to worship by drawing: pictures, images, prayers and words of worship and praise. Post the art where you meet, as a gallery of worship to God.

Media—Turn On and Tune In

Someone once said that computers, television and film are the backdrop of the lives of our students. We believe it. Students are in tune with every new media message out there today. The media may offer good or bad examples, but one thing is certain—examples abound for us to use. Whether good or bad, the use of media is a great tool not only to show spiritual truth but also to evaluate our culture and its view of God.

Movies

There are many practical examples and illustrations that we can pull from current films. Keep your eyes and ears open to what your students are watching. No matter what video clip you may use, be sure to follow two very important rules: (1) Always preview the video clip and make sure it is useable, and (2) make sure that you have a strong point to go with the clip. We can't just use a movie for the movie's sake; there must be a purpose behind it. There are many wonderful resources out there that not only have video clips identified but also have passages, questions or full Bible studies that go along with them.

Music

Music is another excellent tool. Current music reflects the state of culture. Examine the lyrics of songs and the messages they give. This will help students develop a more discriminating taste in the music they listen to.[2]

Print Media

Newspaper and magazine articles provide an opportunity for discussing current events. They can be the source of case studies too. By connecting these events to a biblical base, you allow students to look at their Christian life through the context of the happenings in today's world.

Television

Much like films, television can help us explore current trends, values and messages. Be looking for teachable moments within current television programming. Find out what students are watching and videotape some episodes. More often than not, you'll stumble across a great scene for a future message. Watch and tape newscasts, sitcoms, talk shows and even late-night talk shows. Interviews of current celebrities and newsmakers discussing current issues can always provide great discussion material.

Inductive Bible Study—Digging for Yourself!

A vital part of good teaching is giving students the tools to learn for themselves. Unfortunately, most youth ministries seldom give students the opportunity to learn how to study the Bible—and for the most part, the students are biblically illiterate. They don't know God's Word and have no idea how to dig into it for themselves. The inductive method is a simple tool to help students discover a greater appreciation of looking into the Scriptures.

By equipping our students with the tools they need to dig into and apply God's Word to their lives, we give them the ability to care for their own soul far past the day they graduate from our ministry and move on.

> For a sample case study and inductive Bible study, visit YouthBuilders at www.youthbuilders.com.

CHAPTER 21

Teaching on Sex and Sexuality

Turn on the television, listen to the radio, go the movies, flip through a magazine, open up your e-mail and there it is—sex. There is arguably no other issue so pervasive in our society as sexuality—and perhaps no bigger issue on the minds of our students. I (Jim) was told about a 16-year-old boy who heard that the average male teen will have a sexual thought every 20 seconds. His response? "You're kidding! What am I supposed to think about during the other 19 seconds?"

Our students have sex on their minds; in fact, many of them are in over their heads, having experimented already. With the messages and incredible influences pushing teens toward sexual experiences, we owe it to our students to be talking about the issue of sexuality and their personal lives. They need to know what God has to say about the issue. The unfortunate truth is that most teens have the viewpoint that God is somehow opposed to it, and the thought that God created sex and sees it as good is a completely foreign concept. Even more unfortunate is the correlation between sexual activity and churched youth versus nonchurched youth. The statistics show that the difference is minimal, which leads us to believe that although students are saying that God wants them to wait, that truth has had little impact on their sexual activity as a whole. There is hope on the horizon, though: a recent study found that teenagers who publicly pledged to remain virgin until marriage delayed having sex about 18 months longer than other teenagers, with the longest effect on those who took the oath at age 16 to 17.[1]

One of the needs in youth ministry today is that we continue to help students see the value and benefit of waiting until marriage to experience sex. Students may know it intellectually, but we need to help equip them for the onslaught of messages, influences and pressures they will encounter. Let's consider some important information:

- Statistics tell us that the majority of young people (both male and female) are engaged regularly in masturbation.
- Oral sex is becoming more and more an accepted alternative to sexual intercourse.
- In a recent survey, over 80 percent of teens primarily under the age of 14 considered themselves virgins, yet over 25 percent of them had participated in oral sex.
- Recent surveys of middle school students have found that many consider oral sex as simply another form of making out, so they ask, "What's the big deal?"[2]
- HIV and AIDS are issues that students face with increasing regularity. According to an MTV survey, many young people are misinformed about HIV and AIDS. The poll found that 60 percent of 16- to 24-year-old viewers think they should be worried about HIV and AIDS—but only 24 percent said they knew anything about the disease, and over 12 percent thought it was transmitted by kissing. UNAIDS, the United Nations agency leading the fight against AIDS, says that 50 percent of new infections occur among 15- to 25-year-olds.[3]

These are the issues that face our students today—issues that our students need to be informed about and decisive about their involvement.[4]

Why Discuss Sexuality?

Why should the Church delve into the issue of sexuality? First, people who question sex education programs because they fear that the information itself can be dangerous are simply *mistaken.* Studies have shown that the more positive, value-centered sex education a young person has, the less he or she is apt to be sexually promiscuous. This reason alone is enough to convince us that healthy, value-centered sex education in the Church can prevent future heartache.

Students Are Growing Up in a Sexually Dominated Culture

Television, movies, radio, advertising—and now the Internet—all keep sexuality prominent in the mind of our nation. Like it or not, we can't ignore the fact that our students are literally being bombarded with sexuality at every turn. The Internet has become a major influence—just take a look at some of the e-mail and attachments that are flying around. According to Enough Is Enough, an advocacy group against pornography, a recent study found that 63 percent of teenagers unintentionally found pornography on the Internet.[5]

Students Find Sex Mysterious

The mystery and wonder of sexuality helps keep students attracted to the issue. In fact, many times it is this sense of mystery that leads teens to experiment with it in the first place. Why is it that whenever the youth ministry has a series on sexuality, attendance increases? Because kids want information. They want answers, and Christian students truly desire to know what God has to say about sex.

Students Are Receiving Mixed Messages

The majority of young people receive a "Don't do it!" message from their parents, with little or no accompanying explanation (that is, if their parents say anything about it at all). From the Church, students often hear "Don't do it because it's ugly and dirty—so save it for the one you love!" (which, understandably, confuses them even more). The secular world often focuses on teaching how to do it safely (technique) without discussing sexual values and morals.

Students want someone to be open and honest with them. They

sincerely want to know the truth about their sexuality; they're frustrated because no one seems to be giving them straightforward, honest answers. The Church can be that place. Who better to talk openly and honestly about sexuality and its Creator than the Church? We have the ability, but will we use it?

Students Need Help Integrating Their Sexuality with Their Relationship with God

Far too many adolescents have a difficult time integrating their sexuality with their relationship to God. Many young people believe that God is against sex. They forget that God created sex (see Genesis 2:18-25) and that He sees everything He created as very good (see Genesis 1:25,31). Since we want students to understand that God cares about all aspects of their lives, it is imperative that the Church teach about sexuality from a Christian perspective.

Parents Need the Church's Help

Unfortunately, many parents unwittingly fail to fulfill their proper role in the area of sex education. A professor at Wheaton College told me (Jim) that when he polled his students, he found that only 20 percent had ever had any kind of healthy, positive sex education at home. It was almost nonexistent. The area of sexuality is such a great avenue for us to link arms with parents. Many parents have a great deal of trouble talking about sex with their kids. Let's face it: Many parents (and youth workers) didn't handle their sexuality well as teenagers, so they don't know how to approach sexual issues with their children.

The question is, If parents don't talk about it and the Church won't talk about it, who will talk to today's young people about sexual issues—and what type of information will be conveyed? Parents need help to talk with their children about sex. The Church must not (and cannot) take the place of parents in sex education, but the Church can help parents and their children deal with the topic together.

How Should We Teach Sexuality?

Since this issue is so vital to our students, we cannot remain silent. We need to deal with the issue openly and honestly and with complete transparency. If there is anywhere our students should feel the freedom to ask questions and share opinions, it should be in the context of our youth ministries; and our youth ministries should provide healthy, Christian-based teaching on sexuality.

Biblically Based

First and foremost, we need to expose our students to what the Bible says about the issue of sexuality. Students need to hear that God Himself created sexuality and sees it as very good (see Genesis 1:25,31; 2:18-25). They need to hear that God has created sexuality to be enjoyed within the parameters of marriage (see Matthew 19:4-6; 1 Thessalonians 4:3). God gave us guidelines, not to take away our enjoyment of sex, but so that we could enjoy it to the fullest—without worry of past memories, comparisons and expectations or the consequences of diseases. God gave us guidelines to keep us from getting hurt so that we could enjoy sex for all that He created it to be. Students need to hear that if we belong to Christ, our bodies are the temples of the Holy Spirit, bought with a price (see 1 Corinthians 6:18-20). The picture given in 1 Corinthians 6 is one of a trust—a business term describing an asset is owned by one person but kept and managed by another. The person who is in charge will be held accountable for how the trust is managed. We were bought with a price; our bodies are owned by God but given to us to manage. And in the end we will be held accountable.

We don't need to spend all our time in the thou-shalt-nots of the Scriptures, however. Students are ready to discuss the Song of Solomon and how this explicit book explores the virtues of married love. They need to see how both David and Joseph handled sexual temptation. There are myriad stories and passages that students need to be exposed to. Issues such as lust, forgiveness, homosexuality and consequences need to be discussed from a biblical perspective.

In addition to learning what the Bible says about sexuality, we also need to explore what the Bible *doesn't* say about it. The Bible is silent in certain areas regarding sexuality, but it does give us insight into making right choices and setting boundaries. Aside from sexual intercourse being kept in the confines of marriage, the exact line of how far is too far on a date is not dealt with in exact terms in the pages of Scripture. It does not say, "Thou shalt go this far and this far only on your second date," but it gives us principles that we should explore that give us insight in making that decision. We are encouraged to have respect for one another, because the Holy Spirit lives in us (see 1 Corinthians 6:18-20), and true love is not self-seeking (see 1 Corinthians 13:5). We are reminded not to take advantage of one another when it comes to our sexuality and to refrain from sexual immorality (see 1 Thessalonians 4:3-8). We need to help students look into the Scriptures for guidance on issues that are not directly spoken to and help them find the truth in what's not said as well as what is.

Discussion Oriented

Students learn best when they talk, not when you talk: this adage is especially true in teaching on sexuality. The vehicle of discussion and self-guided discovery is paramount in dealing with the issue of sexuality. Our students need a place where they have the openness to ask questions and share opinions. An open forum is the best vehicle for helping them reach personal conviction in this area.

Small group discussions, anonymous questions, case studies, creating tension, role playing and object lessons all need to be a part of our teaching about sex and sexuality. Rather than giving a monologue, what students need is dialogue. From small-group interaction to allowing students to ask questions anonymously on index cards, students need more than a here's-what-to-believe discussion. They need us to apply the let's-discover-together-what-God's-Word-says-and-how-it-applies-to-our-lives approach. As students are led to conclusions about God's view on sexuality and how that impacts their activities on a Friday night, they will have stronger convictions and ownership.

Relationship Centered

Sexuality training in churches needs to be centered in relationship as well. We need to help students navigate the other dimensions of relationships and intimacy that surround sexuality. Being sexually active before marriage impacts current *and* future relationships in negative ways. One telltale sign of this is the high incidence of divorce among people who were sexually active before marriage.

For most students, sex is not a separate activity, apart from relationship; it occurs in the context of a relationship. Healthy dating and relating to the opposite sex need to be a part of our sexuality teaching. From communication to treating each other with respect and honor, relational issues need to be discussed. How to work on the other areas of intimacy—mental, emotional and spiritual—as opposed to fixating on the physical, also needs to be addressed. Our communication needs to help students focus not only on the short-term relationships they are currently involved in but also the long-term relationships of the future, including the relationships that might ultimately result in marriage.

In our desire to help students make right and wise decisions regarding their sexuality, we also need to help them navigate the seas of relationships in general.

Respect Driven

We've mentioned it a few times, but the issue of respect and honor for the other person in a relationship needs to be held in high regard. Philippians 2:3-4 encapsulates the principle of having honor and respect for others:

> Do nothing out of selfish ambition or vain conceit, but in humility consider others better than yourselves. Each of you should look not only to your own interests, but also to the interests of others.

The respect-driven focus continually looks at the other person's long-term spiritual and emotional well-being. This focus helps make sense of the Christian standard of restraint and control in premarital sexual activity. We need to help students take their eyes off themselves and their needs, encourage them to focus on the other person in the relationship and show them how to honor and respect the other person as a child of the King.

Choice Affirmed

Perhaps one of the most powerful messages we can give students today is a simple yet profound one: Having sex is not a required part of a relationship; they *can* say no. Many educators and researchers are telling us that it's natural (and that we need) to be involved sexually. We're told that it's good for relationship and intimacy, that it helps us find out if we are sexually compatible with our partner, and that it gives us sexual knowledge that is essential for us in marriage. The Christian response to this information is that we don't have to have sex before marriage; it is not a prerequisite for a good marriage—or even for great sex within marriage. Students *do* have a choice!

Many of our students—especially those growing up without much-needed healthy sexual education—can fall into the trap of believing the lie that sex is just what happens in relationships. They need to know that there are other ways of expressing intimacy. There are other ways of communicating love for each other—ways that foster healthy relationship with the opposite sex. They need to be empowered to say no.

Alternative Empowered

The education and training of our students is not complete until we can help them with options and alternatives for being involved sexually. Helping students fight sexual temptation won't work if our teaching only goes as far as telling them to just say no. Our job as youth workers is to help students deal with the realities of sexual temptation and healthy expression of their sexuality. We need to help them do several things:

- **Set Their Sights**—Young people need to make the initial decision to be sexually pure until marriage, whether they are currently a virgin or have been sexually active in the past (see 1 Corinthians 6:18-20).

- **Set Their Standards**—Young people need to be able to answer the question, *How far should I go?* rather than *How far can I go and still be OK?*
- **Analyze Their Situations**—Young people need to look at and evaluate the situations they find themselves in and how those situations impact their sexual activity.
- **Think Through Solutions**—Young people need to develop a list of alternatives and possibilities for staying out of situations that will lead to sexual activity, as well as dealing with actual temptation (see 2 Timothy 2:22).
- **Experience God's Grace**—Young people need to know and experience the freedom of forgiveness in Jesus Christ, even for those who have been sexually active or have made other mistakes in the past (see 1 John 1:9).

Value Centered

In a world where much of the teaching that young people receive is value neutral, the church can provide moral- and value-centered sexual education. It's important to let our students know that everybody isn't doing it, that it *is* better not to do it and that their decisions will affect them in the short as well as the long term.

We can help students set the right standards. Many sexual decisions are made in the midst of an intense emotional environment that is beyond a student's ability to cope. Sexual decisions should not be made at Inspiration Point or in the heat of the moment. We can provide a less stressful environment that will provide young teens with the moral and spiritual underpinnings necessary to properly understand, process and own God's standards for sexuality.

With sexual promiscuity on the rise, the Church is one of the best places to help kids deal with pain and anger and receive forgiveness. In youth ministries all across America, there are many hearts that have been left broken and bleeding by negative sexual experiences. In Christ we can offer forgiveness, hope and a strategy for living out a healthy, constructive sexual life. The Church, rather than the current culture or the media, can and should be the place where kids can find advice, healing and comfort, and people who are willing to talk with them about the mystery of their sexuality.

Need Practical Ideas for Teaching on Sexuality?

Include Parents When Possible

Keep the parents informed about what you will be teaching. This will set their minds at ease and will challenge them to talk about the subject with their children at home. Invite parents to a meeting just for them before beginning a series on sexuality. This will give you the opportunity to share what you'll be teaching about and from what perspective you'll be approaching the subject. As a part of the series you may even want to include a few parents on a panel. This will give you, as the moderator, a chance to ask parents a few questions about sexuality and dating that can help students see things from their parents' perspectives. You may even want to have all the parents there for a parent/student event such as a one-day sexuality or purity conference.

Use the Power of Student Testimonies

Use student testimonies regarding both positive and negative experiences to allow students to hear from their peers. Student testimonies are a powerful way for young people to hear about real-life situations and how their peers integrate their faith with this area of their lives. Another idea is to have a student panel that fields prearranged questions regarding sexuality (this can also be very effective using adults, such as medical professionals, health educators and parents).

Meet with Local Health Education/Sex Education Teachers

Many times youth workers feel they are in opposition to the public school teacher who teaches about sex. This is not always true. Most of the sex education teachers really do care about the students, and although they might be teaching from a value-neutral viewpoint, they are still trying to give the students helpful information. When I (Jim) first met Mr. Dunn, the sex education teacher in our local high school, I expected to meet someone who was trying to convince the students to have sexual intercourse. I was absolutely mistaken. He invited me to sit in on some of his classes. They were excellent; I even learned a few things! After looking at his curriculum, I restructured my series on sexuality, because I realized that I didn't need to repeat some of the positive aspects of the public school system. Instead, I could put more of my time and attention on presenting the positive Christian perspective on sexuality.

Use a Variety of Teaching Venues

Look for opportunities in your program to teach about sexuality. Maybe try a Guys Only retreat where you can talk about the issues of sexuality and being a man of God. Organize a Girls Only retreat where you can look at the issue of sexual purity and being a godly woman. Or organize a seminar and divide the guys and girls into separate groups to address the various issues relevant to their gender. Look at the possibility of doing a one-day sexuality conference, maybe involving other churches in the community.

Explore Various Teaching Methods and Resources

Case studies, role-plays, movie or TV clips, songs, object lessons, dramas and on-site learning can all be creative and effective ways of communicating to students about sexuality. In addition, there are many great resources you can use in this area. Be sure you know what's out there and available; these resources will make your job a whole lot easier.[6]

Bring in an Expert

If you feel uncomfortable teaching in the area of sexuality, find someone (a doctor, nurse, psychologist—even another youth worker) who feels comfortable dealing with these issues. Your church could bring in experts from the community, or a group of churches could organize a one-day seminar. Use your imagination—more great ideas will come your way.

Brainstorm with Others

Ask other youth workers in your area what they have used as illustrations, object lessons, resources or experts to teach on sexuality. Maybe at your next youth workers' network lunch (if you attend one!) throw out the idea during lunch. You'll glean more ideas in 10 minutes by networking than you could in an hour on your own.

Avoid Oversimplistic Answers

Sexuality is not a black and white issue (in spite of what some of us were taught), and it is about much more than having sexual intercourse. Encourage questions and sharing of opinions with your students. Remember that we need to guide students in making their own decisions about their sexuality. If we avoid making decisions for them and instead help them make their own, they are much more likely to take ownership of and follow through with their decision.

Talk About a Variety of Issues

Remember that knowledge can't hurt students and will *not* lead them to promiscuity. Kids really appreciate an open and honest approach that deals with all aspects of their sexuality. Try thinking through some of these issues for your next series:

- How to overcome sexual temptation
- How far is too far? (*How far should I go* versus *How far can I go?*)
- Why wait until marriage to have sex?
- Respect and honor in relationships
- How the culture influences our thinking about sex
- Basic male/female sexual and emotional differences
- How do you know if you're in love?
- Options for pregnant couples (individuals)
- Unconditional love

- Dating and relating to the opposite sex
- Intimacy in relationships
- Conception and pregnancy
- Sexual intercourse
- Masturbation
- Oral sex
- Sexual abuse
- Homosexuality
- Venereal disease
- Birth control
- Abortion
- Peer influence
- Drugs and drinking
- Parties
- Guilt and forgiveness
- Pornography
- Internet
- Sexual addiction
- Lust
- HIV and AIDS

For a comprehensive book on sex and sexuality, check out *Radical Love* (Ventura, CA: Regal Books, 1995) by Jim Burns. You can purchase this book directly from YouthBuilders at www.youthbuilders.com.

Section IV

Personal Relationships—The Heart of Ministry

CHAPTER 22

Building Self-Image in Students

Kim, a junior in high school, summed up low self-image in the following note:

> I don't like my looks. I don't like my actions. I don't like my church. I'm far from excited about my relationship with my boyfriend. I make more mistakes than I do successes, and I'm really not sure why God allowed all this to happen in the past two years. Life used to be so easy. Now it is so complicated and getting worse. I'm coping by experimenting with drugs and having sex with my boyfriend, but I'm still desperately unhappy. The pain runs deep.

Kim is not alone—and not unique. There are many students today who are asking questions and searching for a significance that can only be found in the person of Jesus Christ. There are Kims in your youth ministry. If you take the time to look around, you'll find them. They come in different shapes and sizes, different hair color and have different interests, yet they all have one thing in common—they are searching.

The Search

Identity

Eric Erikson said it best when I (Jim) was a student at Princeton: "The primary task of the teenage years is to construct a strong sense of self-identity." The adolescent years are marked by change: physical, emotional, relational and spiritual. In the midst of all this change, our students are asking life-altering questions of identity: *Who am I? Where do I belong?*

Our students are trying on different personalities, interests and even lifestyles—all in an effort to find out who they really are or should be. That's why a student can be into one style of music one week and another the next, and dress one way this year, only to look totally different next year. They are trying out different images of self, to see which one fits best. Unfortunately, God can become just another piece of their ever-changing wardrobe. Being spiritual or even being a Christian can just be one more identity that students will try to wear in an effort to find out who they should be. The sad truth is that some will walk away from the very thing that gives them their greatest sense of worth and significance—God's heartbeat and design for their lives.

Significance and Meaning

Adolescents are also asking, *Do I really matter? Is there some greater meaning and significance to my life?* This search is based on the deeply felt desire to want to see their lives as a part of a plan—something greater than themselves that's purposeful.

This search for significance can lead students down all kinds of paths. Peer influence and the pressure to conform can be felt most strongly when students are grappling with the question, *Do I really matter?* Involvement in sex, the use of drugs and alcohol, and even eating disorders can all be silent screams of students saying "Tell me by my looks and my actions that I have significance and worth." More often than not, they will search for answers in any other place than the place where they can find real, lasting significance—in a love relationship with the person of Jesus, the lover of their souls.

Healthy Relationships

Young teens are beginning to test the waters of relationships. They are searching for what it means to have a healthy relationship with one another. Whether through dating relationships with the opposite sex or in same-sex friendships, students are learning the fine art of both good and bad relationship building.

Some of those relationships can be unhealthy—based on selfishness and self-gratification. Some of those relationships can be healthy—based on mutual sacrifice, giving, genuine care and concern. If they don't experience what it means to have a healthy relationship in these formative years, it's possible that they never will. One of our roles in youth ministry is to help our students understand, value and learn how to build healthy relationships with each other.

Direction

Students are making decisions that will impact them for the rest of their lives. Their choices regarding their futures, their individual significance, their relationships, sex, dating, drugs and alcohol all have a bearing on their lives. One question remains for those of us who work with students: How are we helping equip our students with the life skills and discernment to make those decisions with the eternal in mind?

Students are dealing at a younger and younger age with the questions and issues we faced in our later years of adolescence or even in young adulthood. Pressure to be sexually active, to drink, to conform and fit in and to succeed and the turmoil of the breakdown of the family all are being felt earlier in the adolescent years. The result is that young teens are making decisions that they are not equipped to handle. As youth workers, we are dealing with students who are in need of decision-making skills and discernment. We may not be able to turn back the clock and undo the things they've been exposed to, but we can seek to help them navigate their decisions with godly discernment and wisdom.

God

This generation is one of the most active in Church youth ministries but one of the least committed to the Christian faith. According to a nationwide study on teenagers, a highly respected research group found that four out of five teenagers say they are Christians, yet only 26 percent claim to be absolutely committed to the Christian faith. When asked to estimate the likelihood that they will continue to participate in church life once they are living on their own, only about one out of three of teenagers currently attending church regularly claimed they would continue to be involved. Placed in context, that stands as the lowest level of expected participation among teenagers recorded in more than a decade.[1]

This should serve as a wake-up call to those of us in youth ministry. We've said it before, but it bears repeating again: If we don't reach students with a life-altering, life-changing relationship with Jesus Christ *right now*, the odds are against them ever being reached. Again, research has borne that to be true. In a national survey, people ages 5 to 13 had a 32 percent probability of accepting Jesus Christ as their Savior. Students between the ages of 14 and 18 had just a 4 percent likelihood, while ages 19 through death had only a 6 percent probability.[2]

We have students' attention—the question is what we will do with it? Students are hungry to know who God is and how He fits into their lives. They are searching. As a youth ministry community, our calling is to help students find what they are searching for in the person of Jesus Christ—not a religion, but a life-changing relationship with God.

The Mirror Problem

As Scott Peck pointed out in the opening line of his bestseller *The Road Less Traveled*: "Life is difficult."[3] This is especially true for adolescents in our society today. Students today are under a greater amount of stress and pressure than ever before, and the roadblocks to a healthy, Christ-centered self-image are many.

Physical Appearance

Our world is caught up with looks and beauty, thanks in large part to the influence of our media-focused society. We are a society that focuses on outer appearance rather than on inner virtue. Unfortunately, much of the Christian culture has fallen into the same trap. Even those in the Church have forgotten the words of 1 Samuel 16:7, where God speaks the prophet Samuel:

> Do not consider his appearance or his height, for I have rejected him. The LORD does not look at the things man looks at. Man looks at the outward appearance, but the LORD looks at the heart.

We cannot underestimate the importance of physical appearance to our students. Adolescents have an incredible need for their physical appearance to measure up to the cultural norm. Many times students feel out of place simply because of their own impression that their physical appearance doesn't measure up to what they consider to be the norm. They look in the mirror and don't like what they see. The desire to measure up to an oftentimes unrealistic and false cultural norm has enormous implications for students. Eating disorders are on the rise in the United States. Five to ten million females (including adolescent girls) struggle with eating disorders and borderline conditions. One million males (including adolescent boys) struggle with the same problem. Add the numbers together and you'll find that the sum is approximately triple the number of people living with AIDS—and at least three times the number of people living with schizophrenia.[4] Oftentimes the mirror can be our own worst enemy, tearing our lives apart by who we think we see.

Not learning to accept our physical appearance devastates our self-image. Think back to when you were an adolescent. What was one of the primary concerns of your life? When I (Jim) was in seventh grade, I received this poem in my yearbook:

> God created rivers
> God created lakes
> God created you, Jim
> Everyone makes mistakes!

For an insecure seventh-grader that poem was anything but funny. In fact, I silently broke away from the kid who wrote it and stopped including him as one of my friends.

We must convey to young people the fact that God's concern is for *inner* beauty; He does not put prime importance on outer beauty. We must help young people understand that beauty and happiness are not necessarily synonymous words. Some of the most beautiful people on the outside are the most unhappy people on the inside—and vice versa.

Sexuality

Students suffering from poor self-image are easily seduced sexually. The number one reason teenagers give for having sex is because there is an intense desire for love and acceptance. The often heard cry is "I want to be loved." Sadly, many students consider sex a necessary ingredient for being accepted and loved. The media portrays it, society affirms it, and unfortunately, our students believe and live it out. I (Mike) remember a young girl sitting in my office, telling me about her Friday night:

> All I ever wanted was to be loved. All I ever wanted was for someone to care about me, and I thought that this was it. One thing led to another and stuff happened, and before I knew it we were having sex. Now I look back, and everything I thought I'd get—the love, the care—it's all gone. Maybe it was never there to begin with. All I know is that all I ever wanted, all I really want is for someone to love me for me.

The culture is changing so rapidly that the church must stand up for biblical values and morals. Young teens need help in forming their moral convictions. In the name of value-neutral education, many parents (and youth workers) have set young people adrift to make up their own minds on important matters, without the proper tools and insight to help them make right and wise decisions. As we help students develop a proper self-image, we will help them be able to choose to say no to the sexual pressures and attitudes that are permeating our society today.

Materialism

I (Jim) can still remember the small group where someone asked the question, "If you could do anything or be anything when you grow up, what would it be?"

One tenth-grader said, "I want to be rich."

I asked him, "What do you want to do to become rich?"

He replied, "I don't care. I just want lots of money."

We must help our students understand that success is not spelled m-o-n-e-y. The Bible warns us that materialism is perhaps the most dangerous "religion" known to humankind.

> No one can serve two masters. Either he will hate the one and love the other, or he will be devoted to the one and despise the other. You cannot serve both God and Money (Matthew 6:24).

Somehow we must convey to our students that money does not bring the happiness, the fulfillment or the acceptance for which they are so desperately searching. We must help students realize the scriptural principle, "Where your treasure is, there your heart will be also" (Matthew 6:21). Students who are struggling with their self-image will constantly seek things in order to fill their need to have worth and significance, often at the expense of deeper and more meaningful qualities of life. Adults too often model the concept that to have things brings about status and meaning–this applies especially to parents and can even apply to the Church. The fact of the matter is that the main reason there are so few churches talking about materialism today is because materialism has infiltrated the Church in America in such a major way. For example, when it comes time to build a new sanctuary or buy a new sound system, it is very easy to fall into the trap of doing it bigger and better than the church down the street.

Peer Influence

The intense desire to belong, to be liked and accepted, is running full force in the teenage years. Students will tell you that there is no greater desire than to be included and accepted by their peers. This powerful force is what causes a 15-year-old Christian girl to become pregnant or a

16-year-old boy to drink and drive. They want so badly to be loved and accepted that they make decisions against their basic values and convictions in a desperate attempt to be loved.

No one wants to be different. There may be people who desire to be more countercultural, but often where they fit in is with others who are countercultural! No one wants to stand out in a crowd. No one wants to be seen as different or odd. All of us have a deep desire and need to fit in and be accepted. If we were completely honest, we'd have to admit that it doesn't stop when we graduate from high school.

Positive Factors

If students sense that there are those who stand with them, they are more likely and willing to stand up for what they believe. This is highlighted in 2 Timothy 2:22: "Flee the evil desires of youth, and pursue righteousness, faith, love and peace, along with those who call on the Lord out of a pure heart."

As youth leaders, we need to not only help students deal with the potential negative influences of peer influence but also be willing to exert some positive influence "along with those who call on the Lord out of a pure heart."

Negative Factors

David Elkind notes, "It is important to remember at this point that peer pressure has no power in and of itself. The peer group is powerful only because there are teenagers with a patchwork self, particularly of the conforming variety, who lack the inner strengths that would weigh against conforming."[5]

His point is important for youth work. Negative peer influence can be overcome when teenagers have positive influences in their lives. Youth ministries can provide positive relationships and affirmation in the lives of students to help them battle negative peer influence. Our students must understand that because the people they spend time with will have a profound impact on them, they need to choose their friends very wisely. They are unique creations of the almighty God who loves them unconditionally.

View of Self

One of the forces most destructive to the healthy self-image of adolescents is not caused by outside influence; rather, it's from falling into the comparison trap. *If only I could look like . . . or perform like . . . or be more like . . . , then I'd be worth something.* When students play the comparison game, comparing their own life, looks, personality and brains with someone else, they will always lose. There's always someone more talented, better looking and smarter.

One of the responsibilities of a good youth worker is to help students understand the power of what sociologists call the self-fulfilling prophecy: You become what you believe yourself to be. If you believe you are a failure, you will most likely become a failure. If you believe (as many adolescents do) that you are worthless, you'll live your life as a person who has no worth. If you believe you can't do it, you won't be able to accomplish the task, no matter what it is. But wait! The opposite is *also* true: If you believe you can accomplish something, you probably will. If you believe you have inner beauty, you will radiate from the inside out; and you will have a beautiful appearance.[6] If you believe you have worth as a child of God, you'll live your life in a way that reflects confidence and joy.

View of God

How students view God plays an extremely important part in their self-image. Students suffer from three major misconceptions about God that have a deep impact on their self-image.

Misconceptions One: God Is Demanding and Unforgiving

One misconception young teens can have is that He is a demanding, unforgiving God. Those who view God this way have a difficult time accepting the concept of grace. They see God as the eye in the sky, constantly looking down and waiting for them to make a mistake, so He can say, "See, I told you. You really are worthless and pathetic." Adolescents fall short of their expectations and even walk away from God at times because they can't meet up to their own misconception of His expectations.

Misconception Two: God Is Distant and Distracted

Another misconception young people can have is that God is so busy running the universe and is so distant and distracted that He couldn't possibly have any time for them. "God, where were You when _______________ happened? I thought You cared about me. I thought You were looking out for me." Anger, bitterness and resentment can well up inside. Their difficulty may be a disrupted family, the death of someone very close to them, etc., but the result is the same: they feel that God has abandoned them or is out to punish them for something. Those who carry this view of God often walk away, citing Him for a lack of care. They live their lives in prisons of bitterness.

Misconception Three: God Is Slow to Forgive

The last misconception some teens may have is that God is somehow slow to forgive. I (Mike) have literally heard students say, "If God really knew what was going on in my life, there is no way He would want to forgive me." Living their lives in shame, these students see themselves as being unforgivable. We must help them see that forgiveness is there for the asking—for anyone, at anytime, for anything. Romans 5:8 states it very clearly: "God demonstrates his own love for us in this: While we were still sinners, Christ died for us." Through Christ's atoning death and resurrection we find forgiveness and freedom.

> Therefore, there is now no condemnation for those who are in Christ Jesus, because through Christ Jesus, the law of the Spirit of life set me free from the law of sin and death (Romans 8:1-2).
>
> If we confess our sins, he is faithful and just and will forgive us our sins and purify us from all unrighteousness (1 John 1:9).

These are timeless truths that students need to hear over and over again.

Healthy Self-Image

Achieving a healthy, Christ-centered self-image is definitely a challenge for students, but it is not an insurmountable task. Youth workers can have a significant impact in the lives of students in this area. There are seven very practical and useful steps you can use to help students in their struggle for self-worth.

Positive Relationships

Students need to be constantly reminded that they will become like the people they spend time with on a regular basis. We need to encourage them to spend time with positive, energetic people who passionately love and follow Jesus.

One of the major goals of any youth ministry should be to provide a supportive community of fellowship. Most youth ministry activities should be planned around the goal of building community. Frankly, the first and foremost reason that students come to a youth group is to make friends, and this is a perfectly acceptable reason. Although many students have a genuine desire to grow in their faith, friendship is usually first on their list. Deepening Christian friendships lead them to grow in their faith.

Attitude Focus

Students are idealistic and extremely hard on themselves. There are many aspects of their lives that students want to see changed that simply never will. Let them know that many of their circumstances will never change but that they can change their attitude—and this makes all the difference in the world. I (Jim) love the prayer of Reinhold Niebuhr: "God grant me the serenity to accept what I cannot change, courage to change what I can and wisdom to know the difference."

Physical Health

We're convinced that at the core of many students' self-image problems are poor or unhealthy physical habits. The youth group should be a place where students can get input on how to care for their bodies. Information on eating disorders, physical balance, proper nutrition, rest, exercise and other aspects of taking care of their bodies need to be a part of our ministries. God made the body, mind and spirit to work together. One suggestion we should give to all our students is to get a regular physical checkup. Some emotional problems may have a physiological source rather than a spiritual one.

Success Experiences

There is nothing better for raising a young teen's self-worth than to have a few successes to build up confidence. Sometimes it might be as easy as being invited to use his or her giftedness in ministry. Find ways to help students experience success. You may need to become a math tutor or to delegate the planning of the youth ministry event to someone who is not only capable of planing a great event but also needs the affirmation of your faith that he or she can do it.

Thankfulness

Thankful people are joyful people. We're challenged by 1 Thessalonians 5:18: "Give thanks in all circumstances, for this is God's will for you in Christ Jesus." A girl came to me (Jim) with an extremely negative attitude about life. For the first half hour of our conversation, this high school senior grumbled and complained her way through every topic she brought up. Although I'm not suggesting that this is always a good counseling technique, I stopped her and asked if there was anything in her life she was thankful about. After a long pause she said, "My cat." I asked her to take a piece of paper and a pencil and write at least 20 reasons why she could be thankful. I'd like to say that she received a miraculous cure from her bad attitude, but what I *can* say is that she walked out of my office a much more joyful person, focusing on reasons why she was thankful. Sometimes students need a reminder to focus on all the reasons in the world why they can be thankful, instead of focusing on their problems.

Counseling

Cathy and I (Jim) were speaking to a large group of single adults on the subject of proper self-image. Cathy shared with the group that in her own life, involvement in a counseling relationship was extremely helpful for her self-image. We were an infertile couple for eight years. After numerous operations and years of frustrating visits to the doctor, Cathy sought counseling to help her through our hurt and pain of infertility. After she told the story, we were amazed at the number of people who came and asked questions about counseling. We were also surprised at the number of people who said, "I'm so happy to hear that a pastor's wife needed counseling too!" When you look at the stressful situations in which students find themselves today, consider encouraging them to take a look at counseling as an important option.

Service

Adolescents with low self-image are also extremely self-absorbed. There is so much going on inside their own lives that they have little desire to reach outside themselves. Yet when those same teens are challenged to serve and become focused on the needs of others, their self-image will improve. Find every opportunity to get students involved in missions and service (see chapter 13 for more information on missions and service projects). One of the greatest benefits of this kind of involvement is that they begin to feel like they are doing something positive with their lives. Everyone needs to be needed, and we believe that everyone has deep within themselves a desire to be used by God in some special way.

The Spiritual Factor

This may seem like an oversimplified viewpoint, but building a proper self-image is a spiritual matter. When students come to understand the true essence of grace and the depths of God's love, they are free to build a healthy self-image that is centered in the life of Jesus Christ their Lord. The spiritual factor of self-image is based in four simple yet profound statements based on Scripture.

We Are Loved Unconditionally by God

"But because of his great love for us, God, who is rich in mercy, made us alive with Christ even when we were dead in transgressions—it is by grace you have been saved" (Ephesians 2:4-5). God's love is the ultimate sacrificial love. In order to have a healthy self-image, students must understand the truth that God loves them, not for what they do, but for who they are. God's love knows no limits. It has no strings attached, no hidden agenda, no surprises and no requirements. The concept of unconditional love is vitally important in a student's self-image and spiritual life, yet it is difficult for students to understand a love with no conditions.

We Are Created in God's Image

The apostle Paul gives us incredible insight when he says, "For we are God's workmanship, created in Christ Jesus to do good works" (Ephesians 2:10). The Greek word for "workmanship" can also be translated "poetry." We must remind students that they are God's workmanship and poetry. They are totally unique. There is no one quite like them in the entire world. They are gifted and different from anyone else because God created each of them from a different and unique mold.

On my (Mike's) desk is an ashtray. I made it in second grade. Now mind you, no one smokes in my family. I think it started out life as a bowl of some sort and just became an ashtray. A few years back my mom came to me and gave me that ashtray. "Here. I want you to have this."

My immediate thought was, *What* is *it?* I took the ashtray and gave it a look. "Why on earth did you keep this all these years?" I asked.

"I kept it because you made it. It's an original masterpiece. There's not another one like it. And if you look inside, you can see your little fingerprints all over it."

Our lives are like that. Each one of us is an original masterpiece, handcrafted by God. There's not another one like any one of us—not even if you're an identical twin. And if we look deep inside our hearts, we'll even see the fingerprints of God all over us. Remind students that they are special—covered with God's fingerprints.

We Are Children of God

Help students understand that once they become Christians, they are children of God, with all the rights and privileges of any of His other children. We are children of the Father and heirs to the throne of God, and He takes care of His children. Nationally known speaker Tony Campolo loves to tell audiences that if God has a wallet, then Tony's picture is in it; and, furthermore, God is proud of that picture (even if it's the goofy one from third grade!). The interesting result is that when people understand they are children of God, they are then liberated to love. They are set free from poor self-image. They are released from being so self-absorbed and can now make a difference in the world. They are free to love as God loves. "Yet to all who received him, to those who believed in his name, he gave the right to become children of God" (John 1:12).

We Are Forgiven by God

Young teens are walking away from the Church because they don't really believe they can be forgiven. When we tell students that they can be a new creation in Christ, they don't understand the concept. Many students today are completely broken down mentally, physically and spiritually because they have never understood or experienced the simplicity of God's forgiveness. It is essential for us as youth workers to help students comprehend the fact that confessed sin is forever forgiven. In the words of God, "[I] will remember their sins no more" (Jeremiah 31:34). Through forgiveness comes freedom. Jesus declared: "You will know the truth, and the truth will set you free" (John 8:32).

CHAPTER 23

COUNSELING YOUTH—COMPASSIONATE YOUTH MINISTRY

Fresh out of seminary and on my first day at the job, I (Jim) was putting all my books on the shelf when someone knocked on my door. There stood a mother, father and their 16-year-old daughter, Wendy. This was no welcoming committee; they were intensely serious. "Can we talk?" was their opening remark, even before introductions. I said, "Sure," and moved some boxes out of the way.

"Wendy has cancer. The doctors give her six months to live." They cried, and I cried. In fact, even as I think about this event, I cry. Wendy died four months later. Until that very hour, I never realized how much pastoral counseling goes on in youth ministry. I was prepared for planning youth programs and leading Bible studies, but the ever-present counseling needs in youth ministry caught me totally by surprise. I had courses on Church history and doctrine, but I never had a course that prepared me for what I faced that day.

"No one ever told me I would spend so much time counseling teenagers in my youth ministry" is an often heard cry. A large part of youth work is counseling. Some youth workers feel comfortable with counseling, but most are terrified.

The truth is that as a youth worker you are a counselor. You are perhaps not trained in counseling and feel inadequate to counsel; but nevertheless at times merely because of your position in the church, students, their parents and even the community at large will look to you for answers.

This chapter is by no means meant to be a comprehensive book on counseling teenagers; it is an overview of one of the most important yet often overlooked subjects—helping students walk through a crisis.

Crisis—Defining the Term

The principal told me I (Jim) would be speaking to the entire student body. They would come in during four different class periods. The public high school was a large suburban upper-middle-class school known for its excellent athletic teams, attractive students and high academic standards. My topic was "Trauma in the Home." As I was being introduced at the first assembly, the principal leaned over and said, "Don't be surprised if you meet some hurting students today." I had asked a psychologist friend of mine to accompany me, just in case. The plan was that she could meet with any kids who needed her help while I spoke to the next assembly.

After the second assembly I wasn't sure we should continue. I had just heard too many horror stories of rape, incest, drug abuse, beatings and a suicide attempt. As I continued to talk about trauma in the home, these hurting students—who looked so together when they walked into the auditorium—continued to tell us story after story of tragedy and pain.

This single experience in my life, more than anything else, reminds me of the fact that we are working with a generation in crisis. All the statistics point to the fact that students and their families are experiencing more crises in their lives than in any previous generation.

"Perception" is the keyword in defining and dealing with a crisis. One fact we need to keep in mind is this: Crisis is self-defined. What you may view as a crisis, I may not see as that extreme. Anytime a person feels that he or she has lost control and cannot effectively cope, he or she is in a crisis situation. Through your work in youth ministry, you will meet a variety of crises: unwanted pregnancy, eating disorders, suicide, neglect, abuse, death, delinquent behavior, runaways, assault, drug abuse, alcoholism, divorce, promiscuity, homosexuality, truancy, rebellion and/or medical problems.

Our guess is that if all the people in your church were asked if they or someone close to them was going through a crisis, the majority would answer yes by their own definition. So it is with our students. Crisis situations are rampant in the teenage years; it seems to be just a part of the territory.

ADOLESCENCE—THE "TWEENAGE" YEARS

In his excellent book *All Grown Up and No Place to Go*, David Elkind contends that our society today has very little place for teenagers, and he calls adolescence the "unplaced years."[1] Young children have a position in life. They have a place in the family and society. Adults have their place, but the teenager is in an ambiguous position with little responsibility and no important place in the American home. Adolescence is a relatively new position in life. Even 50 years ago the transition from childhood to adulthood was much quicker and better defined.

In order to counsel and work effectively with this generation of young people, we must become aware of the thread of common characteristics they are dealing with during these transitional years.

Self-Absorption

Because of the many transitions in the life of a teenager, we often will find them self-absorbed and self-conscious. They are looking inward and often don't like what they see. What appears to be an incredibly self-centered attitude is typically a lack of confidence combined with intense feelings of confusion.

Anxiety

Today's teenagers are often filled with anxiety. They worry about their physical looks, their relationships and their future. It is a time of uncertainty. As teenagers, they know that life is moving rapidly toward adulthood with its greater responsibility, but they may not be sure they are looking forward to this marker in life called adulthood. That inner struggle can produce intense anxiety.

Experimentation

Another common characteristic is experimentation with new behavior. I (Jim) was shocked to hear that Dave and Jay, two of the stronger student leaders in our youth group, got drunk on a Saturday night and then led their small groups the next day. Eventually I asked Jay about their little escapade, and his answer was insightful: "Dave and I were talking at dinner together; we both admitted we had never been drunk. The more we talked about what it might be like, the more we convinced ourselves to try it. So we tried it."

The freedom most adolescents have, mixed with curiosity and the allure of the unknown, results in experimentation with new behavior. Your role as a counselor is to turn the experience into a learning situation without being shocked. The fact is that most teenagers will at one time or another compromise their beliefs and values. They need understanding, accountability and guidance in order to make good decisions the next time around.

Emotions

With the onslaught of puberty also comes a significant rise in emotions. As youth workers, we must realize that teenagers tend to be very emotional. One minute everything is incredible and couldn't be better; the next minute the entire world is coming to an end. Moodiness seems to come with the territory. Students have strong feelings of anger, depression, guilt, failure and passion. We need to keep these in mind, while remembering all the time that "this too shall pass." There is a continual cycle of emotions, and students will often ride an emotional roller coaster. We must take these common characteristics seriously, yet balance the roller coaster with logical thinking and consistency.

Listening—The Language of Love

Most likely you've heard this statement from one or more of your students: "No one ever listens to me." It's common and also very true. The most important counseling technique does not need to be done by a professional. Students will know you are taking them seriously and will open up their lives to you if they know you will listen to them. Listening is the real language of love.

Students do not always need to immediately hear the right answer as much as they need an atmosphere of openness in which they genuinely feel that you are actively listening. Listening communicates value and significance to your students. It lets them know that they are of worth to you. Listening opens doors for students to be ready to hear the advice that they need.

It's been said, "People who give students their ears, capture their hearts." To illustrate this, take out a blank piece of paper. Take just a minute and write on one side of the paper words that express how you feel when you are talking with someone and they don't listen to you. On the other side, write some of the words that express how you feel when you share something with someone and walk away feeling truly listened to. Now examine the words on each side of the paper. When students come to us for counsel, they will find themselves feeling what you expressed on either one side of the paper or the other. The question is, Which side will express what they find in you? As youth workers and counselors we need to communicate and counsel from the second side of the paper. Unfortunately that is not always the case.

Effective Listening Qualities

A good listener is actively involved in the conversation. It takes work to develop the important qualities of listening to young people. One of the special people in my (Jim's) life lives in a little town in Oklahoma. She doesn't have much up-front ability. She'll never be famous. She really doesn't keep up much with the latest music or youth culture trends. Yet when I recently asked one of the students in her youth ministry how he liked the group, he replied with so much enthusiasm. He said, "Sydney is the greatest youth leader in the world. She listens to all of us. She's available, she's not judgmental, and we know she cares." I've probably never known of more students year after year who want to go into full-time youth ministry or the mission field than from Sydney's group. It's not her up-front skills–it's her quiet, gentle listening ear. It's her attitude that really says to the kids "I care about you."

Listening is difficult; it takes energy and focus. However, if we look at the impact that is made by the simple act of listening, the investment and effort are worth it all. Here are some effective listening qualities that every youth worker must keep in mind and practice:

- A genuine desire to listen to your students
- A willingness to accept their feelings and emotions whether they are right or wrong
- A desire to not always be right
- A nonjudgmental attitude
- Eye contact and little distractive movement
- A display of appreciation because you feel honored to have them choose to share their story with you
- A willingness to not only listen but to also keep in touch and be supportive

Problem-Solving

Effective listening does not mean that we never help students work through their problems. Listening comes first. When it's time to help a student walk through a crisis, there's an effective five-step process of problem solving.

Step One: Find the Real Problem

Jumping in and solving a problem too quickly in a discussion can cause us to miss the real problem. It is important to be direct and ask the student what he or she considers the problem to be. This is the time to ask open-ended questions and listen, not give advice. It is a fact-finding mission.

Let's say, for example, you are approached by a student who has a drug and alcohol problem. On the surface, you might be tempted to address the issue with the point of view that the problem is the drugs and alcohol. In doing so, you may miss the real problem. It's important to dig beneath the surface to find out why this student is taking the drugs or using the alcohol. What is the student trying to escape from? What is missing in his or her world that there is a need to fill that void with substance abuse?

Step Two: List Alternative Solutions

Once you have assisted in helping the student to clarify the problem, you can help him or her look at various solution alternatives. For example, if the problem as defined by the student is "I fight with my parents over the use of the car," possible solutions might include a meeting between you, the student and his or her parents to discuss the specific problem; a discussion with the student about what makes his or her parents irritated and development of a plan to alleviate the problem; or the purchase of a used car (which might mean helping the student brainstorm ideas for coming up with the money to buy it, maintain it and provide insurance for it). Remember people support what they create. Don't provide all the solutions yourself; guide the student to come up with ideas too. If the student helps come up with the solution, he or she will own it and have a better chance of following through with the selected course of action.

Step Three: Select a Plan of Action

If one of the alternatives seems to be the best idea, then work on the problem by using that plan. Sometimes it's very helpful to role-play or rehearse the plan. It is important to remember that a plan of action might also include an outside referral for Christian-based counseling. At this stage of the process youth workers often make a mistake by thinking that their counseling job is now over. The process is only half finished.

Step Four: Establish and Enforce Accountability

Good, positive accountability is a loving way of saying "I want to walk with you through this process, but I need you to be completely honest with me." Most action plans with teenagers are not as beneficial as they could be without some method of accountability. You might say, "Since you really want to quit smoking, let me challenge you to stop for a week. Call me if you get the urge. If I'm unavailable, I'll get back to you as soon as I can. Next week let's compare notes after the youth group meeting to see how you're doing." It is absolutely vital to follow through on your promise to hold the student accountable. Remember, a failure to follow through on your promise of accountability is more damaging than the failure to set it up in the first place.

Step Five: Set Up an Evaluation Procedure

We all need to see small chunks of success along the way. As part of the problem solving accountability structure, put together some method of evaluation. Don't look for perfection; instead, find a method that will encourage attainment of the student's goals. A regular phone call, checkup meetings and journaling are all simple evaluation methods. Of course, the more complex the problem, the stronger the evaluation process will need to be (i.e., if a student is chemically addicted to drugs, then the evaluation procedure must be more in line with that particular problem and will probably entail professional help).

Referrals—Professional Perspectives

Some youth workers need to be constantly reminded that they are not professional counselors. Seldom should we be involved in long-term counseling therapy, personality reconstruction or issues in which we have very little knowledge.

A good referral system is one of the most important aspects of youth ministry. It's extremely important to have personal relationships with a few counselors in your area. Make it a habit to have lunch with a counselor at least once a month. In doing so, you will become more knowledgeable in your referrals and can obtain a professional's perspective on different counseling issues. Use that time during lunch to ask questions, seek advice and develop a relationship. It's not likely that a counselor will turn you down—after all, counselors need a network of referrals.

One of the most common questions we receive is "I know I need a referral system, but where do I start?" Usually you can get information from your pastor, other youth workers or members of your church. If this doesn't work, consider universities or organizations that deal with crises, look in the telephone directory or search online.

Keep a file of resources for referral, perhaps cross-referenced by the type of problem or area of expertise. Many youth workers put together a resource directory of institutions, ministries and organizations in their community that have some type of resource or service to provide for people in need. The resource directory could have sections titled Sexual Abuse, Suicide, Family Problems, Drug and Alcohol Rehabilitation, Legal Advice, Medical Problems, and so forth.

As you begin the process of seeking referrals, don't be shy. Ask the hard questions, and don't settle for superficial answers. From the beginning, indicate that you are trying to find good referral resources and would like to know more about this person's approach and practice. Most professionals will be pleased to respond to such requests. Anyone who isn't should probably be avoided for referrals.

Confidentiality—Your Credibility Depends on It

People are giving you an incredible vote of credibility when they confide in you. If you choose to break their confidence, you have not only hurt your credibility with them but also news will travel quickly to the rest of the youth group and church. You will immediately lose the respect of your students and peers, and you will lose the opportunity for more counseling. Many of the worst offenders in breaking confidences are people on pastoral staffs, who share prayer requests as a disguise to tell stories about people in their congregation, ultimately violating their trust. A woman told me recently that she left her church because her pastor had shared her marriage problems as a staff prayer request.

The only time it is reasonable to break confidentiality is when a life-threatening situation is at hand, and even then you should tell the person who you are counseling *beforehand* what you are going to do. A few years ago I (Jim) told a pastoral colleague a personal problem I was having. Two days later I got a call from a mutual friend wanting to help with my problem. This pastoral colleague is still a friend, but that was the last time I ever trusted him with personal problems that I did not want broadcast. An effective counseling ministry is based on trust. Breaking a confidence may destroy your credibility.

Know the Laws of Reporting for Your State

It is essential that you are up-to-date on the mandated reporting laws in your state. Time limits vary from state to state, so be sure to check with the local child protective services.

Know the Balance Between Students and Parents

There is a balance between protecting student confidentiality and getting parents involved for the overall health of the student and family unit. If you encounter a situation in which you feel the need to get parents involved to bring about lasting change and healing, you will want to have a plan that not only protects your confidentiality with the student but also brings the information to light with the parents. Here are three steps for dealing with students in crisis:

1. **Help them see the need to let their parents know the truth.** We need to establish first and foremost the fact that students' parents need to know what is going on in their lives.
2. **Give a one- to two-week time frame for the student to share with parents.** The time frame here should be flexible; depending on the crisis, the time may need to be shorter. This allows for students to talk to their parents on their own terms but still gets them to open up with their parents. This can also be a healing and relationship-building time for the family.
3. **After the set time, check back in.** Asking the student in crisis, "Did you get a chance to talk your parents? How did it go?" and getting an affirmative answer can open the door for you to say, "Great, then I'm going to give them a call and let them know that I'm here to help in anyway I can." If the student doesn't balk, you

can make the phone call and be a part of helping the family. If he or she hesitates at your suggestion, then it's time to approach his or her parents together with the student. If you absolutely feel, because of the nature of the crisis, that you must break the confidence, tell the student what you are going to do. This may not help your relationship with the student, but other students will learn that they can trust you to never talk behind their backs, even with their parents.

Counseling—It's Just a Matter of Time

Your students are going through a tremendous transformation from childhood to adulthood. In the past that may have been an easier transition, but it is not at all easy today. Crisis abounds in the lives of our students. It is not a matter of *if* you will have to counsel students; it's a matter of *when* you will. Keeping this in mind, youth workers have the great opportunity to help students find meaning in life and establish a positive, Christian character that will set a foundation for their entire adulthood. You *are* a counselor, even though most of your counseling won't ever take place in the environment of the office. Your counseling may take place at a restaurant, on the way to camp or after an event. Yet no matter where it takes place, you will have the opportunity to help guide your students toward decisions that will last a lifetime.

> For a comprehensive referral checklist, visit YouthBuilders at www.youthbuilders.com.

CHAPTER 24

WORKING WITH DISRUPTED FAMILIES

A few years ago I (Jim) was away from my youth group for 10 days. While I was gone, three sets of parents of teenagers in my group split up. This experience of divorce within the church moved me to get as much information as I could about working with kids from divorced homes. No one likes divorce, and few if any divorces are easy; but we have to face the fact: there is 1 divorce every 27 seconds. That's approximately 1 million a year. Unfortunately, many of these are within the church. Among people attending mainline Protestant churches, roughly the following percentage of people in each denomination have been through a divorce:

- 25 percent of mainline Protestants
- 29 percent of Baptists
- 34 percent of nondenominational Protestants[1]

We as youth workers are seeing our ministries filled with young people who are dealing with the trauma of split families. We must learn how to work effectively with these disrupted lives.

Consider the following statistics from a study conducted by Arlene Saluter:

- The fastest growing marital status category in the United States is divorced.

- The number of divorced adults has quadrupled from 4.3 million to 17.4 million in the last three decades.
- Today, nearly half of all children in America will witness the breakup of their parents' marriage. Of these, close to half will also see the breakup of a parent's second marriage.
- Within a 25-year span, the number of children living in single-parent families more than doubled, from 12 to 28 percent.
- About 92 percent of the children of divorced parents live with their moms, by either consent or default. Of those who are 11 to 16 years old, 16 percent see their dads once a week; 84 percent see him less than once a week; and 45 percent do not see their dads more than twice a year.
- The average length of a first marriage is seven years, and a second marriage lasts four to five years.[2]

Awareness in the Church is not enough; it takes understanding and at times a special ministry to deal with disrupted homes.

Catastrophic Loss in Divorce

If one thing is clear, it is this—every divorce involves loss. These losses come in all forms, from personal and emotional loss to a more practical loss of living standard.

Loss of Income

When a family splits into two households, there can be a drastic (over 50 percent) reduction in income, since many fathers pay little or no alimony or child support. This is the first loss that young teens may feel.

Loss of Neighborhood

A loss of neighborhood is directly related to loss of income. Many divorced households must move to cheaper housing. This can result not only in the loss of the familiar surroundings of a student's previous home but also the loss of their school—and sometimes even their church.

Even the loss of church comes into play for many students. We once had a girl from our community suddenly begin attending our church and youth ministry. She was wonderful. Not only did she have a servant's heart and know more Scripture than I (Jim) did, but she also brought friends to the group. About two months after Ashley arrived, it dawned on me that she had lived her whole life in our community. This told me that there was undoubtedly another youth worker in the area who was depressed about losing her. I asked her about her church background, and sure enough she said she had been brought up at another church in our community. She didn't give me much information, but she did tell me that her father was an elder at that church.

That afternoon I called the church's youth worker and told him how much I had enjoyed Ashley's presence in our group, but I wondered if I could help her return to his church. He agreed that Ashley was a young, dynamic Christian with a vibrant, radiant faith; but his answer shocked me: "We miss her, but she can't come back right now."

"Why?" I asked with extreme curiosity.

He replied, "Oh, hasn't she told you? Her father and mother are going through a messy divorce, and he is still active here. Her mother refuses to allow her to attend our church."

For Ashley, even the loss of her own church was a direct result of her parents' divorce.

Loss of Emotional Support and Trust

Adolescents can also feel the loss of emotional support, since Mom and Dad are usually less able to give such support after a divorce. Kids feel loneliness, lack of understanding and lack of love.

There can also be a loss of trust. This became painfully real to me (Jim) when Robert, a junior in high school, broke down and cried in my office over his parents' divorce. He had overheard them saying; "We would never have gotten into this mess if it hadn't been for Robert!"

Because of this, Robert found out that 16 years earlier his parents had conceived him out of wedlock.

Loss of Tradition

Each divorce actually consists of myriad divorces and losses. For children of divorce, the extremely difficult decisions of who to live with and where to go to on holidays are sometimes too overwhelming to cope with.

The emotions and reactions of children of divorce are complicated and changing. It's time that we in the Church begin to understand the reactions of and effects on the children of divorced families.

Reactions to Divorce

There are numerous reactions to a divorce. In fact, even within the same family, reactions will vary—and sometimes in a major way. Youth workers need to be aware of common reactions to divorce in order to provide a better support base and help ease the pain. In this section, we've outlined some of the more common reactions to divorce. As you read this section, maybe you'll be able to see some of the students in your group—maybe you'll even see yourself.

Pseudomature Adolescent

One reaction to divorce is to excel in growth and mature quickly. Pseudomature adolescents want to prove that they can do it on their own and take care of themselves. You'll often see this type of person marry early or quit school in order to get a job and take care of the family. He or she has had an abbreviated adolescence at best. They've grown up so fast, they typically don't have much time for normal adolescent activities.

Childish Behavior

This behavior is the opposite of that exhibited by the pseudomature adolescent, yet you may find the two opposing reactions in the same family. This student is very immature. He or she gets stuck and won't go forward in progress and maturity, preferring to be taken care of and making life difficult for anyone who doesn't baby him or her along. Dave's parents divorced when he was 10. He had been an excellent reader before the divorce, but at age 16 Dave was still reading at a 10-year-old level.

Spouse Replacement

A major reaction of many young people is to try to take the place of the missing parent. Their goal in life becomes making Mom or Dad happy. Parents often play into this reaction because they like the attention. Such parents make the mistake of using their children as a replacement for the spouse.

Chris was a 14-year-old 200-pound football player who slept in the same bed with his mother because she got so lonely at night. This was definitely not a healthy situation for his mom or for Chris. When I (Jim) confronted their behavior, they both innocently said, "You don't understand; we aren't having sex." Neither could see any problem with Chris sharing a room with his mother.

Ping-Pong Adolescent

Most adolescents from a divorce feel torn between Mom and Dad. At the same time, they feel responsible and guilty as they try to be good to both parents. The student feels a great deal of tension and stress, especially during the holiday madness of the divorced family. He or she is always busy trying to make everybody happy and smoothing out any problems between Mom and Dad. This student eventually becomes extremely discouraged and unhappy and can often become the jealous adolescent (see next reaction).

Jealous Adolescent

This is the student who begins to sabotage Mom and Dad's new relationships. Rather than bounce back and forth to try and please both parents, this student will play both parents in order to try and break up a new relationship. He or she may tell lies or fail to give phone messages from the new people in his or her parents' lives. The secret hope of this student is that eventually his or her parents will get back together; thus a new relationship stands as a threat and needs to be broken up at all costs.

Money-Wise Adolescent

One of the major problems in the vast majority of divorces is money. Finances are on the minds of everyone involved in the divorce. The money-wise student will work to help out because he or she desperately wants to continue living at the same standard. You'll find that this person is consumed with money problems.

On the other hand, parents (usually fathers) make the mistake of enticing their kids with money. Mom is barely making ends meet, the home is for sale, and they are moving to an apartment. Dad has not sent a support check for three months, and one day the child comes home with a new convertible, stating excitedly, "It's an early birthday present from Dad." The frustration and confusion levels elevate immediately, and the children involved are caught in the middle between wanting the material things they're offered and understanding the importance of budgeting money for necessary day-to-day expenses.

Misidentified Adolescent

Many young people want to feel normal immediately after the divorce. You know the attitude: Dad has moved out of the house and the shouting has stopped, so now let's get on with life. Immediate normality is not the case for everyone. Psychologists tell us that it takes at least three years to feel somewhat normal, to have the custody settled and to have the new roles in place. Often the parents are so emotionally distraught that much of the emotional support from parent to child is not available.

Children of divorce are looking for role models. They want significant adult relationships and a peer group with which to identify. This is where the Church can be a life support to such children. Adults can come alongside, not to take their parents' place, but to provide role models during the transition time.

The youth ministry can be the positive peer influence that the student needs to keep his or her life from falling completely apart. During a time when the misidentified adolescent is searching for role models and a peer group, he or she will keep looking until an identifiable group is found. Unfortunately, many children in this situation choose drugs, alcohol, promiscuous sex and other social groupings instead of the

Church. Often, this is the direct result of a church that did not take time to care, listen and respond to the signals of a young person's searching.

Oversexed/Underloved Adolescent

I (Jim) once read a story by a young woman who had lived a very sexually promiscuous lifestyle as a teenager. It was simply titled "In Search of My Daddy's Love." Need I say more? Oversexed/underloved adolescents are desperately searching for attachment. They want to feel loved and accepted. You'll even find students who start their own families in order to get out of their situation. Unfortunately, the result of an early marriage is often the continuing story of another broken marriage and children from one more divorced home.

Kara never missed a youth ministry meeting. She was the first to arrive and the last to leave. The adult staff affectionately nicknamed her "the clinger." She always had her arm around me (Jim) or one of the other adult male sponsors. It was very uncomfortable, but we really didn't know how to handle her clinging. One afternoon at our adult staff meeting we decided to confront her, and I was elected to do so.

The next evening after youth group I invited her into my office and told her how much I appreciated her, yet the clinging was getting out of hand. She began to weep. She said, "I didn't mean for it to be sexual." My first reaction was to say, "Of course it isn't sexual," but I didn't say anything. I let her regain her composure, and then she kept talking. In the next 45 minutes she unfolded a story of her father leaving when she was six years old. He called the next year on her birthday and never called her again. Eleven times in her life men and much older teenage boys had sexual intercourse with her. Yet she wasn't looking for sex; she was screaming for male attention and had been sexually abused by self-centered men who took advantage of her deep need and searching for her lost daddy's love.

Emotional Fallout of Divorce

Not only do children of divorce react in many different ways, but there are also a number of common results of a divorce that we must be aware of if we are to have an impact-filled ministry with these students.

Loneliness and Isolation

Since Mom and Dad usually can't give much emotionally for the first few years after a divorce—even though they often try—many teenagers become increasingly lonely. You find them withdrawing from friends, relatives and sometimes school or church activities. Distance and detachment surface because these teens often put up defense mechanisms. They've been hurt, and they don't want to get close again.

Sometimes their loneliness comes in the form of depression. Most kids from a broken home will feel depressed at times. They are hurt, angry, confused and even embarrassed. Watch for dropping grades, a personality change or addiction to the Internet or television.

Feelings of Guilt

A common thread in all adolescents is guilt. For many young people there are especially intense feelings of guilt that go along with a divorce. Many young people blame their own misbehavior for the failure of their parents' marriage. They believe that they have failed in some way.

I've heard statements such as, "My sister and I argued too much, and finally my parents couldn't stand it anymore, so they broke up." Christian teenagers with non-Christian parents can be especially hard on themselves. "If only I'd talked to my parents about God more!"

One of the very important things a youth worker can do is to allow students to talk about their guilt. Help them see that they did not cause the divorce. Challenge these students to talk with their parents about their feelings of guilt. Unless a parent is not mentally healthy, he or she will ease the guilt feelings by not placing blame on the children. Above all, let these students know that their feelings of guilt are normal and can be dealt with in a positive manner.

Inability to Trust or Love

Four out of five students are not prepared for the divorce of their parents. Many students will tell you that the separation came as a complete surprise. You'll learn that they feel let down, and don't be surprised to hear that in their minds God let them down. There is a lack of trust in parents, other relationships–even God. As the defense mechanisms go up, there is an overwhelming feeling of not wanting to get hurt again.

You may find some students unable to understand love. Their emotions have been wiped out, yet they are making major decisions based on their damaged emotions. Consider the following statement:

> It is not uncommon for the child of a disrupted home to become hard and callused, seemingly unable to give or receive love. Time usually eases the hurt and heals these emotions. Students can make silly mistakes when they have shut off their emotions. They can reject anyone who reaches out to them. They can pretend that everything is okay.[3]

A student's inability to love or trust can be overcome when significant others stick with them, even if at first they reject all friendships.

Misfit Self-Image

David Elkind writes about a teenager's imaginary audience in his book *All Grown Up and No Place to Go.* He claims that teenagers view themselves as being on stage. Their vivid imagination produces feelings of uncertainty about how other people view them now that their family is divorced. Students from divorced homes view themselves as being watched. Some of them will become very sensitive at church, school and family gatherings. Studies show that kids from broken homes are less optimistic and seek psychological help more often. In a sense they are different, but we need to help them realize that different isn't always bad.[4]

Anger

Anger can be a major emotion in divorce. Some anger can be very healthy, but extreme anger directed at self or family members can be destructive and cause disturbing behavior. Low self-image is a very common result of anger over the divorce. You may see such kids act out their behavior in your youth ministry through withdrawal or disruption or even by being belligerent to the adults in the group.

These feelings of anger, left unaddressed, can result in bitterness and even a lack of forgiveness. These young people are so hurt and so angry that they harbor deep-seated bitterness toward either parent. It could be focused on the parent that left, but it could also focus on the parent that they are living with. They cannot seem to extend grace, and they struggle to forgive the parent they perceive to be at fault.

The anger may cause a real lack of direction. For many teenagers of divorce, hopelessness pervades their life. Their motivation and drive slow to a crawl. There is simply too much going on inside, and their direction in life shuts down for a while.

Poor Communication

Students who have gone through a divorce may also experience a problem communicating with others, especially adults and their own parents. This can be caused by a variety of things. It could be the inability to trust; they simply cannot trust others due to the intense feelings of being let down. It can come from a misfit self-image, and the teenager believes, *No one really understands me and what I'm going through because I'm different.* It may come from the sheer fact that the student chooses not to communicate. Whatever the reason, children of divorce can close up emotionally and lose the ability to communicate. These problems often carry over into relationships with their peers and their future spouses. Whether a choice of the will or just a natural by-product, children of divorce often find it hard to open up and communicate their feelings and thoughts.

Inability to Cope

When problems or stress arise, children of divorce often have a difficult time coping. Many young people who have seen their parents run away as a coping mechanism will choose to do the same in their own lives. They might withdraw, hoping problems will naturally resolve themselves, rather than dealing with the issues at hand. When the problems linger, another set of issues arise. These adolescents will grow up lacking the ability to work through problems on their own, and this can often lead to choosing divorce as a way to cope with struggles in their own marriages in the future.

Cynicism Regarding Marriage

Many students who have witnessed their parents go through a divorce have a cynical attitude toward the idea of marriage. They see the whole institution of marriage as a trial better left alone. Like the adage says, "First there is the engagement ring, then the wedding ring, then the suffering." Oftentimes, that sums up the opinion about marriage of a young person who's experienced the pain of a divorce.

This emotional result comes, not from pure cynicism, but out of fear. Many of our students who have been impacted by divorce are simply afraid that they will end up no better than their parents did. They are afraid of entering into marriage and especially of having children of their own. They truly are convinced deep down that they will end up with a failed marriage that ends in more pain and hurt. The great news is that through Jesus Christ, they don't have to be slaves to their past *or* to the cycle of divorce.

Poverty

Financial loss is one of the major results of divorce. Of all families who get a divorce, 35 percent will move from above the poverty level to below the poverty level in one year.[5] Parents usually try to maintain the same lifestyle with less money. The added stress and extra hours of working usually do more damage than lowering the lifestyle would.

Youth workers must be aware of the added financial strain that church camps and retreats play on many single-family households. If at all possible, develop a fund where kids can work off camp scholarships for church-related events. Try to keep the costs down to insure the opportunity for everyone to attend your event.

Easing the Pain of Divorce

The stark realities of divorce are not easy to handle, and the reactions and results are very real. Yet the good news is that we as youth workers can give hope to students who have been hit by divorce. Be encouraged; you can shine some light on an otherwise bleak situation.

Provide an Accepting and Supportive Community

Stability is a real need for kids of divorce. Life is going crazily in every direction for these kids. Consistent support from you and the youth ministry can make all the difference—your ministry may be the one aspect of a teen's life that in his or her view is not falling apart.

Unfortunately, some adolescents from divorced homes feel like lonely, abandoned, second-class citizens within their church as well. To combat this, develop a peer ministry in which teens learn to care for each other in any kind of crisis. Try to provide adoptive relationships for each student of divorce, in which one adult leader really takes that student under his or her wing. Don't be afraid to refer a student for pastoral or psychological counseling if you sense he or she needs it.

To create an empathic atmosphere in the congregation at large, some churches have sponsored divorce recovery workshops, led by adults and students who have "been there, done that."

Let Them Talk

More than anything, kids going through divorce need to talk about it. Many times, they can't talk about what they're going through at home because everyone else is also feeling the same hurt, anger, pain and chaos.

You, however, can provide a sounding board. Whenever it's possible and appropriate, give these students the chance to talk about their feelings—and make sure you keep current on what those feelings are. One day Jennifer told me (Jim) she was thrilled that her father had finally left the house. The next day she asked me to pray for her father's return. A week later she learned that her father was having an affair, and she never wanted to see him again.

Talk About Forgiveness and Grace

After a disrupted family situation, family members usually experience an inability to trust. They may find it hard to accept the love that you and your caring community are offering. Be consistent in surrounding them with unconditional love, forgiveness and grace. The gospel needs to be continually placed in front of them as their source of hope and strength. Eventually it will seep through.

Don't let any personal conservative theological stance on divorce get in the way of ministering to hurting people. God may not love divorce, but He certainly loves the victims of divorce, especially the children.

Help Kids See the Long View

Adolescents generally have trouble seeing the future, and kids of divorce get especially stuck in the here-and-now. Help them to see that even though life will be different, it will continue to go on. Remind them that their situation may never change, but their attitude can—and that may make all the difference in the world for them.

Model Good Marriages

Students who have witnessed their parents' divorce need to witness married couples who are living out their love for each other and their commitment to make the marriage work. It's part of our ministry to provide those models, even if they're not perfect models. Students need to see people who are working out their commitment to being and staying married.

Cathy and I (Jim) have considered a major part of our ministry in recent years as being a role model of a married couple who aren't perfect but do love each other. At times we've cut back on our own Bible study involvement in order to free up our time to have students in our home. We invite students to our home for dinner on a regular basis. We all prepare the dinner, eat together, do the dishes and then play games or sit and talk. We have found this unstructured time together to be one of our most valuable ministry opportunities as the students get better acquainted with us as a couple. If you're not married, make sure that you have married couples on the adult leadership team who are fulfilling this vital role!

A little preventive maintenance is also a great idea. Provide programs on building a positive marriage. At least 95 percent of your students will choose to get married at one time in their life, and few of them will have had any positive Christian input on how to make their marriage work.

Encourage and Reach Out to Parents

Even though as a youth worker you may be younger than the parents involved, don't hesitate to express your caring for them. Perhaps you can be a reminder to them that the Christian community still loves them.

You can often be the catalyst to help the parents seek counseling. Even if you don't know the family, try to make it a habit to visit whichever parent is still at home with the children. It will give you a better understanding of how to help his or her teenager, and the parent almost always wants to talk. You might even be influential in helping a nonchurched parent make the decision to become a part of the church.

As you deal with teens of divorce, remember that you can make a difference. Your presence, encouragement and listening ear will help more than almost any kind of therapy. I (Jim) asked a recently divorced mother of two teenagers in our church how she was doing. Her reply sums up this chapter:

> It has been the most difficult experience in my life. I'm still a little numb. However, I've never experienced more love, encouragement and acceptance than from this church. I would never choose to go through this, but it has brought me closer to God, and I honestly didn't know Christians would care so deeply for my kids and me. In the midst of our family trauma, I found more intimate friendships than I had ever imagined. I have been given to; now it's time for me to take what has been given to me and help others.

CHAPTER 25

The Crisis of Substance Abuse

In 1999 the Center for Disease Control Youth Risk Behavior conducted a study and found that 50 percent of high school students surveyed reported drinking alcohol at least once in the 30 days prior to the survey—31.5 percent of those drank 5 alcoholic drinks on more than one occasion.[1] This means there *is* a substance abuse problem in your church. Unfortunately, kids become addicted to drugs and alcohol more quickly than adults do.

With so many people in our churches suffering silently from the problems of addiction, we in youth ministry must begin to address these important needs. Many Christian families act as if the problem will go away if we ignore it. It won't.

Why Do Young Teens Use Drugs and Alcohol?

The vast majority of students will at one time or another experiment with drugs and alcohol. The answer to the question of why teens use drugs and alcohol is complicated. Peer influence, boredom and poor self-image are three major factors.

More important than why adolescents use drugs and alcohol is the answer to the question, Why do they *continue* to use drugs and alcohol? Experimentation is normal, but what really drives young people to continue with substance abuse that could ultimately lead to addiction is what needs to be addressed. The answer to this question is alarmingly easy.

Drugs and Alcohol Deaden the Pain

As we've mentioned previously, the adolescent years are filled with transition and turmoil. Oftentimes this leads students to crisis points in their lives. As crisis situations begin to arise, as the turmoil and anxiety of life transitions take hold, often students are looking for a release. They are looking for a relief from the pain and hurt they are experiencing in life. Drugs and alcohol are attractive because, at least temporarily, they are very effective at deadening pain.

Drugs and Alcohol Work Every Single Time

Unfortunately, drugs and alcohol work. That is, they serve their purpose, which is to alter reality so that it's not so hard to deal with. Whatever the substance of choice, more often than not the desired effect is reached—an escape from emotional pain. The person using it feels a sense of relief. Whatever the issue—family struggles, self-image, a relationship—and whatever the pain, short-term relief is found.

Our bodies acclimate to substances over time. Because of this, in order for someone to continue to reach the desired state of disassociation from his or her pain, one of two things will eventually need to happen to reach that high: more and more of the substance will need to be taken or a harder substance will need to be used.

What Is the Impact on Students?

Proverbs 6:27-28 rhetorically reminds us: "Can a man scoop fire into his lap without his clothes being burned? Can a man walk on hot coals without his feet being scorched?" The chemicals students are using have an impact on their bodies, and they cannot escape the consequences and impact that drugs and alcohol have on their lives.

Students Stop Learning How to Cope

When students depend on a chemical high to relieve stress, all other stress-reducing mechanisms in the body and mind take second place to the chemical. Once they come down from their artificial state of relief, substance users will find themselves right back where they started with all the struggles and pressures. As they continue this back and forth process, they begin to lose their ability to cope without the chemical. For them the only way out, the only way to escape and cope with the struggles of life, is through the chemical. Pain is encountered and the chemical is sought. Because they stop learning how to cope with stress in a positive manner at whatever age, they begin to abuse substances. One of the biggest problems of recovering adult alcoholics is having to catch up on what they should have been learning about healthy coping skills during the time they were using.

Students Begin to Change in Predictable Phases

The other natural result that happens to young people when they continue to use drugs and alcohol is that they change in phases. The phases of this change are predictable and can be clearly seen. As youth workers, it is vital to recognize and understand these phases.

Phase One: Experimental Use

This phase often happens in middle school/junior high and can even happen in late grade school. There is an element of mystery about alcohol and drugs. For example, alcohol abuse may begin with an occasional drink at a party or from their parents' liquor cabinet. Before a high school student graduates from high school, there is an 80 percent chance that he or she will have used alcohol, a 50 percent chance that he or she will have used marijuana and a 55 percent chance that he or she will have used any illicit drug.[2]

Phase Two: Social Use

In this phase, adolescents have moved from experimental use to a more regular, relaxed social use. For the most part, they no longer worry about the impact of their use on their reputation. Their tolerance for the substance begins to increase, and their social life—including choice of friends—begins to expand to the use of the substance more than just occasionally. It has now become a more acceptable behavior.

Phase Three: Daily Preoccupation

Teens in this phase are beginning to experience dependence on the substance. They may be experimenting with harder drugs. They begin to think about it more frequently—maybe even daily. Their thoughts and aspirations are bound up in the use of the chemical. Their behavior begins to change. Often their grades will suffer, and to pay for and cover up this expensive habit they may begin stealing and lying. They are getting loaded a number of times a week. Rather than waiting for the weekend to come or for those more natural social settings in order to use, they may begin to use by themselves.

Phase Four: Addiction

In this phase, a person has become dependent on the chemical to cope with life. He or she is addicted and is not using merely for social reasons; the reason has now become that the chemical high is needed simply to function day to day. There is a dangerous preoccupation with getting high. Usually there is a loss of control. Behavior is sometimes radically and noticeably altered. In this phase, users begin to violate their value systems.

Students May Be Dealing with Biological Predisposition

It is almost universally agreed upon that a chemical dependency can be related to a genetic predisposition. Certain people can become addicted much faster than others. The body craves the chemical differently. Alcoholics have a much higher tolerance level. A student may brag, "I can drink a six-pack and do tequila shots and still drive home perfectly fine." That statement is a sure sign that the student may have a predisposition toward alcoholism and a higher tolerance level. This student is a budding alcoholic.

In any drug and alcohol treatment center, more than 50 percent of the patients come from families where a parent is an alcoholic. If both parents are alcoholics, the risk is much higher. Students must take a good look at their own family background, and some will need to realize that they simply don't have the freedom to experiment. Students may say "That's not fair." They're right. Unfortunately, while it may not be fair, it is most definitely true.

What Can You Do?

Is there hope? *Yes.* Chemical dependency is a disease and it can be treated. We can offer help and hope to people because they can change. Treatment is often a necessity, but people can and do change. In fact, many studies show that when you combine God and treatment, people have a very good possibility of recovering from chemical dependency. Although people are seldom permanently freed from the disease, lasting and honest change can and does occur for those who seek it.

Not only is alcoholism a disease, but Scripture is clear that drunkenness or getting high is sinful behavior, "Do not get drunk on wine, which leads to debauchery. Instead, be filled with the Spirit" (Ephesians 5:18). Even teens who are problem drinkers, without being alcoholics, can change. We can keep students from a great deal of pain by helping them choose to steer clear of drug and alcohol use altogether.

Examine Your Own Use

One of the greatest predictors of adolescent drinking and drug habits is the attitude and behavior of parents—and other role models, including youth workers—toward alcohol and drugs. Our attitudes, as well as our behavior, can have an incredible and lasting impact on how young people see and react to drugs and alcohol. We need to look in the mirror and the medicine cabinet while we're there—and consider some vital personal questions:

- *Is my medicine cabinet full of mood-altering chemicals?*
- *Do I medicate myself with prescription drugs or alcohol anytime I feel distress or pain?*

- *Do I have a routine of needing an after-work drink or an after-dinner smoke to relieve stress?*
- *Do I hang on to prescription drugs, just in case, rather than throwing them out when the problem subsides?*
- *Do I laugh at drunken behavior on television or in movies?*
- *How do I react to clothing that has drug-related images or that has alcohol advertisements?*
- *Do I listen to music that glamorizes or trivializes drug or alcohol use?*

Become a Student of the Culture

Every youth worker must obtain as much information as possible about substance abuse. There are some great resources available in books and on the Internet. Read up on the subject of drug and alcohol use. Know what the current trends and thoughts are regarding teenagers and substance use. Every youth worker should attend an AA (Alcoholics Anonymous) and an ALANON (for families of alcoholics) meeting. By far, the greatest percentage of recovery comes when people are actively involved in support. Learn about the various alcohol- and drug-abuse treatment centers in your area. These centers are very helpful and informative.

Talk Openly About the Issue

One of the greatest gifts we can give our students is a safe environment in which they can share their thoughts and struggles. Talk openly with your group about the issue of alcohol and drug abuse. Never show disgust or a lack of love and compassion for an abuser. Continually give students the opportunity to talk with you about their problems or how substance abuse of a loved one is affecting them. Allow students the opportunity to dialogue about the issue and how it is impacting them. Not only do you have students in your group right now who are using drugs and alcohol but a number of them might also be victims of an abusive alcoholic home. Students who live in an abusive environment need just as much help and support as the alcoholic does. Make your ministry a sanctuary of support—a safe place where students can feel safe in sharing their struggles and pains and the issues that drove them to be substance users in the first place.

Recognize the Signs and Symptoms

A first step in dealing with substance abuse is recognizing its many symptoms. The following signs and changes in behavior don't always mean that there is substance abuse, but they should trigger concern:

- Secretiveness, withdrawal
- Disdain for authority
- Disobedience at home, school and youth group
- Withdrawal from youth group functions
- Drug paraphernalia, incense, seeds, other drugs found on him or her
- Rise in school absences
- Violent or noticeably lethargic behavior
- Wide mood swings
- Loss of thought process; strange thinking
- Severe change in school performance; disrespect toward teachers; dropping grades
- Changes in personal hygiene
- Increased interest in heavy-metal music and songs with drug-oriented lyrics
- Unusually late night hours
- I-don't-care attitude
- Tiredness
- Depression
- Inability to concentrate
- Change in appetite; dramatic increase or decrease in weight
- Lack of coordination, clumsiness
- Slurred or garbled speech patterns; rapid speech
- Changes in sleeping habits
- Periods of hyperactivity
- Watery red eyes
- Runny, or drippy, nose
- Loss of interest in hobbies and old friends

Help Families with Prevention

Oftentimes, the people who work in the youth ministry community will be the first ones to see and recognize substance abuse problems. One of our main goals in this area should be one of education. Our students and their parents need to know the dangers and the consequences associated with substance abuse. Assisting families in this area is such a crucial need. Many families see the problem and don't know what to do. Other families simply can't (or don't want to) see the problem in their midst. Parents need assistance and support as they deal with children that are using and abusing various substances. We need to help families recognize the warning signs and work with them once the signs are noticed. Helping families see the surefire indicators and walking with them through a plan to get help can be one of the greatest gifts we can give to our students' families.

Know Where to Go

Quite often treatment is needed to bring health back to a family system. Treatment in its simplest form is the process of bringing people and resources together. Know what options are available in your area for families in need of treatment. Meet the people associated with the treatment center; get to know to whom you are referring your families. The following are a few things to look for when choosing a treatment center to partner with:

- A well-maintained facility
- A referral by someone who has been through the program
- A strong approach to treatment
- Healthy support for a sober lifestyle
- Personal attention
- Family treatment
- Staff attitudes of sensitivity and service
- Support of traditional Christian values

Have a Plan for Recovery

It's too easy to think that our job is over once a student is in the hands of a treatment center or has simply made the decision to stop using chemical or alcoholic substances. On the contrary, it has only begun. As youth workers and family advocates, we need to support the ongoing daily plan for recovery for our students. A good recovery plan will take into account the need for balance and growth in the areas of physical, mental, emotional, social and spiritual well-being and support. As we've said before, one of the greatest gifts we can give families who are in the middle of the stark reality of substance abuse is the gift of continual support. Students didn't fall into their addictions overnight and neither will their healing take place overnight.

> For excellent parent/youth worker and adolescent substance-abuse questionnaires, visit YouthBuilders at www.youthbuilders.com.

CHAPTER 26

THE CRISIS OF SUICIDE

There never is a good time to get a bad phone call, but the timing of this call was ironic. It was a Tuesday night in October, the night before Jim and I (Mike) were supposed to leave to present a YouthBuilders seminar on suicide to youth workers in three different states. It was a seminar dealing with substance abuse, sexual abuse and suicide—what to look for and do, as well as how to take the information into public schools in the local area. I was getting ready to leave the office when the phone rang.

It was Martin's mom. "Mike, can you come over right away? There's a problem. It's Martin . . . and he's . . . well, he's gone."

The words just echoed in my ears, "he's . . . well, he's gone." Here I was supposed to be a part of a seminar dealing with this very issue, and I was the one who had missed the signs. I jumped into my car and drove to the house.

As I entered the house, I didn't know what I'd find or what I'd feel. Just inside the front door I met Martin's mom and dad and was confronted with the harsh reality of what suicide does to a family. The pain was incredible. The atmosphere was something still and haunting. As we sat in the front room in silence, my mind raced back to the past.

Martin was a student in our ministry. He was a guy who had been in and out of trouble and in and out of church. Sometimes he was on the outskirts; sometimes he was involved. He was a face that every one of us has in our ministry. Martin was in pain. Sometimes that pain surfaced; sometimes it was hidden just beneath the surface. The truth was that no matter what Martin tried to do, it seemed that the pain and the hurt never quite went away; it was only a step behind.

Martin tried to hide from his pain with substances. He tried to hide from it in relationships with girls. He tried to find acceptance and power in the occult. Whatever he tried seemed to work for a while, but in the end he was left with his unresolved pain. He did find solace in his music. Martin was a guitar player who loved Nirvana and whose heart was captured by the passion of Kurt Cobain. Martin felt that Cobain's lyrics echoed the cry of his heart: his unresolved pain, his anger, his depression and the lack of hope he experienced.

It was during one of his off-again times with the youth ministry that I received that October night phone call. As I was sitting in the front room of their home, his mom told me about the events of the day. It seems that almost every day, she would come home from work, enter the house and call out Martin's name. She said that in the past few weeks, she had a feeling that his depression was getting worse. She feared that one day, she would come home, call out his name and not hear his familiar reply, "Yeah, Mom?!?" Today was that day.

She had come home, called out for Martin and gotten no reply. She said, "My worst fears were realized when I went into his room."

Martin had killed himself with a single bullet from a small-caliber handgun. Gathered around him were countless posters of Kurt Cobain. Nirvana played on the CD player. This was an eerie fulfillment of a statement made to a friend: "One day, I'm going to do it like Kurt Cobain. One shot and good-bye." (This referred to the way in which the lead singer of Nirvana ended his own tragic and tumultuous life.)

As his parents sat on the couch in tears after the coroner left, I decided that we needed to do something to help them. A friend and I decided that we would go and clean the room, as much as possible to keep his parents from having to go through the agony of reliving that moment in such a way. We climbed the stairs and entered the room.

I wish I could put into words all the emotions that I felt inside that room. Even as I write this, those images come flooding back. I put my back against the wall and let out a deep exhale, one from which I thought I would never recover. The posters that were ceremoniously laid around Martin's body were gone, the music was off, and the CD was left in the open disc changer. The bed in the middle of the room was unmade and stained with the aftermath of the afternoon, as was the floor. We went to work quickly, as if the quicker we were finished, the quicker we could move past the insanity and the emotion of the moment. We pulled the bedding off the bed, took the mattress that was blood soaked and carried everything downstairs and out to the side of the house. We pulled up the carpet and the pad. We found some white paint in the garage and painted the wood flooring beneath the pad, trying to erase the memory of what took place only hours before.

I remember driving home later that night. As I walked in the door, I was met by my wife and my two-year-old son. As I held him in my arms, I started to cry; it was really the first time in five hours that I let down emotionally. How could a life end this way? What kind of impact will this have on the family for the rest of their lives? Every holiday, every family get-together, every October 22 will never be the same. What about his friends, the ones who like me would now look back and see signs of what was to come, such as Martin's giving away his guitar the very morning of his suicide? What would we feel? As I lay in bed, my bags packed for the next day—ready for my trip to talk with youth workers about the very issue I was living that night—I struggled with my thoughts. *Was there something I missed? Was there anything I could have done?*

Students of this generation are killing themselves more regularly than any previous one. The tragedy of suicide is no respecter of economics, geography or status. It is a tragedy that is sweeping all across the nation, reaching into the homes of the richest of rich and the poorest of the poor. Look at these statistics:

- Suicide is the third highest cause of death among students.
- In the United States more than 7,000 students kill themselves annually. (That's an average of 1 every 75 minutes! And this doesn't include the vast number who attempt to commit suicide and fail.)
- The latest research tells us that in the next 24 hours, 1,439 students will attempt suicide. (That's over 500,000 a year!)

- In America, 7 out of 10 students know someone who has attempted suicide.[1]

The sad fact is that many students, like Martin, are seeing suicide as a solution to their unresolved issues. Some of these are students *you* work with. They need to see that suicide is a permanent solution to what is very often a temporary problem and that even long-term problems can be overcome without giving up on life.

Common Myths About Suicide

There are myths so common about suicide that even people in the helping professions assume them to be true. These myths will give you a better understanding of many of the issues surrounding suicide.[2]

Myth One: People Who Talk About Suicide Won't Do It

The truth is that about 80 percent of those who commit suicide *have* talked about it–but weren't taken seriously. Anyone talking about suicide should be taken seriously.

Myth Two: Mentioning Suicide May Give Someone the Idea

Many people are afraid that asking someone if he or she has contemplated suicide will cause that person to consider it when he or she otherwise wouldn't have. This simply is not true. If you suspect that someone is considering suicide, check it out. Ask him or her directly. For example, "As I sit here and listen to you, with everything that's going on in your life and all that you're feeling, I can see how suicide might seem like an option. I just need to know if it is something you are even considering?" If the answer is no, then your reply could be that you're relieved and that if they ever get to that point, then you'd sure like to talk with them. If the answer yes, then you've just opened up the issue for conversation. Talking about suicide with someone who is contemplating it actually works to prevent it.

Myth Three: Suicide Occurs Without Warning

Not only do suicidal people give warnings, but they also usually give many warning signs. Hindsight is always 20/20, and after someone has committed suicide, friends and family are usually shocked when they realize how many warning signs they missed. That was the case with Martin. There were many of us who experienced that kind of shock. The warning signs include moodiness, withdrawal, a sudden traumatic event (especially the breakup with a longtime boyfriend or girlfriend), violent behavior or a history of drugs and alcohol, to name a few. We've included a comprehensive list of warning signs at the end of this chapter. There are usually more than enough warning signs, but those who are closest to the person simply can't believe that a friend of theirs would actually take his or her own life.

Myth Four: All Suicidal People Are Mentally Ill

Too many people believe that suicide happens only to people who are mentally ill, mentally retarded or very poor. They can't imagine that a *normal* person would want to take his or her life. The truth is that only about 15 percent of those who take their lives have actually been diagnosed with a mental illness; the other 85 percent are people who have just lost perspective on their hurts and pain, and in their desperation they see suicide as a viable solution to their problems.

Myth Five: Suicidal People Are Totally Committed to Dying

One of the most common characteristics of adolescents who are contemplating suicide is *ambivalence.* They have a strong desire to end their life and at the same time a strong desire to live. It's been heard from people who have attempted suicide, "I really didn't want to die" and "I just wanted to be dead for a little while." Your best approach is to use their ambivalence and encourage strong feelings about living.

Myth Six: When Depression Lifts, the Suicide Crisis Is Over

Often the lifting of the depression means only that the adolescent has finally decided to take his or her own life. The depression is replaced with a feeling of euphoria or relief now that the decision has finally been made. The relief comes from knowing that after their preplanned date their pain and struggle will all be over. Incredibly, many suicides occur within three months after the person has appeared to overcome the depression.

Myth Seven: Suicidal People Do Not Seek Medical Help

Strangely, research has shown that three out of four people who have taken their lives have seen a doctor within one to three months beforehand.

A Time, a Place and a Method

When someone talks to you about a potential suicide, one of the first steps in getting help is to find out how serious he or she really is. If a person is talking about it, then of course it is important and he or she needs help; however, the situation may not be lethal yet! Rich Van Pelt, an authority on teenage suicide, has given us a very effective method to determine how serious a person really is. He says, "There are three things needed to die: (1) a time, (2) a place, (3) a method. If in your discussion with the student all of the above are present, then the person needs immediate attention."[3]

When in a discussion with a student and it is clear that he or she has considered suicide as an option, begin to evaluate if there is a time (when), a place (where) and a method (how). If a student has all three of these already in mind, then he or she has moved past considering suicide to the point of beginning to plan the act itself.

I (Jim) vividly remember a late-night phone call from two girls who had been in my high school ministry and were now in college. Jenny apologized for calling in the middle of the night, but she said Linda was with her and wanted to kill herself. I asked a few questions and discerned that it was serious. She had a time, place and a method. I invited them over to our house. We talked and sought counseling help the next day. The following weekend Linda called me again in the middle of the night. She had just broken up with her boyfriend. I had to discern if she was suicidal. I didn't believe her to be, so I told her I would love to see her the following day. In the middle of the night, she would not have my full attention. Van Pelt's formula of time, place and method will help you make an accurate evaluation on how serious the potential suicide is.

The Warning Signs for Adolescents

- Abrupt changes in personality
- The giving away of a prized possession
- A previously attempted suicide
- Talk of suicide, including comments and/or notes
- Increased use of alcohol and/or drugs
- Eating disturbances and significant weight change
- Sleeping disturbances (i.e., nightmares, insomnia)
- Withdrawal and rebelliousness
- Inability or unwillingness to communicate
- Inability to tolerate or handle frustration
- Sexual promiscuity
- Neglecting personal appearance
- Theft and/or vandalism
- Adolescent depression presenting itself behaviorally
- Exaggerated and/or extended apathy and dispair
- Inactivity and boredom
- Carelessness and/or accident proneness
- An unusually long grief reaction
- Sadness and discouragement
- Hostile behavior; unruliness in school

- Neglect of academic work
- Truancy and other attendance problems
- Difficulty concentrating
- Family disruption (divorce, death)
- Running away from home
- Abrupt ending of a romance

Dos and Don'ts in Working with Suicidal Adolescents

Dos

- Whenever possible, try to diffuse the plan the person has for killing him- or herself by obtaining and disposing of the method of choice (like a bottle of pills). Don't use physical force to accomplish this.
- Be positive; suggest the most desirable alternatives.
- Remain calm and work at being empathetic (feel the person's pain in your heart).
- Use constructive questioning to help separate and define the person's problems and remove some confusion.
- Emphasize the temporary nature of the person's problem. Suicide is a permanent solution to a temporary problem.
- Stay in touch, both literally and figuratively.
- Urge professional help when beyond your ability.

Don'ts

- Don't sound shocked by what the person tells you (even if you are).
- Don't stress the kind of pain it would cause the suicidal person's family, or even yourself; that may be the exact thing that the person wants to do.
- Don't call the person's bluff, daring them to go ahead.
- Don't get into a philosophical debate with the person.
- Don't belittle or try to shame the person.

- Never try to physically remove a weapon from a suicidal person. You must verbally manipulate it out of his or her hands.

> For a beneficial questionnaire that provides good indicators for suicide potential, visit YouthBuilders at www.youthbuilders.com.

CHAPTER 27

The Crisis of Sexual Abuse

I (Jim) was giving a talk on sexual abuse to a group of youth pastors and made the statement that one out of every four women has been sexually abused by the age of 18 (many authorities now say it is over one out of every three). A young youth worker came to me and said, "I have a high school group of 125 students and we've never had a problem in this area."

I asked him if he had ever brought up or taught the subject to his students, and he replied that he hadn't. I challenged him to talk about sexual abuse to his students within the next month and call me back. Two weeks later he called, amazed and a little stunned at the fact that he had already talked to eight people who were traumatized from sexual abuse. He is not alone. Everywhere I speak on the issue of sexual abuse, people want to talk about their hurt and pain at the hands of sexual abusers. It's almost as if we should put a warning on this chapter that reads "Caution: If you get involved and become knowledgeable in the area of sexual abuse, you will never be the same."

Consider these facts:

- At least 1 in 3 American women[1] and 1 in 6 men[2] will be sexually abused in their lifetimes.
- Fewer than 1 in 3 rapes and/or sexual assaults were reported to the authorities in 1996.[3]

- In 1994, an average of 234,000 convicted rape or sexual assault offenders were under the custody or control of corrections agencies every day.
- Nearly 60 percent of the 234,000 convicted offenders were under conditional supervision in their communities.[4]

Our society's conception is that an abuser is a skid-row bum, smelling of liquor and brutally forcing himself on his victim. However, the facts tell us that *80 percent* of sexual assaults *are committed by someone the victim already knows and trusts.*[5]

The Ugly Truth

As I (Jim) started bringing up the subject of sexual abuse in my own youth ministry, the stories began to come out. Jennifer was baby-sitting for her ex-boyfriend's family. The boyfriend's stepfather came home. He asked Jennifer to stay. They watched a movie together. He said, "You look tired; let me rub your back."

Jennifer didn't know what to say. He first started rubbing outside her sweater and then under her sweater on her skin. He slowly moved his hand to her breasts. Jennifer felt paralyzed. The phone rang, and she ran out the door.

Travis went camping at age 11 with his favorite uncle. Seven years later he told me a terrible story of forced homosexual rape that had been going on sporadically for all those years.

When Lori was nine her father began to fondle her private parts. She didn't like it but thought that maybe she was supposed to let him since he was her father and she loved and adored him. Seven years later (the average length of time for an incest victim), Lori hated her father, was disgusted with her life and wanted to end it all through suicide.

When Debbie's brother would get high on drugs, he would force himself on her. He always left with the same threat: "If you tell anyone about this, I'll kill you."

She believed him. When she finally told her parents, they called *her* the liar.

These are not uplifting case studies. If you could meet each one of these people, you would never guess that they had such major problems. Their stories are similar to the millions of people in the United States who suffer in silence.

Warning Signs

If you are willing to help people who have been sexually abused, there is hope for them. These victims of one of the most destructive of all human behaviors can receive help, though it takes a great deal of time and a willingness to hurt alongside them.

There are specific signals of sexual abuse. Most victims will not come to you right away with their secret. Teenagers may tell you by their behavior rather than their words.

Listed below are a number of signals of sexual abuse, although the mere fact that a teenager has one or more of these behaviors does not always mean that he or she has been sexually abused:

- Learning problems in school
- Poor peer relationships
- Self-destructive behavior; suicidal tendencies; drug and alcohol abuse
- Hostility and lack of trust toward adults
- Major problems with authority figures
- Seductive and/or promiscuous behavior
- Running away
- Fear of going home; fear of being left alone with the abuser
- Severe depression
- Pain, itching, bleeding and/or bruises in the genital areas
- Extremely low self-esteem
- Difficulty understanding the concept of a loving heavenly Father

If you suspect an incestuous relationship, consider the following potential signals for abusive sexual behavior on the part of adults:

- Demands isolation of the child; discourages friendships, school functions and dates
- Enforces restrictive control; allows few social events (actually extremely jealous)
- Displays overdependence; sometimes will depend on the child to fill needs usually met by the spouse or other adult
- Indulges in drug or alcohol abuse

Counseling

If you talk about sexual abuse enough times, someone will seek you out for help. You've touched an issue that is never very far from the abused person's mind and heart. Abused people are dealing with their secret with every sermon, relationship and activity in their lives. When they finally do come to you, there are six principles to help you help victims of sexual abuse.

Believe Them

Few people lie about sexual abuse. There are some false stories, but more often than not, the stories are true. Assume that someone is telling you the truth until it is proven that he or she isn't. Let child protection services do the investigative work. Your job is to simply believe the person telling you the story.

Listen to Them

Let them tell you their stories at their own pace. Clarify, but don't interrogate. Abused people need a listening ear. If you have had a similar situation, you may wish to tell it to them, but do not go on and on with your story. They need to talk.

Support Them

Sexual abuse victims who tell you their trauma will need your support; they need to know that you believe them and that you will care for and help them. They need your time. If God entrusts one of these precious souls to you, you will have to be available to give him or her the priceless gift of your time. At times while listening to the story, we might be tempted to be critical, saying something such as "That was dumb" or "You shouldn't have been so careless." *Don't be critical.* Abuse victims do not need to be reminded of their carelessness.

Recognize Emotional and Medical Needs

Do not overlook their medical or emotional needs when someone is telling you about his or her experience. He or she may need to see a doctor immediately.

Find Community Resources

You cannot handle this problem alone; you will need the help of professionals. Create a list that's easily accessible with the phone numbers for rape crisis hotlines, mental health departments, medical facilities and women's centers at local colleges and universities.

Don't Keep It a Secret

One of the biggest mistakes that youth workers make is that they do not report sexual abuse to the authorities. In many states, the law requires you to report such abuse within a specific time frame. Because of the spiritual nature of church work, youth workers do not follow the law as carefully as educators do. However, the secret has already been kept too long, so tell the abused person of your desire to report the crime. Tell the victim that you will walk through this with him or her. Let the proper authorities handle the legal and psychological problems; your role is that of friend and pastoral support. If you choose not to report the crime—and it *is* a crime—you are hindering the healing process and perhaps breaking the law. Know the specific reporting laws in your state.

Many times after you report a case of sexual abuse, a detective trained in this field will immediately interview the victim, the abuser, yourself and family members, and then make the proper decision about what to do.

God in the Picture

There is no question about the fact that a victim of sexual abuse, can often have a badly distorted view of God as their heavenly Father. Questions such as, "How can a loving God allow this to happen to me?" are very common and need to be dealt with in a professional manner. Although we're not therapists, here are a few difficulties that are often evident in the victim's spiritual life:

> **Fatherhood**—There is difficulty in trusting God as a loving Father. This is especially true in the case of an incest victim. The Father image of God is not a positive image to most people who have been victims of sexual abuse, especially at the hands of their father.
>
> **Unconditional Love**—For victims of sexual abuse, the biblical message of unconditional love is a difficult concept to comprehend. There have always been conditions for love in their lives.
>
> **Forgiveness**—Unfortunately, many victims feel that they had something to do with the problem. They feel dirty and sinful. Understanding God's forgiveness and forgiving themselves is a difficult task. Along with a difficulty in the area of forgiveness, there is usually an extreme struggle with guilt.

You can help victims of sexual abuse by accepting them and their stories. These people need hope and reassurance of your love and God's love. They need to know that the abuse is not their fault and that God truly is our loving Father. You can even help the long process of reconciliation. We're not suggesting that most sexual abuse relationships will be reconciled to normal, loving relationships; however, many people have become spiritually reconciled through prayer. The hate turns to pity and prayer for the condition of the abuser. This does not happen overnight—most likely it takes years.

Education

Considering the statistics at the beginning of this chapter, there *are* students in your ministry who have been down the road of sexual abuse or are currently traveling that road. It is absolutely vital that we address the issue and get help to those students who are suffering in silence. We need to discuss the problems of sexual abuse within our youth ministry, allow time for students to talk about it and become educated about the problem. Students who are suffering need to know the truth, as do their friends. Young people will often confide in a chosen friend to tell their stories. Time and time again, I (Jim) have had two young girls come arm in arm to share their secret. Until they chose to talk to me, only those two had known. Help your students help their friends.

Every student who has been suffering the trauma of sexual abuse needs to know and experience four truths.

Truth One: It's Not Your Fault

Abuse is *always* the fault of the abuser. Many times the abuser will say, "Well, you asked for it" as a way to rationalize what is taking place. That couldn't be further from the truth. The fault always, always, *always* lies with the abuser.

Truth Two: You Need to Seek Help

Don't suffer in silence. Most people who have been sexually abused are afraid to tell anyone. However, they can't get better without help. The pain won't go away by itself.

Truth Three: There Is Hope

The unfortunate fact is that millions have suffered at the hands of sexual abuse. The good news is that many have sought help, worked through their pain and are now living happy lives. There is hope, but they need to reach out for it.

Truth Four: God Cares

Most people who have experienced any kind of sexual abuse will struggle with their relationship with God. In the midst of the struggle, they need to hear loud and clear that God *does* care and that He *does* love them. Perhaps too many people spend their time and energies blaming God instead of being comforted by Him. He cares. He sees. He wants to heal our wounds.

Screening Volunteers

Another very important point to consider in your youth ministry is the screening of your adult volunteers. We can't forget that sexual abusers like to stay close to kids. If you see any behavior that seems abnormal, do not be afraid to confront the person. It is better to be overly cautious than to allow pain and hurt to occur to one of God's precious children. Because of the magnitude of the problem, it would be wise for not only you but also your entire staff to be trained in the area of sexual abuse.[6]

> For general information and education about sexual abuse, visit YouthBuilders at www.youthbuilders.com.

APPENDIX

To find the following documents, visit our website at www.youthbuilders.com and, in the Youth Worker section, click on *The Youth Builder*.

Chapter 2	List of Youth Ministry Organizations
Chapter 6	Family Event and Devotional Time Ideas
Chapter 7	Principles for Contact Work
	Sample Information Card for First-Time Visitors
Chapter 10	Creative Worship Ideas
Chapter 11	Camp and Retreat Ideas
	Sample Evaluation Sheet
	Sample Flow Chart
Chapter 12	Student Leader Commitment Form
Chapter 13	Mission Experience Ideas
Chapter 14	Student Ministry Team
	Application
	Commitment Form
	Expectations
	Reference Form
Chapter 15	Internship Program
	Application

	Evaluation Form
	Job Description
	Personal Goals
	Sample Proposal
	Weekly Update Form
Chapter 18	Sample Student Ministries Event Planning Form
Chapter 19	Sample Teaching Topics
Chapter 20	Sample Case Study
	Sample Bible Study
Chapter 21	*Radical Love* (comprehensive book on sex and sexuality)
Chapter 23	Referral Checklist
Chapter 25	Substance-Abuse Questionnaires
	Adolescent
	Youth Worker/Parent
Chapter 26	Adolescent Suicide Questionnaire
Chapter 27	Sexual Abuse General Information and Education

ENDNOTES

Chapter 3

1. Denis Witmer, "What is Happening to Our Children?" *Parenting Teens*, March 31, 1998. http://www.parentingteens.about.com/library/weekly/aa033198.htm. (no access date).
2. "Every Day in America," *The Children's Defense Fund*. http://www.childrensdefense.org/everyday.htm (accessed April 2001).
3. Walt Mueller, *Understanding Today's Youth Culture* (Wheaton, IL: Tyndale House Publishers, Inc., 1999), p. 41.
4. "Teenagers," *Barna Research Online*. http://www.barna.org/cgi-bin/PageCategory.asp?CategoryID=37 (accessed July 30, 2001).
5. "Family," *Barna Research Online*. http://www.barna.org/cgi-bin/PageCategory.asp?CategoryID=20 (accessed February 2, 2001).
6. Arlene Saluter, *Marital Status and Living Arrangements*, U.S. Bureau of the Census, series P20-484 (March 1996), p. vi.
7. "Christians Are More Likely to Experience Divorce Than Are Non-Christians," *Barna Research Online*, December 21, 1999. http://www.barna.org (no access date).
8. Maggie Gallagher, *The Abolition of Marriage: How We Destroy Lasting Love* (Washington, DC: Regnery, 1996), p. 76.
9. Mike Nappa, "Divorce: Just the Facts," *Nappaland.com*. http://www.nappaland.com/Nappaland-dot-com/Magazine%20Archive%20pages/Divorce,%20Just%20the%20Facts.htm (accessed August 1, 2001).

10. "Youth Risk Behavior Surveillance–United States, 1999," *Center for Disease Control.* http://www.ccdc.gov/mmwr/preview/mmwrhtml/ss4905a1.htm (accessed July 30, 2001).
11. "Teen Sex and Pregnancy," *The Alan Guttmacher Institute*, revised September 1999. http://www.agi-usa.org/pubs/fb_teen_sex.html (no access date).
12. Walt Mueller, *Understanding Today's Youth Culture* (Wheaton, IL: Tyndale House Publishers, Inc., 1999), p. 138.
13. Stephen Arterburn and Jim Burns, *Parents Guide to Top 10 Dangers Teens Face* (Wheaton, IL: Tyndale House Publishers, 1995), p. 69.
14. Walt Mueller, *Understanding Today's Youth Culture* (Wheaton, IL: Tyndale House Publishers, 1999), p. 175.
15. "Sharks," *Enough Is Enough.* http://www.enough.org/sharks.htm (accessed February 2, 2001).
16. Ibid.
17. "The Cyberchurch Is Coming," *Barna Research Online*, April 20, 1998. http://www.barna.org (no access date).
18. "Sharks," *Enough Is Enough.* http://www.enough.org/sharks.htm (accessed February 2, 2001).
19. "Reefs and Rocks: Dangers and Legal Definitions of Pornography," *Enough Is Enough.* http://www.enough.org/sharks.htm (accessed February 2, 2001).
20. *Warning Signs* (American Psychological Association). Call the A.P.A. (1-800-268-0078) for more information.
21. Gary Langer, "Students Tell of Peer Violence," *ABCNews.com*, April 26, 1999. http://www.abcnews.go.com/sections/us/DailyNews/littleton_poll990426.html (no access date).
22. *Warning Signs* (American Psychological Association). Call the A.P.A. (1-800-268-0078) for more information.
23. Ibid.
24. "Scolds and Fundraisers," *ABCNews.com*, May 15, 1999. http://www.abcnews.go.com/sections/us/DailyNews/clintonradio990515.html (no access date).
25. Sharon Lewis, "When Teens Turn Violent: Recognize the Signs Before It's Too Late," *The National Safety Council*, fall 1999. http://nsc.org/pubs/fsh/archive/fall99/teens.htm (accessed August 20, 2001).

Chapter 4

For a thorough curriculum on helping students develop their spiritual gifts, see Jim Burns and Doug Fields, *The Word on Finding and Using Your Spiritual Gifts* (Ventura, CA: Gospel Light, 1995).

Chapter 5

1. Categories taken from James Fowler, *Stages of Faith* (New York: Harper and Row, 1981), n.p. Explanatory comments by Jim Burns.

Chapter 6

1. For further reading, see Jim Burns, *Parenting Teenagers for Positive Results* (Loveland, CO: Group Publishing, 2001); and Jim Burns, *How to Be a Happy, Healthy Family* (Nashville, TN: Word Publishing, 2001).
2. For Bible studies on the family, see Jim Burns, *The Word on Family*, (Ventura, CA: Gospel Light, 1997), written for high schoolers; and Tim Baker, *Home and Family,* Pulse (Ventura, CA: Gospel Light, 2000), written for junior highers.
3. Andy Stanley (speech at the General Session of the Youth Specialties National Youth Workers Convention 2000, Atlanta, Georgia).
4. Ibid.
5. Gail MacDonald, *High Call, High Privilege* (Peabody, MA: Hendrickson Publishers, 1998), n.p.

Chapter 7

1. "Teens and Adults Have Little Chance of Accepting Christ as Their Savior," *Barna Research Online*, November 15, 1999. http://www.barna.org (no access date).
2. Donald C. Posterski, *Friendship: A Window on Ministry to Youth* (Scarborough, Ontario, Canada: Project Teen Canada, 1985), p. 5.
3. Ibid.
4. For a list of youth ministry organizations, visit www.youthbuilders.com.

Chapter 8

1. Bruce Larson, *Dare to Live Now* (Grand Rapids, MI: Zondervan Publishing House, 1965), p. 110.
2. Lyman Coleman, *Encyclopedia of Serendipity* (Littleton, CO: Serendipity House, 1976), n.p.

Chapter 9

1. J. David Stone and Rose Mary Miller, *Volunteer Youth Workers: Recruiting and Developing Leaders for Youth Ministry* (Loveland, CO: Group Books, 1985), pp. 27-32.

Chapter 12

1. For a 12-week study on developing spiritual gifts, see Jim Burns and Doug Fields, *The Word on Finding and Using Your Spiritual Gifts* (Ventura, CA: Gospel Light, 1995).

Chapter 13

1. E. Stanley Jones, *Mahatma Gandhi: Portrayal of a Friend* (Nashville, TN: Abingdon, 1983), p. 27.
2. John Charles Pollock, *A Foreign Devil in China: The Story of Dr. L. Nelson Bell* (Minneapolis, MN: World Wide Publications, 1988), n.p.
3. Dietrich Bonhoeffer, *Life Together* (New York: Harper and Row, 1954), p. 101.

Chapter 14

1. To better understand the issues that challenge today's youth leaders, see the YouthBuilders Training to Go series from Gospel Light (www.gospellight.com).
2. Websites to visit: youthbuilders.com; gospellight.com; youthspecialties.com; youthministryonline.com; reachout.gospelcom.net; sonlife.com; grouppublishing.com.

Chapter 17

1. Paul Borthwick, "How to Design an Effective Youth Ministry Budget," *Youthworker Journal* (fall 1984), n.p.
2. Ibid., p. 25.
3. For more information, see J. David Epstein, *ClergyTax* (Ventura CA: Gospel Light, [updated and published yearly]).

Chapter 19

1. We are deeply grateful to Marlene LeFever of David C. Cook Publishers for her excellent work on learning styles and her practical advice on this section.
2. Mike DeVries, *The Word on the New Testament* (Ventura, CA: Gospel Light, 1996), p.19.

Chapter 20

1. For more ideas, see Jim Burns and Greg McKinnon, *Fresh Ideas: Illustrations, Stories and Quotes* (Ventura, CA: Gospel Light, 1997).
2. For more information, visit www.philchambers.com.

Chapter 21

1. Paul Recer, "Teen Virginity Pledgers Delay Sex," *The Associated Press.* http://www.ap.org (accessed through http://www.aol.com/news, January 4, 2001).
2. *USA Today*, November 16, 2000, pp. 1-2D.
3. "Young Misinformed, Complacent about HIV/AIDS," *Reuters*, November 28, 2000. http://www.reutershealth.com (no access date).
4. For further reading, see Jim Burns and Stephen Arterburn, *Parents Guide to Top 10 Dangers Teens Face* (Wheaton, IL: Tyndale House Publishers, 1995), p.83-98.
5. "Sharks," *Enough Is Enough*. http://www.enough.org/sharks.htm (accessed February 2, 2001).
6. For further reading, see Jim Burns, *The Word on Sex, Drugs and Rock 'N' Roll* (Ventura, CA: Gospel Light, 1994).

Chapter 22

1. "Teenagers Embrace Religion But Are Not Excited About Christianity," *Barna Research Online*. http://www.barna.org (accessed January 10, 2000).
2. "Teens and Adults Have Little Chance of Accepting Christ as Their Savior," *Barna Research Online*. http://www.barna.org (accessed November 15, 1999).
3. Scott Peck, *The Road Less Traveled* (New York: Simon and Schuster, 1978), p. 15.
4. "Eating Disorders in the USA: Statistics in Context," *Eating Disorders and Prevention, Inc*. http://www.edap.org/edinfo/stats.html (accessed March 16, 2001).
5. David Elkind, *All Grown Up and No Place to Go* (Reading, MS: Addison-Wesley, 1984), p. 171.
6. Note that we are not talking about New Age thinking, which says we can become infinite by mental imagery. We are referring to achieving legitimate, God-honoring goals in life.

Chapter 23

1. David Elkind, *All Grown Up and No Place to Go* (Reading, MS: Addison-Wesley, 1984), n.p.

Chapter 24

1. "Christians Are More Likely to Experience Divorce Than Are Non-Christians," *Barna Research Online*. http://www.barna.org (accessed July 2, 2001).
2. Arlene Saluter, *Marital Status and Living Arrangements*, U.S. Bureau of the Census, series P20-484 (March 1996), p. vi.
3. Mike Yaconelli and Jim Burns, *High School Ministry* (Grand Rapids, MI: Zondervan Publishing House, 1986), p. 88
4. David Elkind, *All Grown Up and No Place to Go* (Reading, MS: Addison-Wesley, 1984), n.p.

Chapter 25

1. "Youth Risk Behavior Surveillance–United States, 1999," *Center for Disease Control*. http://www.cdc.gov/mmwr/preview/

mmwrhtml/ss4905a1.htm (accessed July 30, 2001).

2. Walt Mueller, "The Truth About Teens and Substance Abuse," *Youth Culture@2000* (winter 2000), pp. 10-12.

Chapter 26

1. Jim Burns, *The Word on Helping a Friend in Crisis* (Ventura, CA: Gospel Light, 1995), p. 115.
2. Bill Blackburn, *What You Should Know About Suicide* (Waco, TX: Word Publishing, 1982), n.p.; and Mike Yaconelli and Jim Burns, *High School Ministry* (Grand Rapids, MI: Zondervan Publishing House, 1986), pp. 146-147.
3. Rich Van Pelt (speech at a YouthBuilders training seminar, Colorado Springs, CO, February 12, 2001).

Chapter 27

1. Department of Computer Sciences, "Rape Statistics," *The University of Tennessee.* http://cs.utk.edu/~bartley/sa/stats.html (accessed June 22, 2001).
2. Department of Computer Sciences, "Myths and Facts About Rape," *The University of Tennessee.* http://cs.utk.edu/~bartley/sa/mythsfacts.html (accessed June 22, 2001).
3. "RAINN Statistics," *Rape, Abuse and Incest National Network.* http://rainn.org/statistics.html (accessed June 22, 2001).
4. Bureau of Justice Statistics, "Criminal Offenders Statistics," *United States Department of Justice.* http://www.ojp.usdoj.gov/bjs/crimoff.htm (accessed August 20, 2001).
5. Cooperative Extension, Institute of Agriculture and Natural Resources, "Dating Violence and Acquaintance Assault," *University of Nebraska-Lincoln.* http://www.ianr.unl.edu/pubs/family/nf244.htm (accessed June 22, 2001).
6. For more information, see Jim Burns, *Teaching Youth About Sex and Sexuality/Sexual Abuse,* YouthBuilders Training to Go, Vol. 3 (Ventura, CA: Gospel Light, 2000).